'One of the key strengths of this book is that it is written over many years by two extremely experienced clinicians able, through their decades of reflective practice and commitment to their own professional growth, to create a thorough and rich offering to all involved in this complex world of caring for traumatised children. They frequently refer to the use of complex case studies, and, for me, this attention to direct work is vital and gives the book validity and gravitas.'

Di Gammage, *Core Process Psychotherapist, Child Psychotherapist, and Play Therapist, Senior Clinician, Capstone Fostercare, UK*

Foundations, Trauma, and the Child's Voice in Sibling Relationships

Foundations, Trauma, and the Child's Voice in Sibling Relationships is the essential foundation for trauma-informed assessments of sibling relationships in care and in permanence planning. This book provides professionals with the theoretical, legal, and emotional tools to challenge their assumptions and understand the child's context. With rich case material and deep psychological insight, this volume offers a new lens through which to understand what children say, and don't say, about their siblings, and why these insights are crucial to ethical decision-making. The authors' other publication *A Trauma Model for Assessing Siblings* develops from this text to deliver a rigorous, trauma-informed framework for assessing and supporting sibling relationships in a range of care-giving settings. It is an invaluable guide for therapists, counsellors, social workers, child welfare professionals, and indeed anyone involved in making decisions regarding the placement of children.

Tim Woodhouse is a senior trauma-informed therapist, consultant, and clinical supervisor with over four decades of experience in children's social care, psychotherapy, and assessment. He served for 16 years on the NSPCC's Child Sexual Abuse Consultancy and helped set up the first children's SARC at St Mary's Manchester. He is the founder and clinical lead of Tiptoes Child Therapy Services, working nationally across adoption, fostering, residential care, court-directed assessments, and interventions. Tim is a Level III Certified Sensorimotor Psychotherapist, a Level III Internal Family Systems (IFS) therapist, EMDR practitioner, and a BAPT-registered Play and Filial Therapist. He is also a registered social worker and ABE-approved interviewer, known for bridging relational depth with clinical precision.

Norma Howes is a highly experienced and respected independent child protection consultant, therapist, expert witness, clinical supervisor, trainer, and author with over four decades of work in trauma-informed assessments, therapeutic interventions, and children and families social work. Her clinical specialism spans complex trauma, dissociation, forensic assessment, and attachment-focused therapy within foster care, adoption, and high-risk family systems. She is also a Sensorimotor Psychotherapist and an EMDR practitioner.

Foundations, Trauma, and the Child's Voice in Sibling Relationships

The Sibling Paradox

Tim Woodhouse and Norma Howes

LONDON AND NEW YORK

Designed cover image: Getty Images

First published 2026
by Routledge
605 Third Avenue, New York, NY 10158

and by Routledge
4 Park Square, Milton Park, Abingdon, Oxon OX14 4RN

Routledge is an imprint of the Taylor & Francis Group, an informa business

© 2026 Tim Woodhouse and Norma Howes

The right of Tim Woodhouse and Norma Howes to be identified as authors of this work has been asserted in accordance with sections 77 and 78 of the Copyright, Designs and Patents Act 1988.

All rights reserved. No part of this book may be reprinted or reproduced or utilised in any form or by any electronic, mechanical, or other means, now known or hereafter invented, including photocopying and recording, or in any information storage or retrieval system, without permission in writing from the publishers.

For Product Safety Concerns and Information please contact our EU representative GPSR@taylorandfrancis.com. Taylor & Francis Verlag GmbH, Kaufingerstraße 24, 80331 München, Germany.

Trademark notice: Product or corporate names may be trademarks or registered trademarks, and are used only for identification and explanation without intent to infringe.

British Library Cataloguing-in-Publication Data
A catalogue record for this book is available from the British Library

ISBN: 978-1-041-20908-9 (hbk)
ISBN: 978-1-041-20898-3 (pbk)
ISBN: 978-1-003-72479-7 (ebk)

DOI: 10.4324/9781003724797

Typeset in Times New Roman
by Deanta Global Publishing Services, Chennai, India

Thank you to Tim, who has been an inspiration and encouraged me to share our knowledge and write this book together, to his family and mine for their gentle pressure to ensure it was started and completed. Thank you also to all the siblings and their carers who have taught us both so much by allowing us into their lives, thoughts, feelings, and the many, too many, paradoxes impacting them. Thank you to my younger brothers who remember some things as I do. The smiles and laughter as we agree to disagree over some memories as adults reflecting back on who was the boss, who was mum's favourite, who fell off which swing and had the most stiches, the fall-outs and the fall-ins, and realise how lucky we are and were to have had, and to still have each other despite the many paradoxes in our lives. Thank you for reading this book, for the thinking and planning you will do, and for the relationships and insights you will have with siblings whose trauma-filled lives, with so many intolerable and misunderstood paradoxes, need understanding now and in the future.

Norma Howes

First, thank you to my wife Kim who believed in this book and enabled it to be written by holding Tiptoes steady at the helm. I know it consumed me, thank you. Thank you to our children Ellie and Nia, who continue to teach me so much about sibling relationships. Thank you to my parents: my mum, Shirley, and in memory of her siblings Brenda, Margaret, Joyce, Stella, Ralph, Eileen, Jean, and her surviving younger brother Jimmy; and to my dad, Gary, and in memory of his sister Diane, DiDi. Thank you to my sister Kirstie and our ongoing sibling relationship. Thank you to all the children and families who have allowed me into their lives since 1984. They have taught and challenged my beliefs about sibling relationships. I carry their memories with me as I continue to endeavour to support others who come after. Finally, thank you to Norma, who has been a lighthouse, helping to navigate stormy waters and ensure safe passage. It's been quite a voyage.

Tim Woodhouse

Contents

Foreword	*xi*
Acknowledgements	*xiv*
About the Authors	*xv*
Prologue	*xvi*

Part I
Foundations: Values, Attitudes, Beliefs, and Biases — 1

1 One Hand Clapping: Coherence in Fragmented Practice — 3
2 The Mirror in the Room: Self-Awareness in Sibling Decisions — 13

Part II
The Children's Context — 23

3 Siblings in the Shadows: When One Child Suffers — 25
4 Shattered Bonds: Trauma's Impact on Siblinghood — 35
5 Between the Lines: Children's Voices on Sibling Relationships — 48

Part III
Evidence and Ethics: Research, Law, and Policy — 55

6 The Myth and the Measure: What Research Really Tells Us — 57
7 Law and Paradox: Policy, Courts, and Sibling Futures — 64

Part IV
Trauma and Development: Body, Brain, and Behaviour   71

8 Incubated in Terror or Held in Mind?: Attachment, Regulation, and Developmental Trauma   73

9 Brains under Siege: How Trauma Shapes Development and Behaviour   83

10 Bound by Fear: How Trauma Hijacks Attachment   98

11 The Quiet Parts Loud: Children's Voices in Sibling Decisions   107

Part V
Hearing the Child: Listening, Validating, and Understanding   125

12 Between Truth and Survival: Forensic Neutrality, Therapeutic Empathy, and the Discipline of Hypotheses   127

13 Conversations on the Edge: Staying within the Window of Tolerance   137

14 Entwined and Unravelled: The Dynamics of Sibling Conversations   148

15 Hold the Adult, Help the Child: Conversations with Parents and Carers   159

16 Between the Ship and the Anchor: The Pull of Sibling Ties   166

17 Echoes of Separation: Adults Reflect on Siblings Lost and Togetherness   175

References   *189*
Index   *202*

Foreword

At the end of Shakespeare's 'Comedy of Errors,' twin brothers separated from birth, find one another again and celebrate their renewed relationship:

'We came into the world like brother and brother, and now let's go hand in hand, not one before another.'

(Shakespeare , 1594/2025 Act 5, Scene 1)

Despite their different experiences and life paths, they acknowledge their shared identities, seeking mutual understanding as they start the next phase of their lives, with a new awareness of one another. As a twin myself, I loved this quote when I first heard it, but more so following the death of my twin brother some years later, when it connected me with the loss involved in going 'one before another' and reminded me of how my own ongoing identity continued to be affected by my relationship with him.

This quote came to mind when I was asked to write a foreword to these two books on the sibling paradox. For many of us, sibling assessment touches both our personal and professional lives. Personally, I grew up in a family of four siblings and have come to understand over time the significance and potential benefits of these relationships for my own life. Professionally, I have worked with many groups of siblings as a social worker and therapist and contributed to assessments and decision-making about siblings' short- and long-term placement decisions, often struggling with the complexity of these decisions and my own conflicting emotions about them. Such work has included seeking the views of children about their potential placement with family members and siblings, while paying attention to their age and understanding, their individual histories and shared experiences, and seeking to represent their views honestly and directly to decision-making forums. Or supporting sibling groups when they have been separated, working to help siblings to say goodbye to one another and to acknowledge the loss and sadness involved. Or preparing children for contact with siblings they have not seen for some time or may not know at all. All of this work is emotionally charged, requiring our skills as practitioners in communication, empathy, and exercising professional judgement, alongside our own self-awareness and ability to acknowledge our personal beliefs and values about sibling relationships and how these have shaped us.

These two volumes make a welcome, much-needed contribution to our understanding of a complex area of theory and research, and in support of our application in practice when assessing siblings. Reading through them, I was struck by the depth of therapeutic understanding that underpins every chapter and the empathy and compassion with which even the most complex of practice dilemmas are explored. Norma and Tim bring a wealth of experience as practitioners, therapists, and supervisors to their writing, drawing on their considerable experience to inform the key ideas explored within the texts. Most significantly, the books develop and enhance previous practice guidance (Lord & Borthwick, 2008; Beckett, 2021), integrating existing understanding of attachment theory and placement planning with a theoretical understanding of trauma, to present a clear framework that can support practitioners across disciplines when undertaking sibling assessments.

This is no simple task, and the two volumes presented here reflect the complexity of the challenge through the range of theoretical and practical issues they consider. The first volume helpfully begins with reflections on theoretical coherence and how we can sustain our own intellectual and emotional coherence as we practice within this complex, contested field. The authors challenge us as both organisations and individuals to reflect on the decisions we make and to recognise the constraints that sometimes shape our practice, shifting our focus or diluting our conceptual thinking. At the heart of the first volume is a theoretical presentation of how attachment relationships and brain development can be affected by traumatic experience and how this may affect each child uniquely. Throughout, the child's voice and identity are brought to mind, through research and rich case examples, drawing on the authors' combined therapeutic experience and practice wisdom to demonstrate how theory can be applied to children's experiences both as individuals and within sibling groups. The case material supports the reader to really engage in applying and understanding the concepts being discussed. The final section of Part I focuses directly on listening to and understanding the child through a trauma-informed lens, encouraging us as practitioners to make meaning out of presenting behaviour and conversations with children, to put these into context, while checking out our understanding with the child themselves and honouring their experience and perspectives.

Volume two continues the authors' theoretical framework in more detail, applying their ideas to specific areas of practical issues such as decision-making about keeping siblings together or placing separately, evaluating the benefits and potential risks of sibling contact, and understanding the implications of life story work within a trauma-informed framework. The authors also present their distinct, integrative model for trauma-informed practice, offering practitioners a template for future sibling assessment. An additional strength of this work is how the experience and voice of the child is threaded through each discussion, urging the reader to consider each child's distinctive developmental needs within the wider decision-making framework. Throughout, the authors sustain the coherence of their own practice model, balancing their analysis through both attachment and trauma-informed lenses, integrating relevant research evidence from a wide range of disciplines and sources to inform their discussion.

Finally, the book returns to core issues of self-awareness and self-care, highlighting the importance of developmental, reflective supervision and the obligations of employing organisations and managers to help sustain staff who are engaged in this field of practice, highlighting the potential risks of vicarious trauma and moral injury for practitioners who work without appropriate support mechanisms.

I feel renewed awe and respect for the authors when I consider the scope and ambition of these volumes. Readers searching for a simple checklist approach to assessment will be disappointed. The texts provide a comprehensive framework for sibling assessment, mirroring the complex, multi-dimensional nature of practice in this field, while integrating complex theoretical ideas and practice examples with humanity and authenticity. The authors acknowledge the potential challenges and dilemmas of sibling assessment with compassion and congruence, offering many helpful strategies to improve and support our understanding and decision-making. As such, they provide an innovative and illuminating addition to the practice literature and a valuable tool to inform our growing understanding and practice in this complex area.

Dr Peter Ayling
University of Worcester

References

Beckett, S. (2021) *Beyond Together or Apart: Planning for, assessing and placing sibling groups. Good Practice Guide*. London: Coram BAAF.

Lord, J. and Borthwick, S. (2008, 2014) *Together or Apart? Assessing Siblings for Permanent Placement*. 2nd edn. London: Coram BAAF.

Shakespeare, W. (1594/ 2024) *The Comedy of Errors (Oxford World's Classics)*. Oxford: Oxford University Press.

Acknowledgements

Our thanks to our publisher, Routledge, with particular appreciation to Alice Maher, Manon Berset, Anna Moore, and Prisha Revar; to our team at Tiptoes Child Therapy Services; and to all at the British Association of Play Therapists (BAPT).

We are inspired by those who have taught us, including John Briere, Colin Ross, Ellert Nijenhuis, Cathy Steel, Melanie Watt, Janina Fisher, Virginia Ryan, Pat Ogden, and the Sensorimotor Psychotherapy Institute, Anne Bannister, Ann Cattanach, Eliana Gill, Richard Schwartz, and all at IFS Training UK, Rise Vanfleet.

Special thanks to Peter Ayling, Di Gammage, Ruth Lazarus, Lorna Hauff, and Martin Calder who believed in this book.

About the Authors

Tim Woodhouse is a certified advanced sensorimotor psychotherapist, social worker, play therapist, and internal family systems therapist who is trained in a wide range of associated therapies. His social work career started in 1984, working with children with disabilities, terminal illness, and developmental issues across residential, field work, adoption, fostering, investigation, and court assessments before specialising in all aspects of sexual abuse and sexual harm. He worked on the NSPCC, Child Sexual Abuse Consultancy, helped establish the UK's first children's SARC in Manchester, and was an investigating officer on the Waterhouse Inquiry. He is the founder and a director of Tiptoes Child Therapy Services, a specialist service for children, siblings, and families affected by sexual abuse, sexual harm, and developmental trauma.

Norma Howes, CQSW, ADSW, DCFS, MSc, has worked as a social worker, child forensic psychologist, and is now a sensorimotor psychotherapist and EMDR practitioner. She started her career as a trainee social worker in 1970 in Strathclyde. She is now involved in training agency staff and other therapists on all aspects of childhood trauma, specialising in assessing/treating victims and perpetrators of sexual and physical assault, a clinical supervisor, author, provider of clinical governance and governmental advice nationally and internationally. She has a private practice working with adults and children who have experienced significant harm as children and/or as adults. She values working with both adults and children as this enables the adults' articulation to help the children and the children's voices to help the adults. She is especially interested in the impact that trauma, abuse, and domestic abuse (in childhood and then across the lifespan) has on attachment, the survival strategies needed at the time, and how these inform consequent relationships and behaviours (especially between siblings).

Prologue

Norma and Tim met in the mid-1990s sharing a belief that children who have lived through developmental trauma needed services designed and delivered with depth, humility, and rigour. The title 'The Sibling Paradox' reflects a simple truth of trauma-informed practice: paradoxes appear everywhere, especially when deciding who should live with whom. A parent can be both a haven and a hazard, a sibling, a closest ally, and a fiercest rival. Naming these contradictions matters. When we map a child's extended chronology, the paradoxes which surface can help guide planning, rather than distort it.

Before any assessment, practitioners must notice their own starting points, 'siblings should always stay together' or 'separation is safer.' Either stance narrows vision and reduces possibility, whereas maintaining an open mind invites the full vista and the possibility of opportunities.

Human cognition seeks confirmation of pre-existing beliefs and avoids the dissonance of contradictory evidence. Serious Case Reviews and Public Inquiries, including the Cleveland and Orkney, show how questions can be framed to fit a belief, producing fragile conclusions. Lord Clyde advised a neutral stance of neither belief nor disbelief of views, but being able to hold both sides of a paradox that can withhold scrutiny. Even today, following the collapse of the Carl Beech case, public statements implied officers were trained to believe allegations. In fact, for decades, child-interview training has emphasised neutrality. The paradoxes abound: Was adult-focused training different? Were officers not following protocol? Was the Commissioner poorly briefed, or expressing a personal belief? Only by acknowledging and exploring these paradoxes can sound conclusions be reached.

Sibling assessments require the same discipline to identify, question, and weigh-up the paradoxes lived by children and embedded in our assumptions, research, and statutory guidance. Only then can we make informed, potentially life-changing decisions.

Some repeatedly found paradoxes include:

- Internalised coping/externalised behaviours
- Attention-seeking/attachment-seeking

- Together/apart
- Best friends/sworn enemies
- Age-appropriate grief/trauma bonds
- Clinging to damaging contact/rejecting all ties
- 'Contact'/'family time' or 'golden time'
- Parents' needs/child/ren's needs
- Prioritising one child's needs/keeping siblings together
- Stability of placement/need for movement or therapy
- Life story work as integration/triggering trauma/dissociation
- Hopes/fears
- Adoption/long-term foster care
- Staying with extended family/starting anew
- Children's needs now/adults' reflections on their own sibling histories
- Lived experience/professional expertise

Engaging with these paradoxes openly and reflectively leads to more ethical and balanced recommendations.

Both authors began as Local Authority social workers and now work in the independent sector. Frontline experience matters because most decisions about children's futures are made there. The context has shifted markedly over 40 years. Local government cuts were already well underway in the 1980s and have persisted, reshaping and cutting services to critical levels. Smaller workforces carry higher pressures and a greater chance of burnout, then requires accessible, easily understood, and implemented high-quality guidance that aids professionals in gathering, analysing, decision-making, and relaying information that will echo across each child and their siblings' lives.

Social work delivery models have cycled through generic, specialist, patch/area models, long and short-term teams. Teams have been replaced with 'hot-desking' and working from home. Balanced multi-experienced teams have often been replaced by fluid agency staffing with the undesired effect of inconsistency and change. The context, support systems and the beliefs of the individuals and teams vary considerably, so too their value base and world views. To promote consistency, a clear framework, one that keeps outcomes anchored in reflective practice and current knowledge and not in an individual's untested preferences.

Service divisions, prevention, child protective/safeguarding, investigative/court, placement teams (fostering, adoption, residential), therapeutic services, and leaving care bring different foci and beliefs about 'what works.' Decisions can shift with changes of practitioner or team reorganisations, creating further instability for children.

As Blom-Cooper's enquiry into the death of Jasmin Beckford noted, weaknesses in training, supervision, and allocation have far-reaching consequences. A transparent format for how decisions are made and what support will follow helps families and professionals understand reasons, conditions for review, and thresholds for change, even if those decisions are disputed.

Specialist Local Authority trauma teams have dwindled. CAMHS provision for looked-after children in some areas has been dismantled entirely, and other services reduced whilst facing increased demand. With fewer specialist colleagues or services to consult, practitioners can be left floundering for support with the many controversial and difficult decisions they have to make.

Much training has shifted towards online delivery. There is a paradox here too. Whilst virtual connection increases capacity to see other people, its lack of human presence further feeds into isolation and disconnection. The learning which builds reflective capacity, tolerates or invites challenge, and integrates left-brain knowledge with right-brain empathic attunement is impossible to achieve behind a screen responding to slides and quizzes. The further we move away from creative, experiential, challenging, multidisciplinary, face-to-face human learning and relationship building, the harder it becomes to render coherent judgements about human care relationships, including siblings. It has to be lived and experienced.

So Why This Book?

Their shared curiosity is not only about the strengths, gifts, and needs of individuals, but about why children and families sometimes present in chaotic, rigid, inconsistent, stuck, dangerous, or baffling ways. That curiosity led them to deepen their therapeutic training across multiple contemporary modalities, whilst continuing to assess and report for Magistrates, County, and High Courts.

This led to undertaking and continuing with training to gain further therapeutic qualifications and current knowledge in this rapidly expanding field. Both now work primarily as therapists and have a joint experience exceeding 80 years. They also assess and report on family functioning for Magistrates, County, and High Courts.A comment about the need for more informed assessments and planning when considering whether siblings could live together or may need to be split, followed by the need for any future contact to have a clear purpose, became this book.

Increasing numbers of children are being seen whose plans have been shaped by assessments which were descriptive but lacked analysis, where trauma-informed questions were not asked, where behaviours were not understood as distress responses, where contact lacked purpose and structure, where sibling placements lacked a coherent formulation, and where multiple therapeutic programs were implemented without goals, reviews, or analysis of change, regression, or stuckness. Placements threatened by the legacy of decisions not reviewed in the light of new information became increasingly commonplace.

The combination of social work and robust therapeutic training alongside professional longevity offers a perspective on the pressures practitioners face when making decisions which may shape a whole life. Work with families requires holding paradoxical, competing needs in mind while keeping the child's welfare paramount. Listening carefully to all siblings' wishes and feelings, including when they disagree or seemingly agree.

This volume aims to deepen understanding of developmental and complex trauma and its impact these have on a child, sibling, or adult's capacity to:

- Take in information, process, understand, or present a view.
- Develop a deeper understanding of the limitations of Gillick or Fraser competence.
- To understand what must happen for lasting change to occur.
- Consider wishes and feelings, make the distinction between wants or needs, and use this to inform decision-making.
- Consider the developmental age/ability of the child to determine a timescale for the outcome.
- See the paradox in the 'ability' of a number of young people who can sometimes be seen as having competence and the danger in not seeing the 'sometimes.'
- Recognise a sibling placed with the wrong sibling or with the right sibling in the right or the wrong or the least-worst placement.
- Seriously consider the impact of siblings joining late or being removed early and other changes in the sibling group.
- Avoid arranging contact with no clear purpose, plan, or content.

It also invites practitioners to:

- Weigh developmental age when setting timescales.
- Recognise when siblings are with the right/wrong sibling, in the right/wrong/least-worst placement.
- Consider late entrants and early removals in sibling groups.
- Avoid purposeless contact; define goals, structure content, prepare, and debrief participants, and review intervention impact.

This book is neither pro- nor anti-sibling contact. It is pro-purposeful contact aligned to assessed needs, with content designed to support safety, regulation, relationship, and refection.

Sources and Stance

The foundations of this book are enduring social work texts, enriched by research on trauma's impact on children, siblings, adults, families, and practitioners; by child development, psychopathology, and neuroscience; and by therapeutic literature that challenges assumptions. Above all, the heart of this book centres on the lived experiences of children and families across eight combined decades: siblings well-matched and thriving, siblings together who should not have been, siblings apart who may have flourished together, reunifications made too early or too late, and separations made too early or too late.

This book is not about blame. It will not blame individuals, teams, organisations, governments, or finance. This book is about curiosity and challenge. Challenge of beliefs, views, values, sentiments, and maybe, even cultural, faith, or other personal identity markers.

This book uses each child's gender pronouns where known; otherwise, language is kept in a non-gendered format. Where quotes are used, the original author's terms are used.

It is hoped this book will become essential reading for anyone meeting children where conversations touch the complex, often paradoxical territory of sibling relationships, together or separated, and those who plan contact. May it support clear, courageous, reflective practice, and help all of us hear what is said, unsaid, and not yet sayable in children's words, behaviours, and silences.

Afterword

These two volumes are filled with case examples. They are based on real people from a combined 80-plus years of practice. To preserve the anonymity and confidentiality of service users, all case material in the book has been altered, and pseudonyms are used throughout. Where actual case material is used, explicit permission for this has been given. Other examples are composite case materials which have been developed. After giving a recent keynote, an attendee came up afterwards and stated that she and her colleague were still working with a family that was given as a case example in the presentation—it was not the family being presented, it just felt like it to the attendee. These case examples will resonate because there are only a finite number of circumstances that can be presented, a lot for sure, but finite.

Part I

Foundations
Values, Attitudes, Beliefs, and Biases

Chapter 1

One Hand Clapping
Coherence in Fragmented Practice

Social work in the UK has become polarised, particularly in the realm of safeguarding and the court system, resulting in the frequently asked question 'Are you child or parent focused?' which is more often delivered as a statement. This leads to a judgement on how one is seen to carry out a particular intervention: 'She/he is child focused/led,' 'She/he is parent focused led.' Without apology, this book will have the siblings at the forefront, centre, and heart of the focus.

Dr Seuss's (1954) iconic line 'A person's a person no matter how small' could represent the microcosm to remember children are not a different species, and yet, it is true, they are treated differently. In some ways, a great job is done in protecting children's status as vulnerable seedlings that require nurture and attention in an optimum environment and then paradoxically do something really crass and behave in ways no-one would dream of behaving with an adult, for example, send them to their bedroom, the naughty step, bellow at them, or even smack them to teach them about consequences.

The macrocosm, therefore, may be represented by Mandela's address at the launch of his children's fund in Pretoria on the 8th of May 1995, 'There can be no keener revelation of a society's soul than the way in which it treats its children.' When he talked about the 'National abuse of a generation by a society it should have been able to trust' ironically, and perhaps unbeknown to him, he was talking about the very behaviour that causes trauma bonds in families. It is an incoherence such as this that led the statesman Frederick Douglass, in 1885, to hold a series of dialogues with slave-owners who could not or would not see the immorality slavery represented when he said, 'It is easier to build strong children than to repair broken men.' When it is known that the outcome of a poor start in life, littered with adverse childhood experiences, increases poor outcomes in adulthood, and yet there is nothing done to prevent these from occurring in the first place or to put in the reparative work required. The result is future generations who will continue to experience the same outcomes.

DOI: 10.4324/9781003724797-2

Scott Peck in 1978 stated

> The feeling of being valuable – I am a valuable person is essential to mental health and is a cornerstone of self-discipline. It is a direct product of parental love. Such a conviction must be gained in childhood. It is extremely difficult to acquire it in adulthood.'

The growth in knowledge of the impact of trauma suggests he was right and therefore governments need to shift their emphasis to develop safer societies whilst simultaneously investing in both prevention and reparative services. Neuroscience, 'child development, and trauma studies have advanced significantly over the last 40 years, and, as a result, we now know there are not just explanations for, but greater evidence that, different types of parenting, both positive and negative, impact on all aspects of child development which have implications for their outcomes in later life.

Being child-centred does not negate the ability to work with parents and carers; on the contrary, it demands it and enables the child to be seen within that hurt or hurting adult. If the behaviour or needs of the parent/s are ignored, there can be no expectation of change in the life experiences of the siblings. The ability and capacity to work effectively with all the members of the household is needed, or as Richard Schwartz helpfully reflected, 'Imbalanced systems, whether internal or external, will tend to polarize' (1997).

Case Example: Mike and Simon

Mike, aged 10, and his brother Simon, aged 6, were placed together long-term with first-time foster carers. This was their third foster home. On the third visit, the male foster carer asked to speak with the social worker about his growing anger towards Mike. He admitted he disliked himself for feeling this way and, worse, that the previous day he had found himself wanting to hit Mike. The social worker immediately wondered whether Mike should remain in the placement and said she would speak with her manager. By chance, before speaking to her manager, she spoke with Mike's therapist about the likely disruption to the placement and the possibility of Mike moving, with or without his brother. The therapist grew curious about the carer's feelings and agreed to speak with him to assess any immediate risk and explore whether a resolution could be found to keep Mike in placement.

The therapist began by asking for a detailed account of the moments before, during, and after the carer wanted to hit Mike, pausing frequently to reflect on and locate that feeling in the carer's body. What emerged was that the carer was, in fact, a deeply empathic man, desperate to show Mike that someone was truly there for him, something the carer had lacked in his own childhood. He described Mike entering the room and standing silently, not responding to questions about his day or how he felt, only wearing what he called a 'stupid' grin. The carer wanted an answer, not that 'empty feeling' radiating from Mike in powerful waves. He recognised that same feeling from his own childhood and, rather than sharing that connection, intensified his questioning, hoping to show he cared and as a result, this pushed Mike further away.

The carer suddenly stood up and said, 'That's when I wanted to hit him. But I didn't. I went into the kitchen,' and sat back down. The therapist took a breath and slowly released it, consciously modelling the need to pause, breathe, and reflect. She invited him to consider the tone he used when questioning Mike. He was startled to recognise the depth of his anger and how this might have sounded. He also realised how frightening it must have been for Mike when he stood so suddenly to walk away, effectively abandoning him.

More importantly, he recognised that whilst his feelings were triggered by Mike, they did not belong to Mike. They were his own: feelings of emptiness, helplessness, hopelessness; anger towards his father for the harm he caused; anger towards his mother for failing to protect him. All were stirred by that empty, 'stupid' grin he saw on Mike's face, and also anger with himself, for hearing and almost echoing his own father's threat to 'smack that grin off your face,' a phrase he had vowed never to say to a child. Individual sessions and then couple work with the carers, alongside Mike's therapy, enabled the placement to safely continue.

Fundamentally, social work decision-making juggles the differing needs of all the family members. It is the lens through which the family situation is viewed, and the outcome will vary accordingly (Reamer 2013). There is a direct correlation between how the world is seen, how interventions are initiated, the impact on the siblings and their family, and ultimately the outcomes for those siblings and those around them.

In one Local Authority where the services had been split into areas or 'patches,' there was an obvious split between two areas in how their interventions with children were delivered. Whilst in one area this was driven by the pervading belief 'keep children in their families at all costs,' in another area the unspoken belief, 'remove children at all costs,' was practiced and the contrast in decision-making and practice was clearly evident.

The co-existence of these two paradoxical views resulted in service users having very different outcomes. Interventions offered were based on little more than a postcode lottery. Services lacked continuity, held opposing rigid beliefs, and lacked model coherence. When one service manager was off sick and the other covered, the pressure to change service delivery on some particular cases completely changed the direction of the intervention, only to be reversed again when the usual service manager returned.

The service managers here held core beliefs that were demonstrated in their employee candidate interviews, which started with the question, 'Are you a dove or a hawk?' pertaining to the use of statutory powers to remove children or to provide support to keep children in families or to being either parent or child-centred. An analogy that is separatist, somewhat fragmented in its existence, and actively supported the continuation of this divide. The notion that it is even healthy to be so polarised is anathema. Being in the middle of these two positions, as another service manager was, put her in danger of being hailed a 'fence-sitter.' This middle ground, from a positive viewpoint, holds the most capacity for movement and flexibility, but arguably from the negative view is where the most danger of indecision and drift can occur.

The personal view of the service manager influenced the views of the team managers who were already selected for their general outlook and how they would serve their area. In turn, their views influenced the direction of the social worker's views through selection, supervision, and training. Kadushin and Harkness (2014) state, 'Because most social workers perform their professional functions within an agency, they find themselves in a bureaucratic structure in contact with the supervision that a bureaucracy requires,' and further, 'Social workers are valued in terms of their identification with, acceptance of and adherence to agency policy and procedures.' Regular supervision and training are essential requirements for social workers, but how they are used can significantly influence individual social workers and maintain agency outlook.

There was contact between the service managers, but there was little opportunity for team managers or social workers from the other areas to meet, creating fewer chances for open discussion, debate, reflection, challenge, or change, and thus the status quo remained. Personally held views can dictate the whole direction of service delivery. This can occur at any point in the provision of a service.

Case Example: Becky and Tom

Siblings Becky (12) and Tom (10) were placed together in an independent fostering agency (IFA) placement with two foster carers, Cicely and Emmett. The children had lived there for two-thirds of their lives. They lived in the same family environment and, as far as could be known, had the same family experiences. Yet they coped in very different ways. Tom internalised his distress; Becky externalised hers, often the reverse of what is expected in 'gendered responses.' This difference is not unusual, but it is not gender-based. It makes sense that they developed different strategies. If both had used the same strategy, their chances of survival would not have increased. Neither child would have had their needs met. They would have remained in direct competition with each other. These strategies were not consciously chosen but were subconscious survival methods in a dangerous environment.

The siblings were so embedded in their individual coping styles that they could not connect with each other, or their carers, in a meaningful or transformative way. For change to occur, their experiences and resulting strategies needed to be understood so that the support necessary for change could be implemented. They needed parenting that was essentially loving and authoritative, but also trauma-informed.

Emett believed that childcare, whether for his own or foster children, was Cicely's responsibility. He came across as dismissive, detached, and indifferent, giving the impression he held no strong views about the children. Cicely was anxious and compulsively talked. She both complained about her husband's indifference and yet defended him fiercely. There was much to consider about their relationship: She was overly positive about 'her Tom,' whilst she scapegoated Becky. She couldn't see that both children were struggling. Only Becky's externalising behaviour was viewed as problematic.

The couple did not support each other; Emmett lacked the will to support his wife. She was riddled with anxiety and self-doubt, which led to swings between irritation and emotional collapse. This created inconsistency in her responses and her availability to the children. Although the placement was physically safe, several factors got in the way of the children's progress. They had been removed from danger but had not yet been helped to process or release their experience of danger. This limited their ability to grow individually or to form a healthy sibling relationship. They were cared for by foster carers who, due to their own unmet needs and the toxicity and co-dependency of their relationship, could not model a healthy relationship or empathically attune to the children's needs.

Becky was at risk of a placement disruption. If this occurred, then difficult decisions would follow: Should Becky move alone? Should both children move? Could or should they be placed together? Each possibility carried potentially lifelong consequences.

The supervising social worker, tasked with supporting the family, carried multiple tensions. Although her remit was to support the foster carers, she did not lose sight of her responsibility for the children's well-being. She could clearly see the oppressive relationship between the carers and their individual needs. Despite considerable work, she could not facilitate lasting change. Emmett was passive in his resistance but also at times passively aggressive. Though he was often booked onto in-house training, he never attended, suggesting he was displaying disguised compliance. He took part in supervision, offered platitudes, and continued his belligerent behaviour. Cicely was inconsistent with the children and repeatedly voiced her frustrations about Becky and Emmett and was unwilling or unable to take or maintain advice.

The social worker felt stuck. She couldn't create change for the children because she could not effect change in the carers, either individually or as a couple. It became impossible to determine how much of the children's behaviour was due to past or current trauma, how much their relationship had been shaped by that trauma, or how much the carers' behaviour and relationship were preventing progress.

Tensions then emerged with her team manager, who insisted the carers should be sent for more training. This was arranged and whilst Cicely attended and had moments of insight, she continued to complain about both her husband and Becky. It was no surprise that Emmett continued to fail to attend. The team questioned why the supervising social worker could not create change or reduce the ongoing risk of the disruption Cicely continued to threaten. The team manager escalated the case to the service manager, who was adamant that this was a long-term placement and must not break down, a view that may or may not have been about the child's needs. Two interventions were proposed: that the supervising social worker must be failing and therefore should be sent on further training and that respite care be arranged for Becky, without discussion of the possible contra-indications of such a provision.

This agency like every service—be it public, voluntary, or private sector—has its own raison d'être. It will largely be directed by that aim or goal through its statement of purpose, associated values, and fundamental beliefs.

These fundamental beliefs are in place to reduce the impact of further harm on those worked with, not only on the children, their families, and friends but also on the professional systems that surround or support them. This system of having an identified work-based culture, once popular in the 1980s, appeared to have lost favour in the changing faces of both social work and schools of therapy and perhaps is one of the reasons why there is a struggle with decision-making, but it is returning in the 'new' concept of Contextual Safeguarding (Firmin 2020). Model Coherency (Wolfensberger 1999) provides a clear framework that allows us to look at where decision-making can become impaired by views that are compromised, dogmatic, rushed, assumed, delayed, confused, acrimonious, entrenched, or significantly blaming. Positively viewed, in 1973 Wolfensberger had already asked, 'Does the service provide a coherent program in which a number of variables combine harmoniously so as to meet the specific needs of each client at this particular time of his life?' This is not just about a service being fit for purpose but life-enhancing.

Using the Model Coherency approach with this IFA example, the lack of progress in the children's recovery can be understood in how the protagonists are viewed or understood. This can then create various potential working hypotheses:

Is Becky:

1. Experiencing intrusive experiences as a result of her traumatic past?
2. Or being triggered by living with her brother as a result of shared past experiences?
3. Resentful of her brother's positive attention from Cicely?
4. Is she seen as a 'non-compliant/problem/difficult/bad' child? (These words are often used when people cannot make sense of the behaviour they see in a child.)
5. Responding to Emmett's distant and dismissive nature?
6. Reacting to Cicely's inconsistency and scapegoating behaviour?
7. Or affected by the foster carers' relationship?
8. A combination of the above?
9. Or indeed something else?

Hypothesis would have to be developed for Tom, Cicely, and Emmett. Would these be the same or different questions? How each person is viewed is likely to impact the type or level of support they receive, if any.

The requirement is to separate the needs of the children, how and why they react individually, from how and why they react together is evident. If these behaviours are triggered, intensified, regressed, or skewed as a result of their carers' responses, behaviours, or beliefs, this becomes vital information which will inform and become part of the assessment of the children's needs. An assessment or re-assessment is a difficult time for carers and parents who are already struggling to cope. To become carers or adopters, they have already gone through their own assessment and may feel resentful, fearful, or bewildered as a result.

How the children are viewed through these hypotheses will be directly linked to how they are treated and responded to. A child who is co-operative, compliant, or able is more likely to be seen as trying, or worthy, and more likely to have their actual unmet needs missed with the predictable mantra: 'Oh, she's fine.' 'Oh, he's okay.' A child who is seen as resistant, controlling, rejecting, harmful, aggressive, and/or failing is prone to be scapegoated, labelled, or blamed. In this example, neither child was 'okay' or 'fine.' There was no understanding that the children's Internal Working Model, the way they developed their strategies to manage their early experiences, was informing their view of and understanding of the world. This was being expressed in their presentation. Perry (1995) calls this 'emotional states becoming behavioural traits.' Their coping strategies, necessary at the time, were the answer to the problem and not the problem. It is regrettable tmany years can be lost in recovery when the focus of work and interventions are on the child's or adult's answer to the problem rather than by resolving the problem, making the answer redundant.

It's not mandatory to like every child, young person, or adult. This wouldn't be realistic, and it would also put an unnecessary burden on the parent, carer, or professional to achieve this. It could evoke incongruence if people believed this was necessary. Incongruence leads to incoherence and is therefore contrary to this model. Being authentic and having the ability to talk openly and positively about the feelings and views being held enable exploration and understanding.

Case Example: Joel

Joel, age seven, was one of the first children worked with by the therapist in a then-new attachment service. This service, developed in the mid 90s, had been designed to provide integrated services for children with disorganised attachment patterns. On meeting Joel for the first time, the therapist was immediately struck by an unwelcome feeling of dislike for Joel. This was uncomfortable on several levels. The therapist, entering the field of children's services over ten years previously was as a direct result of wanting to make a difference in the lives of children and not to contribute to the harm they had experienced by self-generated negativity. Having achieved internal permission to notice feelings (acknowledgement), there was then a reliance on colleagues' generosity and acceptance to be able to 'confess' having these strong feelings. This allowed these feelings to be explored individually and with the team.

'Disorganised' children can be difficult to like. They are so scared and discombobulated by their belief that danger is all around them and have no workable strategy to manage that danger. A coherent response to danger is to stay away from it. But when the experience of danger is from the adults the child depends on to be looked after and cared for, the child cannot escape from the danger. Children innately require safety and trust. A way must be found to keep that perceived, ever-present threat at bay. The best way to reduce the proximity of others is to present in ways that provoke dislike.

The therapist's initial feeling of dread and the internal thought, 'How am I going to survive the next three years of therapy with this child' (the average duration of a disorganised child's therapy when placed in a solo placement without contact issues, court or police involvement and secure supportive carers) resulted in feeling, 'I must be a bad person/therapist,' was transformed to a sense of relief that having these feelings was actually a natural response to Joel's strategies. How could this be a therapist's, or indeed any adult's natural response, to not liking a child? One answer is that disorganised children experience proximity, caregiving, or kindness as dangerous, and use their perfectly honed responses to that danger in ways that are most likely to succeed in repelling it. On seeing and understanding behaviour as purely a survival strategy, feelings of dislike make sense. They are coherent and can then be discharged, enabling how the child is viewed to shift.

Becky and Tom's placement was not the cause of their survival behaviour strategies but did little to ameliorate them. Without understanding the context in which the children are placed, their presentation and relationship cannot be fully understood, especially when these may vary in differing contexts or placements such as school or respite. Assessing any sibling relationship cannot be undertaken in isolation from their current environment. How their carers are viewed is also likely to result in the type or level of support they are given, and then how well they receive and act on that support.

Case Example: Jayne and Saul

Jayne and Saul were new to fostering and had their own birth daughter aged eight. The couple met whilst Saul was on holiday in Jayne's home country. Jayne had experienced neglect and abuse as a child. She was effectively a prisoner of her own family history and had previously been unable to move away from them. Saul did not know at that time how Jayne viewed him as periodically her ticket out of entrapment, her knight in shining armour or her soul mate. Saul grew up in an environment where others' needs were more important than his own and that sense of responsibility essentially required reliability. His job, for 20 years, was a metaphor for both the need for reliability and his requirement to look out for the needs of others. Jayne was equally unaware of her husband's need to rescue and neither saw how those truths would impact on how they saw their relationship.

Six-year-old Abbey, who experienced Fabricated or Induced Illness (FII) at the hands of her mother and sexual abuse by her mother's boyfriend, was placed with them. Abbey ignored Jayne, was overly focused on Saul and targeted their birth daughter. Jayne saw Abbey as sexualised towards Saul, a behaviour he minimised. Saul saw her as a little girl who needed reassurance and love and felt, due to her background, she had missed so many positive experiences. He believed it was his responsibility to help her recover. As the situation deteriorated, Jayne saw her husband as a rescuer who was over-focused on Abbey. This made her question their relationship. He was no longer her knight in shining armour. She realised three things: that theirs was not a healthy relationship, he had failed as her knight, and he was choosing Abbey over their family. She gave the ultimatum to choose between his wife and child or Abbey. Saul then went into an existential crisis. His belief system was that Abbey needed him to be reliable and dependable and therefore he should never give up; paradoxically, on the other hand, to carry on would mean losing his family.

The reality was that the depth of the foster carers' experiences was not fully assessed. The current assessment processes in either adoption or fostering do not go to that depth. When either the carer or child assessment processes or both are flawed, then so too will the matching processes. How much more complicated then would placing two or more siblings be?

Becky and Tom's foster carers were being supported by their supervising social worker, who was following her child-centred practice. She could hold the apparent needs of both children so far as she could see them but found it hard to understand the sibling relationship as a result of the foster carers' presentation. Despite increased supervision, spot checks, and the availability of training and support groups, she was unable to make any changes. The placement for Becky was becoming untenable. The supervising social worker began to blame the carers. The response she received from the management team became increasingly reactive in blaming her and counter-productive in their strategy of providing respite care. The social worker felt judged and then increasingly judged the carers, mirroring how Cicely was behaving towards Becky.

Children are not brought into the care system when everything is ok; they are brought in when something has gone significantly wrong at home, either by omission or commission. Their experiences are often toxic, and that toxicity spreads between people. They are removed from a place of danger, but what is often forgotten is that the place of danger has not been removed from their heads, their consciousness, their bodies, or their beliefs. It is quite literally carried in them. They are then placed with carers, adopters, connected carers, or in children's homes, where this carried toxicity is allowed to spread to other people. Research shows those drawn to the caring professions, frontline carers, social workers, their managers, or those in connected supportive roles are more statistically likely to have faced ACEs and therefore are at greater peril of having carried their own exposure to toxic experiences with them.

Public, voluntary, and private sector agencies develop a rationale for their service. Their sector status is not necessarily an indicator of how they will function in terms of values, attitudes, or ethics. The significant factor is how they respond to situations such as those outlined above. Where the agency is unknowingly overtaken by that toxic soup, a mix from its own practitioners, providers, and the children's experiences, it can start to mirror the chaos in the children's own birth families.

Model Coherency requires a seamless flow of continuity from the lead of the organisation through to the children and families for whom they provide a service. Their statement of purpose is not a lifeless document but one that is believed and practised by that organisation's members. When a child or group of siblings comes to the service with a presentation that suggests they have been harmed, they require carers who are insightful enough to separate their own experiences from those of the child and who are then able to develop a sense of emotional containment, trust, and safety for that child. This can only occur when those parents or carers are supported by all the involved practitioners who are able to be insightful enough to recognise and acknowledge the difference between their own pain, the carers' experiences, and those belonging to the siblings.

In order to do this, practitioners also need to be supervised and supported by a management team that can add their own positive or negative experiences into the mix, whilst 'containing' the practitioner. Managers need the same consistency from their directorate. This is not the end of this cascade, as the views of Society, OFSTED, and Government also place an external pressure that will always be fluid, inconsistent, challenging, or oppositional. This is where the Directorate needs to hold the line in a manner that helps change attitudes, informs, and challenges policy whilst maintaining service integrity and protecting its service providers and service users in equal measure. Regrettably, this flow can and often does get blocked at any point in that cascade.

To make the most informed sibling assessment requires the most informed and coherent service delivery. To understand Becky's needs, it is not enough to work with just Becky or just Cicely. That doesn't create the sound of clapping but of one hand waving to no purpose. Intervention with only one aspect or 'hand' in the work needed results in one hand waving to no purpose. To be able to celebrate success needs two 'hands' to make the sound of clapping, to create an ovation needs the inclusion of Tom and Emmett.

Chapter 2

The Mirror in the Room

Self-Awareness in Sibling Decisions

The previous chapter outlined Model Coherency as a container for safe practice. It demonstrates that enabling children to be cared for by their parent or carer requires human consistency throughout the organisation. To create positive systemic change, care must be modelled to the carer by the practitioner, to the practitioner by the manager, and then throughout the organisation, and then modelled by governments and society. If Model Coherency was fully embedded in society, the required behaviours would be modelled back to organisations. The following example demonstrates that this does not always happen:

A practitioner, social worker, or therapist shares responsibility for the wellbeing of a child with their parents or carers. As discussed in the previous chapter, this is rarely possible in isolation. Yet many child therapists, particularly in educational settings, continue to see only the child. This is neither coherent nor congruent, though occasionally necessary. The practitioner plays a pivotal role in helping adults understand and respond to their child. Where the carer is open, this may be straightforward, but where there is resistance, it becomes more complex. Yet even this tension between modelling and resistance may not be the only challenge. A practitioner's assessment of a child's needs may be contested by a manager or by a school lacking understanding of the child, disagreeing with the practitioner's view, or struggling to accommodate the child's needs. Regardless of whether the practitioner is right or wrong, if unaware of this tension, complications are sure to follow.

The Team Around the Child (TAC) were one of the strongest ways to ensure a child's needs are met. It cannot be coherent if individuals' or teams' needs are overlooked. A team is only as strong as its most fragile member. This is not a judgement of individual competence, but a recognition that team members may carry gaps in knowledge or be triggered by a client's history resonating too closely to their own experience, other stressors, or life events, sometimes all at once. The 'weakest link' is not a fixed point. As Personal resilience fluctuates.

TACs were typically multidisciplinary, time-limited groups composed of professionals who may never have worked together before and my not meet again. These groups often function well, until they don't. Disruption can come from conflicting professional models, individual belief systems, or different ways of seeing the child. One essential challenge is knowing how to manage a professional argument. Another, equally vital, is knowing how to support a colleague who is stuck, defensive, or rigid, and to recognise that same state in oneself. This issue is notably explored in several serious case reviews and in the Beckford Inquiry (Blom-Cooper 1985), where serious professional disagreements were concealed to preserve a false sense of unity.

The first mission for each TAC member was to assess their own readiness to be a strong, empathic, knowledgeable, supportive, yet humble and curious advocate for the child or siblings. This is no small task when those engaged in social responsibility come from such varied and diverse personal and professional backgrounds.

Every human life experience varies and shapes how a person sees the world, often in subtle or unexpected ways. Parents' histories are a starting point. Their experience of care—who provided it and how it was received—shape generational patterns that can be both helpful and harmful (Fonagy 2004). Factors include ethnic origin, identity, ability, disability, health, faith, sexuality, gender, and how each of these was navigated. Added to this are their histories, how the couple met, compromised, and how their relationships were shaped by family, community, and geography. Whether a child is parented by birth parents, stepfamilies, grandparents, or others adds further layers to how the world is understood and experienced.

Self-awareness requires returning to one's own early experiences and understanding how these were internalised and normalised, whatever 'normal' means. Developmental experiences, the type of care received, family structure, friendships, financial circumstances, and place of upbringing all contribute to how adversity or resilience plays out.

The following three brief case studies explore how lived experience may influence what someone, who has chosen to work in social care, brings into a TAC meeting, should they choose to work in social care.

1. **Hannah and Devon** were raised in loving, working-class, financially stable families. Although their community faced social challenges, it remained cohesive, with a strong sense of identity and mutual support. On the surface, they appeared quite different; Devon became a gifted engineer, while Hannah entered social care, where she excelled and completed a PhD. Devon was quiet and laid back, yet quietly organised. Hannah was effusive and openly organised, but quietly laid back. They complemented one another and shared a deep love. But this was not a fairy tale; they disagreed and quarrelled but worked through their differences, knew each other's needs, and made space for both togetherness and individuality. They had four children later in life and were financially secure enough to enjoy parenting. They created structure and boundaries, attended school events, went on holidays, and sustained their personal interests.

When the children were in latency (six years to puberty, Freud 1905, 2010 ed.), Devon died suddenly. The family was naturally devastated. Despite this inconceivable loss, Hannah didn't fall apart, not simply because she would not, but because she could not; her children relied on her. She was held by a strong network of family, friends, community, and employers, which enabled her to hold her children in turn. In time, the intensity of grief subsided. The children missed their father, but they did not collapse. As young adults, they remained well-balanced, creative, empathic, articulate, and loving.

A history of safety, emotional literacy, and consistency enabled the siblings to cope. Grief-stricken, Hannah was resilient enough to keep going. She neither denied nor was incapacitated by her grief. She embraced it and enabled her children to do the same, giving them the space to experience it, own it, and grow from it. They could draw upon the resilience they developed before their father died.

2. **Alison and Mark** came from markedly different backgrounds. Mark grew up in a deprived working-class neighbourhood. His brother died in infancy. His childhood was overshadowed by domestic violence. His father was dominant, angry, and intolerant, and his mother was beaten into submission. Mark survived by retreating into books and gardening. Alison, by contrast, was raised in an upper middle-class academic family in a quiet, affluent village in Middle England. She was one of three siblings and thrived educationally. She and her siblings all turned away from careerism and profit, but they lived in comfort. Alison became pregnant young during a holiday romance but never saw the father again. Mark had married young and became a father. Contact with his son ended when the relationship collapsed.

Alison and Mark met when Alison's son was six. Their relationship developed, and they eventually married and had a child together. Their political leanings were socialist, and their outlook was liberal. Their parenting reflected this: perhaps not fully permissive but certainly marked by blurred and inconsistent boundaries. Their parenting styles fitted together like mismatched puzzle pieces. Alison's parenting resembled the tolerant, academic approach of her upbringing. Mark's was shaped by a fierce determination not to repeat his own childhood experience. They avoided restriction, abhorred discipline, and shied away from authority. In their desire not to exert power over the children, they also avoided setting expectations or enforcing consequences. They overcompensated, offering the children the freedom and material comfort that Mark, and to some extent Alison, had lacked.

Their three children had divergent outcomes. Mark's son grew up angry at the world, directing his rage outward, particularly towards his girlfriend. Alison's son internalised his anger. He became moody, intolerant, and irritable; his coping strategy turned inward. Their youngest, the child they had together, was both introverted and depressive. As an adolescent, he self-harmed and required significant support from mental health services for much of that period, which included several hospital admissions. Their sibling relationships became fractured and, as adults, they seldom stayed in contact.

3. **Carla and Marcus**. Carla was born into a British-Asian working-class family and raised alongside her three younger sisters. Her father worked long hours, often extended by post-work drinks at the pub. Her mother, a full-time parent, suffered from severe mental health difficulties. As a result, Carla increasingly took on the responsibility of caring for her siblings during an unforgiving, overtly racist, and intolerant period in time. Her husband, Marcus, was raised in an aspirational, middle-class British white family, with two brothers. His parents were university-educated, financially secure, and caring, though not emotionally demonstrative, arguably veering towards cold and detached. Carla and Marcus appeared to be a perfect match. They had a long courtship, moved in together, and eventually married. In time, they had two children, and Carla loved them both, although in truth, she favoured one.

She was highly organised and boundaried, but also strict, at times almost authoritarian. She shouted her expectations, offered little discussion, relied on concrete thinking, and could not comprehend why her children sometimes failed to meet her demands. Marcus was clear-thinking, quiet, and competitive. He was warm, but not demonstrative. He spent a great deal of time with his children, but in ways he understood, mainly through competitive sports, rather than imaginative play or relaxed engagement.

When a parenting challenge arose, Carla and Marcus would talk, debate, and sometimes argue. Marcus usually capitulated verbally, then continued parenting in his own style. Their two daughters succeeded academically, rarely tested boundaries, and complied with expectations. Both, however, presented as socially awkward, emotionally contained, and somewhat aloof. The favoured child went on to live abroad, but the other struggled to leave home. As adults, their sibling relationship resembled that of respectful colleagues, distant but polite, and largely disconnected.

Each of the parents described above worked in human services, most within social care. Parents and children alike bring their histories to their membership of TACs. Their experiences formed individual blueprints for caregiving and care-receiving relationships, a map of how their world is seen, and the structure of their belief systems.

People test their beliefs with siblings and friends, occasionally with colleagues, and most often in new relationships. How much is shared, challenged, or accepted can influence, but may not guarantee, change. This shapes the consistency of their parenting as parenting styles vary between authoritative, authoritarian, or permissive. But even where the style differs, consistency is less frightening than unpredictable inconsistency. To trust, children and siblings must not only be safe; they must feel safe. Inconsistency, chaos, and rigidity each threaten that felt sense.

Every professional in a TAC team had the potential to learn from families on how to reflect on their own value base. It is worth asking: How does each team member respond to the families they work with? What beliefs and experiences shape that response?

In Model Coherency, the mantra might be: If you would not value it for yourself, your child, or someone you love or respect, what makes it acceptable for anyone else? Then ask the questions:

Where do you place your values?
Which of the families described would you value for your own child, or the child of someone you love?
Do you have concerns? Are they about the parent, the child, or both?
How would you respond if one of the families presented to foster, adopt, or connect with others?
What if they were already fostering, and their history had not been disclosed?
What if one of these individuals were your colleague?

When a belief resonates with personal experience, it may create, for want of a better word, a blind spot. The refrain, 'It never did me any harm,' often used to justify physical punishment, illustrates how a person may internalise a harmful practice as normal or acceptable, particularly when their parent believed it too. Generationally shared experiences do not make them true; if they did, there would still be the birching of children or drowning of witches.

The role of the practitioner is not to judge but to be a conduit for change, and that cannot be done from a position of superiority. Immersion in the families is required to support them; this work is heuristic, almost having to breathe it. Carrying a stone in one's pocket, a quiet reminder from scripture, 'Let the one among you who is without sin cast the first stone' (John 8:7), can help guard against judgement and cultivate empathic curiosity over intrusive scrutiny. Bob Marley's lyrics in Judge Not (1962) echo this spirit of congruence and coherency.

When someone's choices harm another, especially a child, then judgement and intervention are not only warranted but essential. Doing nothing is not a neutral act; it is a decision with its own weight. Where action is required, it must be empowering for the individual, and herein lies a paradox. When a parent's choices harm their child, who needs empowerment? The law says the child. This is not a simplistic view; it is complex beyond measure. The consequences of empowerment, when there is no or little authority to safely put this into practice, need to be thought through. This is seen in well-intended work with victims of sexual or physical abuse who are coached to say 'no' when returning to unsafe situations. If no equivalent work has been done with the perpetrator or the protective adults, this strategy may place the victim at greater risk. Little children do not have the strength or weight, and older children do not have the power or authority to protect themselves. Self-safety work without complementary adult intervention does not make children safer. Worse, when 'no' fails and further harm follows, the child will carry more blame, feel responsible for the failure, and become less able to disclose further abuse.

Intolerable adversity does not build resilience, but low-level tolerable adversity, buffered by care and connection, can. Something must shift in the parent, in their parenting, and in their partnership. If the change needed cannot be made in a time frame that aligns with the child's needs, or if it does not make enough difference, then alternative care must be considered.

At some point, what may need to be said, honestly and compassionately, is:

'This is just ok enough for this child and parent,'
'This is the least-worst option,'
'It is no longer tenable for this child or parent to live like this, it is not ok.'

Equally, when one life impacts another positively, it should be recognised and celebrated. To engage in this work, as Marley reminds us, self-awareness of our own lived experience is vital. Everyone is driven by what has been lived. How do we know when we are ready to take on work that will change the trajectory of a family's life, affecting each member differently and deeply? When are we ready to make decisions that will send ripples through lives we may never see again? When are we ready to sit in a room with a parent or child, a TAC team, or a court of law, and either align with consensus or stand, alone, against it?

The starting point must always be the individual, I. Not 'I' as in ego, but as an internal compass, what I think, what I feel, what I believe. It means undertaking the work of surfacing those beliefs, understanding where they come from, about ourselves, and about others.

Each of the individuals described, Hannah, Alison, Mark, Carla, Marcus, would bring a different outlook when they entered this work, whether as a therapist, social worker, teacher, or support professional. Each would carry the imprint of their lived experience into every decision they made about the lives of children.

What is the personal work that needs to be undertaken? Alison and Mark provide an understanding of how their view of the world impacted on their own parenting experience. They need to be considered individually, even though they shared some of the same values. They both developed the belief that social intervention was inherently damaging, and that 'over-parenting' was oppressive and suffocated the free will, creativity, and natural curiosity of children. The result was Alison continually 'laughed off' her children's transgressions and boundary violations, made statements such as, 'Boys will be boys,' 'They are only children' and 'What harm can it do?' When her children crossed a boundary that resulted in them causing harm, she took it personally and felt violated herself. Her feeling that she had failed meant she then became stuck and found it hard to understand her children or to reconnect with them, resulting in them experiencing emotional neglect and abandonment. Mark's father was violent. His brother died as a result of what the family believed was an unnecessary medical procedure. Mark too developed the outlook that social intervention of any kind was something to be suspicious of and generally to be resisted. When life became too challenging for him, he retreated into his books and again, the children experienced abandonment and emotional neglect. Their children needed a sense of safety. The lack of parental boundaries and their consistent withdrawal contributed to their sons' presentations.

Carla and Marcus were almost opposite to this. The lack of safety in Carla's own childhood resulted in her becoming controlling in everything she did. Her own parenting style was not just inflexible but rigid. Where Marcus did not agree with Carla's decision-making, he took the line of least resistance, 'Anything for a quiet life,' and therefore did not provide any balance to his partner's parenting style. At work in her teaching role, Carla was irritated and opinionated about the young children she taught and was unable to be nurturing to them or others. She was left brain dominant; she could plan, process, analyse, store, and retrieve facts but was dismissive of anything that might relate to emotion, stating she did not have time for that. Not having time for something may mean that this is actually too scary to acknowledge or face. If she was able to accept the impact of her father's absence and her mother's mental health issues, she would then be compelled to acknowledge how she felt about having to take on the caretaking role of her sisters when she was still a child herself, followed by how having to do this had influenced her thinking, beliefs, and behaviour then and now. Carla would then have to acknowledge what she had missed out on in her childhood and review how she viewed her parents. As a result, she would have to see her world differently, question her relationship with her partner, and how they were raising their own children. Not investing in and not undertaking this work was underpinned by her subconscious fear, 'What if I am not strong enough to manage viewing my life experience differently?'

There is a refrain, 'You can't give to others, that which you have not received yourself.' This is probably to sweeping a statement and brings to mind the earlier quote by Peck, 'If you don't feel valuable through feeling loved, how do you emulate it for your children?' Children are congruence detectives; they can spot a lie. How often is the question, 'How are you?' answered with 'I'm fine, OK, alright' when feeling far from it? Or the question, 'Are you angry with me?' answered with, 'I'm not angry,' when actually filled with overwhelming rage.

Case Example: Finding and Using Self-Awareness

Karen was a health visitor, happily married, with a seven-year-old daughter. At work, she was hard to dislike, but colleagues often felt inadequate around her as she always completed her visits and paperwork, was efficient, and compliant with her agency's protocols and expectations. One day, she came home to find her daughter's toy out of place; it was in Karen's bedroom. When asked why, her daughter disclosed sexual abuse by her father. Though devastated, Karen's response was efficient and faultless; she contacted the Police and Social Services, ensured the medical was arranged at the Local Sexual Assault Referral Centre (SARC), and that the Achieving Best Evidence interview was on track. She contacted a therapy agency and reassured her daughter, keeping her informed of what would happen and why. She also took the necessary steps to prevent her husband from returning to the home.

In pre-therapy consultation, Karen described herself as, 'Fine.' But given the circumstances, the therapist suspected 'fine' meant she did not want to delve too deep, or indeed, let anyone in. With a gentle smile and nod of acceptance, the therapist offered the interpretation used by a survivor's charity, that 'fine' may mean feeling fucked-up, insecure, neurotic, and exhausted. Karen relaxed as the empathic delivery landed. She had been heard at the level she needed, allowing the assessment to begin. Had she not relaxed, time would have been needed to explore her resistance.

Karen completed the Trauma Symptom Checklist for Young Children (TSCYC, Briere 2005). The results were valid, neither over nor under-scored, but indicated a level of trauma suggesting her child would be presenting as highly dysregulated. What her child experienced was significant and it should not have happened. It should not have been perpetrated by her father, someone who should have kept her safe. Karen believed this was a one-off assault and whilst statistically unusual, no information to the contrary emerged. The therapist agreed the experience would have had an impact but questioned the dissonance between the scores. Karen had not described behaviours that would be congruent with such extreme dysregulation suggested by the scores, and the school would have raised concerns. With permission from mum, the school was contacted. They described a bright, articulate, popular child, recently somewhat withdrawn but not 'bouncing off the walls.'

These opposing views were gently shared. Some parent-scored assessments are accurate. Others reflect subconscious resonance with the parent's own history, and this can compromise their ability to manage or read their child's coping behaviours. Karen was asked to complete the TSI (Trauma Symptom Inventory, Briere 1995) to help distinguish what related to her and what related to her daughter, which she agreed to complete. Her results showed above-average dissociation, possibly at the level of a dissociative disorder, and the results required sensitive discussion. Sharing the outcomes was not framed diagnostically, but as a prompt to consider what made her scores look this way. Karen's response was to say: 'You think I'm mad, don't you?' The wrong response would have been, 'No, of course not.' Instead, the therapist took a breath to slow down and avoid rescuing her from her pain, then allowed a short pause to externally regulate her distress and hold her in her 'window,' and then in using her word, 'mad,' she was empathically told, 'There are no 'mad' or 'not mad' results, no rights or wrongs, only results that are what they are, and need our understanding.'

This gentle holding allowed Karen to cry. She disclosed her father had been a violent alcoholic, and her mother had a life-debilitating mental illness. She had cared for her mother and sister because neither could care for themselves, let alone her. She kept the house immaculate, meals ready, and tried to avoid anything that would trigger her father's wrath. But his wrath came anyway. She described stealing money from his pockets while he slept to buy food for the next day. On one occasion, in fear for their lives, she hid her mother and sister. Her father demanded to know their whereabouts and threatened to kill them, lifting Karen off her feet by the throat, pinning her to a wall. She was 9 years old and still refused to tell.

The therapist acknowledged the terror, bravery, and tenacity of the child she once was, and the loneliness she endured. Then she affirmed that no little girl should carry so much responsibility or danger, that all little girls should be loved and protected. Karen wept again. She remembered how, in the face of her father's violence, her body would freeze, a hyper-aroused response. She could not afford to feel and said that if she did, she would have been unable to do what needed doing, so she cut off her feelings. She paused, then said, with remarkable insight, 'But those feelings never came back, and that is not going to help my daughter.'

Consistent with how she presented (self-reliant and industrious, over-focused in her character strategies), she stated she wanted to read something so that she could work on herself and could be as present as she could for her daughter. The irony here was that, being self-reliant and industrious—over-focused, she was assuming responsibility for herself to change on her own instead of accepting the appropriate relational therapy she needed. However, the support offered was accepted.

Months into a difficult and harrowing therapeutic journey, she said, 'I feel so much more connected, truly connected to my daughter, and it's beautiful, but I have a problem at work. My work has fallen behind and I can no longer finish everything by the end of the day.' Invited to explore this, she said, 'It feels like almost every time I do a home visit, some young woman discloses something; domestic violence, sexual abuse, mental health fears, things that never happened before.'

Karen had been split. She had relied on her left brain to plan, organise, complete tasks, but in doing so, had cut off her capacity to connect. Her husband's actions re-confirmed her belief that the world was not safe. As therapy progressed and she realised this was 'old stuff,' her right brain came back online but she did not lose her left brain; she gained balance. She began to connect with service users; they felt it, they trusted her, and then they disclosed. Karen sighed and said it was a better way to live, even if it meant falling behind on her agency's recording requirements... something which may resonate with the reader. Karen had a long conversation with her sister during which her sister disclosed she had been sexually abused by her father. It seemed she had a felt sense Karen was now able to hear her. Karen was now able to support her daughter's therapy without becoming triggered herself; she could be present, truly present.

Returning to the words of Peck (1978) in thinking of Hannah and her children, who had experienced love, nurture, and emotional balance before Devon's untimely death, it is possible to add, as Peck does:

'When children have learned through the love of their parents to feel valuable, it is almost impossible for the vicissitudes of adulthood to destroy their spirit. This feeling of being valuable is a cornerstone of self-discipline because when one considers oneself valuable one will take care of oneself in all ways that are necessary. Self-discipline is self-caring.'

When we can recognise and meet our own needs in healthy ways, it becomes far easier to support others to attain wellbeing.

It is equally important to undertake self-work/personal therapy even when life appears to have been charmed, because what seems charmed may, on closer reflection, have been emotionally or relationally limited. Just as surviving adversity can make it harder to withstand the vicarious impact of this work, so too can the absence of adversity. Both scenarios can reduce resilience and inhibit understanding of how trauma splits minds, families, and siblings.

Society still places greater value on academic achievement than emotional literacy, on writing about human connection, rather than building it. Assignments may be graded A*, or C– (A star is a top mark, C– a mark just above a fail). It is harder to measure the depth of meaningful human connection. Some courses do include placements to promote experiential learning, but workplace environments are increasingly task-led. Some courses now mirror this trend, focusing on 'doing' rather than 'being with.' The shift to online learning, accelerated by the COVID-19 pandemic, has compounded this. The resulting disconnection risks reinforcing a culture of emotional disconnection.

Experienced social workers who trained years ago and later undertook therapeutic training often fare better in relational work. Their social work grounding provided essential exposure to children's lived experiences and their therapeutic practice relied on empathic connection. They understood the impact of trauma, not just on clients, on colleagues but also on themselves. It is not uncommon to see newly qualified or more experienced practitioners, like social workers become undone, emotionally overwhelmed, when attempting to apply a task-led model to deeply relational work, particularly when their supervision is equally task-led and focused on meeting agency and inspection demands. Conversely, practitioners coming from therapeutic backgrounds may excel in individual relationships but struggle to contextualise a child's experience within the complexity of family or family of origin. Those who operate from only one approach, therapeutic or systemic, can feel unanchored, adrift in a vessel without rudder, sail, engine or oars.

To begin making decisions about the future of siblings means first having, and then continuing to build, the knowledge, experience, and self-awareness required. This includes understanding where one's motivations and world views come from. It means staying empathically curious about the work, but most of all remaining curious about oneself.

Part II

The Children's Context

Chapter 3

Siblings in the Shadows
When One Child Suffers

Detailed in Chapter 2 is the need for every practitioner to have a coherent narrative about their own history and to be alert to any unconscious or preconscious decisions or actions that may unwittingly be made. These decisions are informed by each individual's developed belief system rather than a clear understanding of the child's or family's experience. Such unwitting responses can resemble procedural reactions to certain events or stimuli, much like learning to drive a car. When learning to drive, a left-brain mode of learning is used; listening to information from the instructor, processing, analysing, and storing it so it can be retrieved. Initially, each step is undertaken with deliberate steps: mirrors checked, clutch engaged, indicators used, handbrake released, and then the car stalls. The brain's two hemispheres have not yet integrated the task into a seamless process.

Arguably, at this moment, a personal belief system kicks in. The children of Hannah and Devon might take it in their stride, knowing that practice eventually brings success. Mark's son might explode with frustration, whilst his younger son might withdraw in defeat. Carla and Marcus' eldest daughter may remain confident due to meticulous preparation, while the younger child might be tripped up by self-doubt. A year later, all may drive smoothly without conscious effort, as driving by then is procedural.

How each individual reacts under pressure whilst driving may cause them to revert to type. For example, in a minor traffic accident, each young person will have their own emotional response, intensified by the added stress. Mark, hijacked by his four-year-old self, the child who felt the injustice of the world, who was not heard, whose needs were not met, reacts by screaming with road rage. A four-year-old's reaction in an adult body behind the wheel is not what is needed to deal with an accident.

The process of learning to drive is not dissimilar to the journey therapists take in learning their therapeutic technique. Every modality has its own unique rhythm and rules, often taught through a left-brain lens, but must then be practised through right-brain to right-brain connection. One might know how to drive a car, but there is a world of difference between driving a Fiat 500, a battle tank, or a Formula One car. Each one is subtly or very different and demands adaptation and may feel like starting from scratch.

DOI: 10.4324/9781003724797-5

In the United Kingdom, quick-fix models of therapy are proliferating. Many are not research-based or trauma-informed, require minimal training, and are favoured by agencies seeking inexpensive upskilling. These offer some left-brain learning and may include some right-brain awareness, but they do not equate to becoming a therapist. True therapeutic training involves years of academic, personal, and supervised clinical development, somatic awareness, and relational depth.

Therapists are trained to connect at the deep emotional level described by Schore (1994, 2003). The challenge many then face lies in being able to analyse and make sense of their client's experience and to translate this right-brain material into a left-brain format that is then accessible for recovery work or written reports. Some therapists, depending on their training, modality, or inclination, struggle to see their client in the wider context of family, community, or geographical setting, often because they have not witnessed the raw contextual harm that social workers encounter daily.

Social workers face a different but equally demanding challenge. They witness the child's lived experience within their family context but often lack the time to build a deep relationship (Firmin 2017). Communication is vital to their role, but their training is typically information-focused: 'Are these children safe?' 'Are their needs being met?' 'Is this the right placement?' and 'What do parents, carers, or teachers think?' Their learning increasingly leans towards the didactic, with less space for experiential growth. The advantage social workers hold is their ability to see the environment in which the child has developed, the missing developmental stages, the impact of harm and trauma, and the children's positive elements of experience too. Social work training does not typically include the 'right brain to right brain' connection needed to truly enter a child's inner world.

A powerful combination would be social work training paired with deep therapeutic training, not to be confused with aforementioned surface-level therapeutic models, which offer structure but not the internal shift that fosters true insight. This integrated preparation would enable practitioners to begin recognising and working through the ways in which their own childhood experiences may have resulted in blind spots, unhelpful stress responses, avoidance patterns, or behaviour justifications.

These issues are evident in society's long-standing responses to children (Kempe et al. 1962). If asked, what did the following 19 children have in common: Dennis O'Neil (1945), Maria Colwell (1973), Jasmine Beckford (1984), Tyra Henry (1984), Heidi Koseda (1984), Kimberley Carlile (1986), Doreen Mason (1987), Leanne White (1992), James Bulger (1993), Rikki Neave (1994), Chelsea Brown (1999), Victoria Climbié (2000), Lauren Wright (2000), Ainlee Labonte (2002), Daniel Pełka (2012), Liam Fee (2014), Arthur Labinjo-Hughes (2020), Logan Mwangi (2021), and Sara Sharif (2023). The answer, which may come to mind, is that they are children who were murdered. They were killed by a parent, step-parent, guardian, or, in some cases, by other children. Most endured horrific levels of neglect, abuse, and torture. What is less well known is that each of them had siblings.

These children's deaths span more than 70 years, a period in which our knowledge of child development, legislation, and safeguarding guidance has grown exponentially. Children in the United Kingdom still die at a rate of approximately one a week as a result of abuse or neglect (NSPCC 2024). This awful statistic persists despite decades of research, inquiry, and reform; the ability to prevent such tragedies has still not been realised. In the past two decades, the understanding of trauma and neuroscience has expanded dramatically, and the conversation has slowly shifted from focusing solely on 'What was done to the child,' the external abuse, to 'What did it do to the child?' the individual internal impact. There is now a greater recognition that early harm affects lifelong development and that adults who were once abused may unknowingly raise children in similar ways. Yet despite this awareness, we remain unable to halt the generational repetition of neglect and abuse.

These cases also highlight a persistent blind spot, the failure to consider the wider family system. What must it have been like for their siblings to grow up in those environments? What were the long-term repercussions for their futures?

In 1945, 12-year-old Dennis O'Neill was killed by his male foster carer. Dennis had been placed with his 9-year-old brother, Terry, while their younger sibling, 7-year-old Frederick, was placed elsewhere (O'Neill 2000). The rationale for this separation remains unclear. The siblings had all been removed from their birth parents due to neglect, and this took place during a period when awareness of children's experiences was gaining momentum, but understanding the impact of abuse on individuals, siblings, and their capacity to relate to others was still limited. There also appeared to be little meaningful assessment of the children's unmet needs or of their carers' ability to meet them. The boys likely arrived at their foster home in a state of fear. However neglected or mistreated they had been, their home life was at least familiar, and familiarity is often, mistakenly, equated with safety. The unknown, 'safe' foster carers and their home may have felt more frightening to them.

Historical published reports suggest that removing the boys from their parents was necessary and justified. Tragically, they also indicate that the boys' fear of their foster carers was not just due to unfamiliarity. Their experience had taught them that the very people meant to care for and nurture them, their parents, were capable of abuse and neglect. They then might anticipate worse from strangers, who had no connection and did not love them. When this fear of strangers proved justified, the psychological impact must have been devastating. They had no way of knowing if their new circumstances would mirror or exceed the danger they had known. It is likely their fear manifested in their behaviours.

Arguably, Dennis and Terry may have been mourning both the loss of their parents and the separation from their younger brother, Frederick. Given their early experiences, they will probably have developed a trauma bond, that connection forged through fear and adversity, resulting in behaviour that was complex and difficult to manage. Tragically, their carers' relationship was itself dysfunctional, with reported domestic violence and a failed attempt by the female carer to leave her husband. It is reasonable to assume the boys sensed this tension and were affected by it. The carers scapegoated Dennis, beat him with a stick, starved him, and locked him in a cupboard. At 12, he weighed under four stone, the average weight of a seven or eight-year-old. It was reported that his feet were ulcerated and his legs chapped. He was regularly stripped naked, beaten, and made to watch the family eat while he starved.

The immediate concern, both then and now, is rightly focused on the horrific abuse Dennis endured. But what of Terry? The psychological harm he suffered from witnessing his brother's torture may have been equally damaging. To see and hear what was done to Dennis, helpless to intervene, will have been as traumatic as enduring the abuse firsthand (Galston 1998).

Nearly 30 years later, in 1973, 7-year-old Maria Colwell died. She was one of six siblings, three half-brothers and two half-sisters. Maria's early life was marked by instability, with multiple transitions and losses. Taken into local authority care when only a few months old, she was later moved to live with her aunt and uncle, where she was reportedly happy and settled, then returned to her mother and new partner. Maria was scapegoated by her stepfather, who favoured his own children. He forced Maria to watch them eat while she went hungry, echoing the abuse inflicted on Dennis O'Neill. She became so malnourished that she was described as a walking skeleton. The psychological impact on her siblings, who witnessed this prolonged cruelty, must have been profound. The relationship between her mother and stepfather was also reported to be violent and oppressive. One night, fearing her partner's return home drunk, Maria's mother kept her awake. Whether this was for company or protection is unclear, but that night, he kicked Maria so savagely she died the next day. Twenty-three professionals had visited the family in the two weeks before Maria died.

In 1984, Jasmine Beckford was starved and beaten to death by her stepfather and neglected by her mother. Jasmine had a younger sister, Louise, who had previously been brought to the hospital with a broken arm and retinal bleeding. Again, the question must be asked, 'What was worse for each child, being physically harmed, or witnessing a sibling being harmed?'

That same year, Tyra Henry also died at the hands of her father. He had previously been convicted of assaulting her brother, Tyrone, but was later released. Tyrone was reported to have suffered a fractured skull, bruised thighs, retinal haemorrhage and brain damage with lifelong consequences. Professionals involved in the case later admitted they were afraid of the parents. If the professionals were afraid, how much more terrifying must life have been for those two children?

Heidi Koseda was also starved to death in 1984, and her stepfather was convicted of her murder. Heidi's mother, detained under the Mental Health Act, was found guilty of manslaughter on grounds of diminished responsibility. Before Heidi's death, the couple had two more children, James and Lila. All three children were neglected, and both Heidi and James had multiple bruises. The family apparently avoided professional scrutiny through denial, deceit, and lies. The full extent of what life was like for these siblings will probably never be known; however, as Heidi's body was kept in a cupboard for two months, it is reasonable to believe James and Lisa lived in fear.

Three-year-old Leanne White was killed in 1992 by her stepfather. Leanne was reported to have a younger half-sibling, Ben, the child of her mother and her stepfather's son. She died two months after Ben's birth. Her mother alleged Leanne had soiled and smeared her faeces and had tried to throw Ben on the fire. Whether these claims were true will never be known. If the claims were true, they would indicate a highly distressed child, or a child being scapegoated, or a parent seeking help in a chaotic, dysfunctional way, or some combination of these. A psychiatrist who saw Leanne and her mother remarked, 'She was a little girl who had not developed a close relationship with her mother' (NACPC 1994).

In 1994, six-year-old Rikki Neave was found strangled in a wood. Although unsolved for many years, an unrelated man, aged 13 at the time, was convicted in 2023. Rikki's mother admitted cruelty to him and to two of his three sisters, for which she received a seven-year custodial sentence. The public record contains little about the abuse Rikki experienced, how this compared to that of his siblings, or the nature of their sibling relationships. This also raises important questions about the boy who killed Rikki, who was known to have had a 'difficult and troubled childhood,' and had been in foster care shortly before the murder and maintained contact with his father. The report did not mention whether the child who killed Rikki had any siblings.

In 1999, two-and-a-half-year-old Chelsea Brown was murdered by her father. Her body bore 47 injuries to her head and body. Her father blamed her for falling, then blamed his wife, and even blamed Chelsea's 17-month-old sister for her injuries.

Victoria Climbié (Anna Kouao on her false passport) died in February 2000. Her murder by her maternal great-aunt and the aunt's boyfriend led to sweeping reforms of the child protection system in England and Wales. The Inquiry identified twelve missed opportunities to prevent her death. Victoria had six siblings who remained in the Ivory Coast when she was taken to Europe for a supposed 'better chance.' She lost her parents, siblings, culture, and ultimately, her life.

Lauren Wright, aged six, was fatally assaulted by her stepmother. Life had already been difficult as her parents' volatile relationship left little space or time for Lauren. Her stepmother scapegoated her, fuelled by 'resentment and antipathy.' The Chief Superintendent described the father as having 'abdicated' responsibility, while the wider community remained in denial. Lauren was one of at least five half or step-siblings across the two families and, according to media reports (Judd 2001), was scapegoated by both her mother and stepmother. Despite the abuse, Lauren appeared to idolise her stepmother. The violence she endured was witnessed by her step-siblings, and the final assault that ended her life was witnessed by her stepbrother.

Peter Connelly (Baby P, Child A) died in 2007, aged 17 months, after suffering more than 50 injuries. He had 3 sisters.

Daniel Pełka, aged 4, was murdered in 2012 by his mother and her partner. He was reported to be the middle child of 3 siblings who lived with him.

In 2014, two-year-old Liam Fee died from blows that caused a ruptured heart. His autopsy revealed 30 injuries. His brothers were also beaten, locked in a cage, given cold showers, and subjected to 'abuses too appalling to detail' (Anderson 2016).

These events show a repetition of common criticisms from Dennis O'Neil to date in relation to agency learning:

- Agency or professional confusion
- Staff shortages
- New carers
- Miscommunication/poor interagency communication
- Failure to see children alone
- To see, really look at or examine children. Beckford was significantly malnourished and had 40 injuries, Henry had 40 bite marks, Labonte/Walker was starved to death, Brown had 47 injuries, Connelly had 50 injuries, Climbie had 128 injuries, Pelka had 22, Fee had 30 external injuries
- Misguided decision-making to return the child to parental care
- Failure to witness a child's distress. This was also seen in Pindown records (Levy and Kahan 1991)
- Conflicting professional viewpoints
- A failure and/or delay to investigate, poor investigation, and/or poor analysis, or to see a child
- Inadequate training of social workers who lacked the skills and judgement
- Lack of supervision of the family
- Agency 'siege mentality' or lack of interagency working
- Services failing to see the child
- Listening to and hearing parents/carers, not the children
- Parent focus rather than child focus
- Poor assessment and/or poor analysis
- Change of plan or closure with change of staff
- Practitioners being overly trusting of, compliant towards, or manipulated or bullied by the parents
- And in every enquiry the supervision of the social worker was inadequate or missing

Between April 2020 and March 2021, during the COVID-19 lockdown in the United Kingdom, there were 223 child deaths linked to suspected abuse and neglect. How many of these involved sibling groups is not known. Arthur Labinjo-Hughes, aged six, was one of those children who died. He was abused and neglected by his father and stepmother. He was removed from the bedroom he had shared with his stepsiblings and then made to sleep in the lounge. He stood in the hallway for fourteen hours a day, was given water laced with salt, and was covered in one hundred and thirty bruises showing the extent of the beatings he endured. He was scapegoated, starved, excluded, isolated, and tortured while his siblings were loved and cared for. His life ended when his stepmother repeatedly struck his head against a hard surface, causing unsurvivable brain injury. No public comment has been made about any assessment of his siblings, their needs either before or after his death.

It was reported that professionals believed Tyra Henry's mother had ended her relationship with her abusive partner, when she had not. Services struggled with the idea that people lie. The real issue is not the lying itself, but the response to the lie. The response is often oversimplified, and followed by judgement, blame, and shame towards the person who lied, rather than a deeper curiosity about the person's reason or need for the lie. To understand a lie means visiting the liar's internal world.

Terence O'Neill lied in court. Whether he lied in his first account or under later questioning is a moot point. What is known is that his brother Dennis had been tortured and murdered. In that process, Terence too had been tortured. Lying is often a tool to protect against overwhelming shame, to hide fear or anxiety, to conceal feelings of inadequacy, or to preserve a fragile sense of self-worth. A trauma-informed lens sees lying not as the problem, but as the answer to a problem. The bigger the lie, the bigger the problem it is trying to solve.

Children who have experienced trauma, abuse, and neglect are often blamed when they lie. Lying is frequently accompanied by stealing and other behaviours interpreted as deceitful. Dennis stole milk directly from a foster carer's cow, he drank it from the teat, and ate a raw swede. How else was he to survive? Terence lied, but was this a deliberate deception, or a version of events constructed to help him survive? He had witnessed his brother's brutal suffering, whilst also experiencing his own. Was his account a calculated lie, or a fragmented recollection shaped by fear, confusion, and dissociation? All typical responses to trauma. Perhaps he was shamed and blamed for what others saw as dishonesty, when in reality he was unable to articulate what had happened to his brother, or to himself. People lie when they say 'nothing happened,' or 'it only happened once,' or 'it won't happen again,' or no-one knew, when to not have known would be impossible.

Archer and Gordon (2006) encapsulate this well when they stated, 'Truth is a misnomer for dissociative children with a skewed Internal Working Model (IWM); they have a genuine information gap and as such have difficulty in the recall of events. Survival means forgetting.' It is worth reframing the word 'forgetting' as 'not remembering,' a conscious or unconscious way of managing actual or remembered pain—an unconscious, dissociative response as a mechanism that allows the too-painful experience to be not remembered but then cannot be forgotten (Chu 2011).

How often is there frustration or impatience when a question is answered with, 'I don't know,' 'I don't remember,' or 'I don't care?' That frustration shifts with trauma-informed understanding into being heard differently, as, 'I do know. But both then and now I must not know to stay alive, sane, or attached,' or 'I do remember, but to survive I must not remember,' or 'I did, and do, care so much, but to remain alive, sane, or attached, I must not, I cannot care.'

This response does not only apply to a real and present danger, but also to perceived danger, which can feel equally real. A child draws upon the same survival template in a new or even safe situation because they do not, or cannot, feel safe, even when they are. Just as Terence did, so too did Claudette, Tyra's mother, lie. Whether she lied because she was terrified of her partner, or afraid of the Local Authority's power to remove her children, or because she had participated in the violence, or failed to protect, or felt culpable, or even, though some may struggle with this possibility, chose to lie and liked it, may never be known. Unless people are given the opportunity to explore their world, their 'truth' will remain unknown, and therefore their lie will never truly be understood.

If children can be scared of their parents, so too can professionals. This fear can lead to avoidance, ingratiation, conflicted feelings, lack of clarity, confusion, and denial. These dynamics are documented in numerous Serious Case Reviews:

- Professionals being scared of their clients.
- Louis Blom-Cooper (1985), following the death of Jasmine Beckford, observed: 'We fear that their [social workers'] attitude in regarding the parents of children in care as the clients rather than the children in their own right may be widespread among social workers.' This comment helped shift the focus to the child, prompting additional training in communication with children. He went on to assert, 'Thou shalt not, not intervene.' Proactive protective services were to be wrapped around children, and professionals were to be clear, the children, not the adults, were their clients. Social workers were directed to seek out endangered children and discover what those children had to say about their lives.
- Professor Munro's 2011 review of child protection called for, 'Council leaders to take more responsibility for giving Social Workers the right conditions to practice effectively, and Ofsted to focus inspections on social work practise, not just paperwork.'
- In many cases, there were known concerns about siblings. Jasmine Beckford died despite earlier concerns that her younger sister, Louise, had been assaulted by their stepfather (Edinburgh University). Chelsea Brown's father had prior convictions for child assault. Similarly, Dennis O'Neil and Maria Colwell had been known to the authorities for extended periods. Olive Stevenson (1986) wrote of Maria's case: 'There was a manifest failure to see the child sufficiently often and properly to appraise her physical state, in particular to use her weight to check her wellbeing.' While it is undisputed that a child's physical

condition must be monitored, little was publicly discussed, or even considered, about the psychological impact on her siblings, their emotional presentation, their relationships, their futures. Jasmine's sisters, for instance, not only endured her death but also the imprisonment of both their mother and stepfather. This silence may be understandable in 1986, when knowledge of the neurological, physiological, and emotional effects of harm was still emerging. It is troubling that even in more recent reports in the 2020s the focus remains on a single child, with little or no reference to their siblings.

- Also relevant are the cases of Susan Aukland (died 1975) and Doreen Aston (died 1989), where it was known that their parents had previously killed a sibling (Reder et al. p. 53). This is included as a reminder to practitioners who might claim that these cases are historically irrelevant or that such oversights could not happen now. In fact, they still do. In 2020, a referral was made for 7-year-old Martin to begin therapy. He was living with his mother, who had a diagnosis of schizophrenia. Further information gathering by the therapist uncovered that Martin's mother had killed his sister when the sister was 9, two years before Martin was born. The girl had been drowned in a bath, dressed, and placed in bed, where she was eventually discovered. Therapy was initially refused, on the grounds that unless this information informed a reassessment, Martin could not be deemed safe. The reassessment which followed concluded that Martin should be removed, and he was placed in foster care. A little over a month into therapy, Martin disclosed sexual abuse by his mother's boyfriend. The man had silenced Martin by threatening to let his mother do to him what she had done to his sister.

Taking Dennis O'Neill's death in 1945 as a notional 'ground zero' of children's deaths at the hands of parents or carers, the learning should have been that appropriate and ongoing training is essential for all practitioners, including how to communicate not just with the child, but also their siblings. Training must encompass the complexity of child development, signs and symptoms of abuse, the impact of experiencing and witnessing domestic violence, neuroscience, attachment, psychoeducation, grief and loss, each grounded in trauma-informed practice.

Alongside this must sit clear policies, procedures and guidance, regular case management supervision and clinical supervision, structured team meetings and reflective time, a workforce whose caseloads match the demand, clear lines of communication internally within agencies and externally across multi-agency teams. A TAC must allow professionals to share concerns and manage disagreement in the interests of the child and siblings. Perhaps Local Authorities failing OFSTED inspections could demonstrate the impossibility of doing this work with the catastrophically deficient governmental support. These measures might not eliminate child deaths, but they would certainly reduce them. Warning signs would be more visible, and protective steps could be taken, not just for one child, but for all the siblings. None of this is new as these measures appear in every Serious Case

Review and yet history shows that the repetition of recommendations has not prevented the repetition of these outcomes.

Every child death inquiry includes some comment about the quality, frequency, or absence of supervision. Clinical supervision is a known protective factor, and both worlds of social work and psychotherapy recognise its vital role in supporting individual casework. Yet it is often replaced by managerial oversight supervision, focused on performance metrics and agency protection rather than therapeutic reflection. In the United Kingdom, one major fund-holder for adoption support, via the Regional Adoption Agencies (RAAs), has been the Adoption Support and Guardian Support Fund (ASGSF). Historically, ASGSF allowed one clinical supervision session per 25 therapy sessions, equivalent to one every six months, way below professional guidelines. In 2025, this was rescinded entirely, and then further funding cuts made even that level of support unfeasible. The result is that some of the most vulnerable children and families are being supported by therapists and social workers who are themselves left unsupported and, in defiance of repeated recommendations, the opposite of model coherency.

These 'individual' cases where things have gone wrong are no different from other high-profile reports where children have been lost in the system. For example, the children in Rochdale vulnerable to Child Sexual Exploitation, children in care in various or unregistered education settings, children out of school being educated at home, Satanic and Ritual Abuse crises, and so many others. The issue these 'lost' children often have in common is the presence of siblings. In order to understand a child's experience, there must not be reliance on what one child has to say but what and how it is said in the context of the family's and their siblings' reports. This work is paradoxical, complex, and forensic. It requires a questioning mind, not only from social workers but from every professional involved, to plan for the best, or least-worst, future for children who have faced adversity in the presence of siblings.

The children described here sit at the extreme end of a continuum of harm, but none of these children suffered alone. Each had siblings, some of whom were directly abused, others deeply affected by witnessing the abuse or its aftermath. Even Victoria Climbié, who came to the United Kingdom without her siblings, left behind brothers and sisters who later read of her torture and death in the press. The trauma of hearing about such events, particularly involving a sibling, can be as, or even more, damaging than direct experience. Global responses to events such as the 9/11 attacks and ongoing Middle Eastern conflicts have illustrated the profound impact of indirect exposure to traumatic events.

Sue Gerhardt (2004) reminds us, 'The children of today are the parents of tomorrow and will look after us in our old age.' What becomes of siblings who share these histories; through direct experience, family memory, or through assessments and research? What shapes their worldview, their beliefs about caregiving and receiving, their capacity to resolve conflict without violence, the nature of their adult relationships, and the kind of parenting they will offer in turn?

Chapter 4

Shattered Bonds
Trauma's Impact on Siblinghood

At birth, the connection between mother and child is abruptly biologically severed. A flood of experiences follows the birth: breathing, changes in light and sound, rough textures, defecation, urination, handling, thirst, and hunger impact the child's senses. Children are arguably born fragmented into the pain of the world, and it is initially the mother who connects her right-brain limbic system to the baby's, enabling regulation and helping the child make sense of their needs. As Putnam (1997) first suggested and others now agree, this begins the process of associating and integrating thoughts, emotions, bodily sensations, and behavioural responses. The mother does this through empathic attunement, her behavioural and emotional response to a simple cry. She must then quickly work out if the cry signals hunger, thirst, pain, tiredness, need for a nappy change, proximity, love, or a combination of factors. Sometimes she gets it right, sometimes wrong, but both the empathic attunement and the timely repair of any errors contribute to mentalisation, association, and the developing window of tolerance and social regulation. Fosha (2003) notes, 'The roots of resilience are to be found in the sense of being understood by and existing in the mind and heart of a loving, attuned, and self-possessed other.'

It is the process of having their needs met in a calming manner where the mother and/or father become empathically attuned by creating a holding environment (Winnicott 1971), recognising and responding to the subtle difference in cry, and speaking in the melodic lilt of motherese with right-brain to right-brain limbic attunement (Schore 2003) that produces 'the most comprehensive and integrated map of the body state available to the brain' (Damasio 1994, p. 66). Many authors comment on attunement without using the word empathic. This is important as a parent using attunement without empathy may be meeting their own needs.

For example, a mother who needs peace and quiet becomes annoyed when the baby cries. The baby attunes to her feelings and cannot tolerate the uncertainty and withdraws into silence. The mother then smiles and relaxes; the baby mirrors her response and stays quiet. The baby does not *know* what has just happened but feels the shift from arousal to calm approval. Meeting the mother's needs by ignoring his own needs then becomes a habitual pattern. As an adult, distress regulation may then rely on external sources by meeting others' needs whilst neglecting his own, through career choice, drugs, or alcohol, rather than internal resilience. If there is a paradigm shift from an addiction model to a trauma model, assessments and interventions would then frame this as habitual behaviour, to meet unmet needs rather than addiction. This may also explain why so many people drawn to social work, social care or therapy are then vulnerable to vicarious traumatisation.

Empathic communication (mentalisation) is not only what is said but the way that it is said. This allows the verbally driven left brain to connect with the non-verbal right brain so that hunger, tiredness, the need for proximity, or other discomforts are met with holding, rocking, singing, and regulating both body and mind. Such calming experiences teach that pain or discomfort has a name and can be soothed (Winnicott 1971). In this act of containment, the parent takes the child's projected feelings, be they positive, negative, or neutral, and returns them in a manageable form (Klein 1975). Schore (2001) clarifies the impact of developmental trauma when he writes,

> Early abusive memories are stored in the right hemisphere outside of conscious awareness, and this realm represents the traumatic memories in imagistic form along with the survival behaviour employed as a result of the abuse. The cortical hemispheres contain two different types of representational processes and separable, dissociable memory systems, and this allows for the fact that early emotional learning of the right hemisphere, especially of stressful, threatening experiences can be unknown to the left hemisphere.

Therefore, relying solely on verbal dialogue with a developmentally traumatised child or adult is less effective than approaches engaging the right brain through body-orientated therapeutic interventions (Ogden et al. 2006, Fisher 2021, McConnell 2020). In safe touch, play, and sensory interventions, timely empathic re-attunement teaches that whilst the behaviour is unacceptable the child remains loved and lovable, something not achieved by punitive isolation in 'naughty step' time (Hughes et al. 2017, Hughes 2012).

There are qualitative differences between attunement, empathy, empathic attunement, and sentimentality.

Case Example

Jenny, aged 16, was in therapy working on her strained relationship with her mother, a tension deliberately created by her criminally abusive father, who was serving a long prison sentence by that time. Whilst describing her difficulties with her mother, she began comparing this relationship with the one she had with her father. She missed him, loved him, could talk to him about anything and, above all, stated, 'He was so empathic.'

Empathic? Knowing his psychopathy surely, she misunderstood the word but rather than telling her she had used the wrong word, she was asked to give some examples. Her descriptions sounded empathic: he understood her, always knew what she was thinking, could 'get inside her head' and change her mood. When he was sad, he would look at her, and she would know how to make him happy. He had taught her, through attunement, how to read his moods, and so did whatever it took to please him.

Several challenging but genuine empathically attuned conversations helped her realise what she had experienced with her father was attunement without empathy. True empathy primarily meets the other's needs, not one's own. Feeling this for the first time, she not only understood the difference intellectually but experienced it and recognised his behaviours as manipulative, controlling, harmful, and designed to meet his needs and not hers.

Distinguishing manipulative, negative attunement from empathic attunement can be difficult, sometimes because the practitioner is being manipulated too. This can be achieved by asking the question, 'In this situation whose needs are being met at the expense of another's?'

Empathically attuned behaviour regulates, but more than that, it shows that feelings of discomfort are not parts of the self to be rejected, but embraced, focused on, and accepted. This allows integration of overwhelming experiences or parts. In 'good-enough' families, where warmth outweighs criticism and Adverse Childhood Experiences are few, this integration and association is a major developmental task in the first four years of life. From an empathic relationship with the primary caregiver, a template is then created for building empathic relationships with others.

In the Positive Internal Working Model, Bretherton (1992) describes this as:

Positive Early Experiences	**Self Experienced as**	**Others Experienced as**
Loved	Lovable	Loving
Valued	Worthy	Interested
Regulated	Effective	Responsive

The better the quality of our early attachment experiences, the greater our capacity to tolerate distress as we develop into adulthood. Our capacity for affect tolerance, self-soothing, and an integrated sense of self later in life depends on self-regulatory or self-soothing abilities acquired during the first two years of life.

(Fisher, 2017)

Recent research has overturned the earlier view that failure to develop these skills before age two caused irreparable damage. The brain retains its capacity for change throughout the lifespan. When someone says, 'I can't change,' it doesn't mean change is impossible. This is a belief, and not a fact. The next step is to explore the reasons for this belief which may include a fear of loss, failure, loss of respect, or love, often in situations where staying the same is, or was, necessary to remain in a dependent relationship.

The variations in the success of developmental integration become evident when a child in the United Kingdom starts school at the age of four. Most of the children need help to be socially regulated by the teacher or teaching assistant. Some can self-regulate within a predictable routine whilst some, to varying degrees, struggle under any circumstances. Differences may reflect the children's chronological age: an August baby will be just four on entry, whereas a peer in the same class born in September the previous year is nearly five. Developmentally, the five-year-old is going to have an advantage by being more socially regulated or self-regulating compared to their younger classmates.

The child's temperament, experienced parenting style, and consistency of care also influence integration. Children who achieve homeostasis display markers of integration, sometimes referred to as 'self-energy' or the 'wise-self' in Internal Family Systems (IFS) literature. Schwartz (2001) describes this as embodying the 8 Cs: Compassion, Creativity, Connectedness, Clarity, Confidence, Courage, Curiosity, and Calm. Spiegel (2017), a child IFS therapist, adds three more Cs: Commitment, Consistency, and Contentedness, and then 5 Ps: Patience, Perseverance, Presence, Perspective, and Playfulness.

An integrated child has:

- The capacity to play with others without disruption.
- The ability to communicate, especially in a symbolic way.
- Respect for others (and respect for self) and awareness of other people's gifts and achievements.
- Capacity for tolerating envy in respect of other people's gifts and achievements.
- Has no need for total attention.
- Doesn't need to be the protégé or scapegoat.
- Can experience empathy for self and others.

Having achieved integration or homeostasis, the child then needs a period of relative stability in which ongoing positive experiences reinforce the belief that adults and others are generally good. Children's sense of self is continually reinforced so that when the major developmental task of identity formation arrives in adolescence, they are better prepared to deconstruct or shed childhood norms and to reconstruct themselves as the adult they eventually become. 'Individuation is to divest the self of false wrappings' (Jung 1967).

The more adversity a child faces in their early years, the greater the risk of negative outcomes. Yet, as research shows and therapists know from experience, these consequences are reversible.

Some children experience neglect, physical, sexual, emotional abuse by commission, while others endure emotional neglect by omission. Where these and other stressors such as domestic abuse, loss, disruptive transitions, change, and ACEs are present, it becomes harder for them to be 'present' in the classroom in a meaningful or helpful way. The more unmet needs and ACEs experienced, the greater the negative impact, and the children are more likely to struggle globally. It also becomes harder for those around them to understand the children's behaviour, whether it is dysregulated or, paradoxically, exceptionally well controlled (Felliti et al. 1998; Bellis et al. 2015).

All children, especially siblings, present themselves according to how they have interpreted the world and experienced their care-receiving. Trauma fragments people and relationships. If trauma occurs in or following an optimal childhood, the resulting fragmentation matches the trauma's impact. Integration develops when parents provide good enough care in the first four years of life. Experiencing and having the ability to remember being integrated makes it easier to return to that state if later trauma causes fragmentation.

There is an individual saturation point where returning to the developmental track of integration is impossible without support, even long after removal from the abusive situation. How often have adopters and foster carers said, 'It must be me, what am I doing wrong?' This child has lived with me longer than they lived at home. Herman (1992) writes, 'When neither resistance nor escape is possible, the human system of self-defence becomes overwhelmed and disorganised. Each component of the ordinary response to danger, having lost its utility, tends to persist in an altered and exaggerated state long after the actual danger is over.' Perhaps carers and workers expect too much change too quickly in a child's ability to integrate and without this the impact on behaviour. Being safe will not necessarily equate to feeling safe. New experiences may further reduce that feeling of safety. Previously necessary coping strategies and behaviours will remain in place and are often used to test this new 'safe.'

> Our brains will take in new information and construct new realities as long as our bodies feel safe. But if we become fixated on the trauma, (for example we continue to experience trauma, or are asked about our trauma experiences during multiple assessments or when undertaking Life Story Work) then our ability to take in new information is lost, and we continue to construct and re-construct the old realities.
>
> (Van der Kolk 2014)

These 'old realities' include the strategies used when trusting was not safe, kindness preceded harm, quiet was the calm before a storm, and waiting for something to happen meant taking some control over when it would happen by making it happen. This is challenging for one child, more complex when a sibling is being treated differently, uses or used different 'realities' to survive.

Lack of integration results in behaving differently in different contexts: home, school, therapy, carers, games, with siblings, and friends, signs or indicators of a lack of integration or dissociation. 'Dissociation is the essence of trauma' (Van der Kolk 2014) and, 'Where there is trauma there will always be dissociation' Briere (1992). Nijenhuis recognises, 'There is a spectrum of dissociative disorders,

(2015), whilst Putnam (1997) notes, 'Greater severity and repetition of trauma increases both the likelihood and degree of dissociation, reflecting the child's compensatory response to overwhelming stress.' Each sibling's unique experience of the same trauma-filled environment will require different degrees of dissociation, influencing not only individual thinking, learning, and behaviour but also, in their like or dislike, appreciating, dismissing, or hating their own and each other's ways of relating and surviving.

Lack of association and fragmentation in the early years becomes a problem in later or latency years. The longer fragmentation remains, the more 'hard wired' it becomes. Fragmentation, which becomes procedural, creates an environment where the internal structures of the brain organise themselves around this disorganisation. This, in turn, encourages those early belief systems to 'hard wire.' As the brain is an anticipatory organ, it is never fully in the present; it looks out for what it knows and what it has had to acclimatise to. When this was in response to a then trauma, and a now situation triggers the same feelings, the first response is to look for anything which looks like danger and not to look for any safety which would balance or change the now response. Catastrophising, expecting, anticipating, or creating more trauma feels the safest way to live. How can adolescents safely experience developmental deconstruction having never experienced integration? How does one know what wholeness feels like having never experienced an integrated state? How can one know what the possibilities are when not knowing how to get there? 'The world will ask who you are, and if you don't know, the world will tell you' (attributed to Jung). How often are positive adjectives applied to teenagers? How often are adolescents in alternative care described as difficult or disruptive? Would a parent's complaint about their adolescent's behaviour immediately result in placement disruption?

The Negative Internal Working Model

Negative Early Experiences	Self Experienced as	Other's Experienced as
Unloved	Unlovable	Neglectful
Ignored	Uninteresting	Rejecting
Abandoned	Unvalued	Unresponsive
Dangerous	Ineffective	Hostile

It can be too easy to forget that children and young people affected by extreme neglect and violence have not only been awash in violence and apathy but have also lacked the psychological, emotional, physiological, safety, and security needed through a consistent, empathic, and loving manner noted by Maslow (1954). Siblings may have needed, or competed with each other for, whatever care that was available. Each may develop self-reliance, pseudo-parentification, and/or an inherent belief that they control their destiny: a skewed self-actualisation. But because this self-sufficiency is built in an insufficient way, it is not possible to adequately meet their own or their siblings' needs. This wobbly, insecure, often disorganised position is Maslow's hierarchy of needs triangle, not on its secure wide base but inverted on its point.

Siblings develop coping strategies to adapt to this maladaptive situation. These survival-ensuring behaviours become their answers to such problems. When siblings are removed, these maladaptive responses—memories, thoughts, emotions, and body sensations—remain active and will not change until each, in their own way, feels safe. Each child must learn, by experiencing their previously unmet needs being met, a new set of responses, how to trust and adapt to this new situation. Behaviours then, and now, are their language for what was felt, then and now. All behaviour arises from a state of stress. Negative behaviour does not arise from a conscious state.

> Negative behaviour arises from an unconscious state and therefore does not stem from a place of conscious intent but a place of unconscious fear, unconscious survival: scared children do scary things. These survival ensuring behaviours are only present with feelings of fear or threat.
>
> (Schore 2003)

Children's behaviours need to be addressed from a physiological and emotional level rather than 'top down' cognitive interventions. Children are conditioned to behave in the way they do through repeated negative experiences. Only through the repetition of new positive experiences, whilst simultaneously processing trauma, can different behaviours emerge. When caregivers do not understand, or have not been helped to understand behaviours, they struggle to see the triggers or causes. They then either start to blame themselves or one or both children together or alternately. When a child is blamed, a child experiences the new carer in a frightening or negative way; these feelings are familiar and require the tried and tested response; this then reinforces the behaviour rather than changing it. If the adult blames themselves, children experience the carer as someone who is scared. Frightened parents and frightening parents are equally scary to children who still need to rely on the very people who scare them to ensure their needs are met.

> The child's experience of allowing the carer to be in charge is to suffer an absence of care, protection, and emotional regulation. It is simply too frightening to allow helpless/hostile parents be in control…as a result children driven by anxiety and fear, begin to boss the parent, belittle her…even attack her. This behaviour makes the parent feel even more helpless.
>
> (Howe 2005)

These dynamics teach children the world is unsafe and escape impossible. Siblings experience paradoxes where one may align with the abusive parent, another may resent being dependent on their sibling for protection yet also hate being their sibling's victim or protector.

In order to understand a child or young person's behaviour, their behaviour must not be seen as the problem, but their answer to the problem. Once this has been accepted, then, and only then, is it possible to ask, so what was, or still is, the problem that requires this answer? Trainee managers have to learn to manage an annual appraisal where a member of staff's behaviour is raising a cause for concern or their presentation is creating a problem. Before deciding how to deal with it, the manager needs to apply the BASK test, to find out if this problem is the result of a lack of knowledge (K), or a lack of skill (S) to put the knowledge into practice, or there are both knowledge and skills, but the issue is an inappropriate attitude. Useful then to wonder if the presenting behaviour is the practitioner's answer (S) to a problem they experienced as a child or as the staff member they are now, knowing from experience (K). Then how their belief systems (A) needed to ensure their survival, as a child, remains fixed at the age they were when it happened and raises the issue if this is a supervision need or a need for personal therapy. Hence adolescents and adults alike often hear the accusation, 'you are behaving like a 2-year-old.'

Behaviours and their answers can also be seen in the cycle depicted in Figure 4.1.

What Was Done

Done equates to (a) what was 'positive-done?' (b) what was 'negative-done?' or (c) what was 'not done or missing?'

'Positive-Done'

In order to physically survive, basic needs must be met: fresh clean air, food in the shape of a balanced healthy diet with fresh uncontaminated produce, interspersed with 'happy food' that is not so great, but feels good or special, safe uncontaminated fresh water, the required hours of sleep for the age group in a place that feels safe and holds the trappings of their identity, clean and safe sanitation, all building a sense of self. Age-appropriate provisions are required to meet developmental needs including physiological, psychological, emotional, educational/cognitive, as well as sexual and identity support, which lead to homeostasis and a widening of the window of tolerance. The consistent availability of family, body security, educational or employment needs, resources to build good health and healthcare, a safe space to inhabit, a code of ethics to live or be brought up by, routine, boundaries, and limits, all leading to safety and a felt sense of safety. Nurture, love, and belonging, being believed in, the development of self-esteem, self-confidence, self-efficacy, achievement, the opportunity to face appropriate adversity in order to build resilience, and the development of mutual respect. If basic needs are not met,

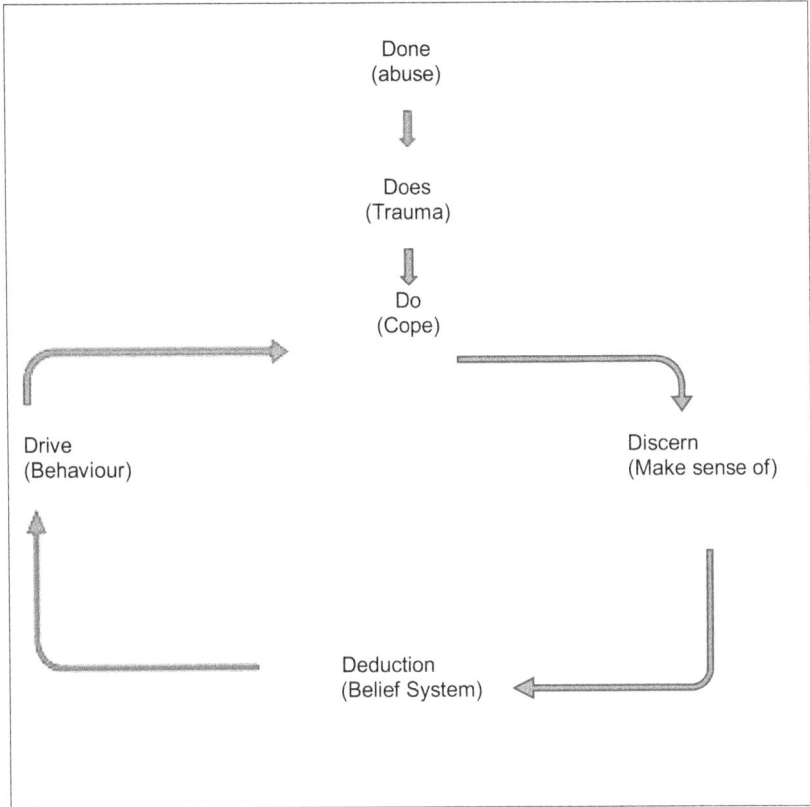

Figure 4.1 Behaviour is the answer not the problem.

optimal outcomes are compromised. When the first four of Maslow's preconditions are met, there is a foundation which increases capacity to face adverse life events.

'Negative-Done'

The abuse includes: physical, emotional or physical neglect, sexual abuse, witnessing or experiencing domestic violence, and/or exploitation. In addition, multiple transitions and moves out of context to family or community norms. The difference between a travelling family moving from place to place as a community lifestyle is not comparable to a woman fleeing domestic violence with her children into a refuge where life's mementos and pets are left behind. The former, a cultural norm where, when this happens, is accepted by that community and has the foundations Maslow requires. The latter, with its lack of safety and loss, does not. One experience of transition cannot therefore be compared to another, and in a similar way, one experience of abuse cannot be, nor should be, compared to another.

'Negative-Not Done or Missing'

Often, the abuse seen overshadows the fact that the positive things that children require, as depicted in Maslow's hierarchy of needs, are also absent, or other developmental issues are missed.

The impact of abuse is multi-faceted, shaped by the presence or absence of protective factors such as 'good-enough' or positive parenting, fulfilment of Maslow's hierarchy of needs, and innate temperament. Innate temperament, originally defined in three types: easy, difficult, and slow to warm up have been expanded to include activity level, distractibility, intensity, regularity, sensory threshold, approach/withdrawal, adaptability, persistence, and mood (Chess and Thomas 1995). Larzelere et al. (2013) add further influences: age of onset (pre-age 4), disability, chronic illness, family mental health, prematurity, and parenting style, which can be authoritative, authoritarian, disciplinarian, permissive, indulgent, or uninvolved.

What is 'done' too often becomes the focus of Services. The danger is that people are labelled or diagnosed by the behaviours that are, in fact, survival strategies. These behaviours then become the target of the intervention rather than being understood as necessary responses to what the experience did to the person. How often does the question, 'What is wrong with this child?' lead to a diagnosis of a disorder such as ADD (attention deficit disorder), ADHD (attention deficit hyperactivity disorder), ASD (autism spectrum disorder), ODD (oppositional defiant disorder). Or later, an adult seeking mental health services is told, 'I will ask you lots of questions to find out what is wrong with you,' and is then given one or many possible diagnoses: depression, BPD (borderline personality disorder), or EUPD (emotionally unstable personality disorder), bipolar, early onset dementia, schizoid, or schizophrenia. A trauma-informed assessment or intervention instead asks child or adult alike, 'What has happened or not happened to you?' This shift in focus can be seen in the following examples:

Case Example: Siblings Lacey Aged Four and Eleanor Aged Three

Lacey and Eleanor were removed from their mother following neglect, multiple moves and numerous caregivers. 'The more placements children have experienced the more they are likely to have, and frequent moves or placements are a cause of insecure attachments' Finkelhor (1995). Their mother lived with depression, exacerbated by domestic violence. Where domestic violence is present, vigilance for signs of physical and sexual abuse, emotional neglect, or abuse must be maintained. The absence of consistent supervision, boundaries, limits, and inconsistent care left the girls with multiple injuries, being found wandering the streets having escaped the dangerous home environment. Their experience directly mirrored their mother's own childhood.

What 'Did'/'Does' the Trauma Do

Intolerable events traumatise each individual, and each is affected by their individual experience of trauma. Their coping strategies are then seen as the problem.

Lacey developed an insecure avoidant attachment style but demonstrated signs of insecure ambivalence.

Where both avoidant and ambivalent themes are present, a disorganised attachment pattern emerges. 'Disorganised behaviours are considered to be indicative of an experience of stress and anxiety which the child cannot resolve because the parent is at the same time the source of fright as well as the only potential haven of safety. In the face of this paradoxical situation, the organised strategy is expected to fall apart' (Van Ijzendoorn et al. 1999). The internal working model becomes the template for how children understand relationships, especially in care-giving and care-receiving. This template cannot be erased but can be overlaid with the development of a healthier alternative. As the new veneer strengthens, the original template diminishes.

Eleanor presented an insecure-ambivalent attachment pattern with avoidant components present, suggesting an emerging disorganised attachment style.

This is demonstrated by the use of multiple insecure strategies that fail to reduce stress, an inability to assuage anxiety, and restricted capacity to relate to others or have needs met by recreating a familiar sense of chaos. Causes of insecure attachment include physical and emotional neglect, any persistent abuse (including blurred sexual boundaries and domestic violence), traumatic experiences, maternal depression, alcohol and/or substance misuse, and lack of empathic attunement. In addition, Cole and Putnam (1992) argue that 'Secure and stable attachments are crucial in the process of healthy development; but when the parent figure to whom the child has a fundamental attachment or bond becomes simultaneously a figure of imposing abuse, the developing integration of self may be profoundly disturbed.'

Do (Cope)

Whilst developing relationships with the carers, Lacey and Eleanor's original blueprint of disorganisation resurfaced during stress, inconsistency of care, or reminders of their mother's parenting. Like other 'disorganised' children, they developed aggressive self-reliance and controlling behaviours, denying internal states of helplessness, vulnerability, or need for comfort. This increased their misuse of power and control, which in turn heightened their anxiety and dysregulation.

Lacey had developed a pseudo-parentified role, ensuring Eleanor ate, even giving food from her own plate. Eleanor, on the other hand, fought for attachment and survival by keeping Lacey away from caregivers by throwing toys for Lacey to fetch so she could secure unhindered proximity. Lacey, whilst preoccupied with meeting her sister's needs, then missed the love she required from her carer.

Meanwhile, Eleanor's preoccupation to monopolise the carer meant she could not relax enough to receive the love she so desperately sought.

Which child had the greatest chance of recovery?

Discern (Make Sense of It)

Lacey and Eleanor both fought for survival, instinctively knowing they were responsible for their own survival. Having experienced adults who failed them and/or caused them harm, they 'knew' no one else could protect them. As the elder, Lacey could sometimes find food or shelter, becoming as resourceful as any desperate four-year-old could. Eleanor lacked physical or cognitive capacity but sought human contact while closely watching her sister. Eleanor soon learned that Lacey would attempt to meet any demand she made.

Deduction (Belief System)

Despite her young age, Lacey believed she was responsible for her own and her sisters' welfare. If she could not meet her own survival needs, how could she meet Eleanor's? Lacey eventually gave up fighting for attention; she no longer anticipated or expected it. Eleanor believed her mother, and therefore all mothers, did not have enough love to go around. She fought off competition for whatever love was available, keeping her sister at bay whilst still relying on Lacey to meet her demands. Eleanor may have recognised her sister's capability to fend for both of them. This capability also posed a threat because Lacey might take away adult attention, so Eleanor worked even harder to exclude her.

Drive: The Behaviour Which Became the Answer

Lacey presented with violent and sexual behaviours towards others. She used sexualised language suggesting she had at least witnessed physical and sexual violence. She tried to induce vomiting by putting her hand down her throat. She took on a pseudo-parental role with her sister.

Lacey withdrew when her sister became dominant and later presented with so-called 'attention seeking' behaviours in foster care. This term, however, carries a negative value judgement, so reframing it as attention needing or attachment seeking moves closer to understanding, as simply changing words can reveal the truth. Despite everything, there is still hope in these behaviours. Lacey was unable to self-regulate and had difficulty being regulated by others. She both pushed people away and sought attachment through paradoxical behaviours, hyper-kineticism, anger, opposition, defiance, and disproportionate or absent reactions to injury.

The social worker noted that Eleanor dominated Lacey. On entering foster care, Eleanor presented with urine-retentive behaviours, stomach upsets, and temper tantrums beyond those expected of a child of her age. She bit herself and pulled out her hair, and she struggled to be regulated by others and was often in a highly aroused, distressed state.

This case reinforces 'Discern' and how sense is made of their experiences, entering into a self-defeating vicious cycle continually reinforcing and justifying behaviour and beliefs in repetitive or avoidant behaviours which were then and continue to be the answers needed to enable coping with what 'Done Did.' Focusing on the answers, rather than resolving the underlying problem, leads to blaming the child or adult, attaching a diagnosis, or imposing interventions aimed at stopping the behaviour, instead of recognising it as an answer to a problem requiring understanding and resolution.

Chapter 5

Between the Lines
Children's Voices on Sibling Relationships

How often does a lecturer begin by quoting from the Oxford English Dictionary (OED) a definition of their topic? When this happens, those listening may sigh and perhaps may not expect any riveting new insights or information. However, for clarity in a changing world of who is connected to whom and how, the OED defines a *sibling* as (1) a relative and (2) each of two or more offspring of the same parent or parents. This prompted a look at the definition of a *relative*: 'a person related to another by blood or marriage or a connection between people arising out of the ties of blood or marriage.' Neither definition helps define a *sibling*, a difficulty recognised by other authors, assessors, and researchers, when thinking about children's views on who is, or is not, a sibling in their paradoxical, complex, and often confusing families and lives.

Monk and Macvarish's socio-legal review (2018, published 2019) asked the key question: 'Who is a sibling?' Their analysis mapped over 100 statutes referencing siblings across multiple legal domains yet found no consistent definition across statutes. Terminology ranged from 'sibling' to 'brother and sister,' with some statutes specifying 'blood' relationships only. Edward Timpson MP, in his foreword to the Young Person's Guide to the Children and Families Act 2014, mentioned growing up with 'foster brothers and sisters' (DoE 2014, p. 1). However, the Children Act 1989 (Schedule 7, Paragraph 3) specifies that the only circumstance in which a foster placement can exceed the limit of three children is when 'the children concerned are all siblings with respect to each other.' This wording implicitly excludes foster siblings who are not biologically related, indicating that those relationships are not legally recognised as siblinghood, even if they exist in practice, leading to a lack of clarity and ultimately inconsistency.

Research and reviews of sibling-related issues in social care consistently highlight the lack of clarity and consistency in how the term sibling is defined. This variability makes it difficult to compare findings across studies or apply the results effectively in decision-making. In many cases, the term is not defined at all (Rees Centre, 2017), or it is only briefly and inconsistently outlined (Tarren-Sweeney and Hazell 2005). In their conclusions, Wulczyn and Zimmerman (2005) acknowledge the limitation in their study by using only siblings linked through a maternal blood tie. Another study identified children to be siblings only when they shared a parent

DOI: 10.4324/9781003724797-7

(or other caregiver) and had lived together (Leathers 2005). The double criteria of sharing a mother and having the same home environment were used elsewhere (Drapeau et al. 2000, Linares et al. 2015). Albert and King (2008) identified siblings as those children who shared the same address. Hegar and Rosenthal (2011) used children who considered themselves to be siblings. Other more recent studies have embraced a similarly broad definition by asking the participants about who they considered to be their siblings. Richardson and Yates (2014) used full, half, step, and adoptive siblings. McDowall (2015) asked the young people to identify their siblings from their birth family only. Confusion can arise again when talking about one's foster sibling when this may relate to another non-related foster child or a birth child of the foster family.

The complexity of ascertaining children's experience can be seen in the Office for National Statistics (December 2011) research to gather information about the make-up of families in the UK. They found that the percentage of families with dependent children in the UK who had only one dependent child in the household increased steadily from 42 per cent in 2000 to 46 per cent in 2010 a statistic that on its own is not very helpful. It does not mean that 54 per cent of children therefore live with a sibling because it does not define a sibling, nor does it help us know if or how many older children have moved on to university, their own homes, or where families have separated, taking a child or children each.

Siblings referred to in this book are similar to those identified by James et al. (2008):

> Children who were thought of as siblings by their parents or carers, including biological, step, half and siblings acquired through placement in care, extended family disruption, boarding school, or even a neighbour. The blood-tie is only one factor in assessing whose needs are best met by living together or apart.

A 'Sibling' assessment must therefore also include other children who were important to the child and the loss of whom may cause greater grief than an actual sibling. For example:

i. The 12-year-old boy in his third foster placement, who was asked who he missed most, immediately recalled with love, smiles, and then a deep grief the loss of the 14-year-old son of his first emergency foster carers. A place he had only lived for four months when he was five . He genuinely could not recall that he had a blood-tie older brother.
ii. The non-related, 'difficult to place children with challenging needs' are placed separately from their blood-tie siblings in a foster home for four years from birth and are then found separate adoptive families.
iii. The 11-year-old who is sent to a 52-week boarding school despite their three siblings remaining at home.

iv. The 13-year-old whose adoption disrupted no longer lives with his two 'adopted' siblings but has had and continues to have letterbox contact with his two birth siblings placed in separate adoptive families.
v. The two 10-year-old unaccompanied minors 'rescued' together from a camp in Syria.

In none of these cases had any consideration been given to the importance or otherwise of these 'connected' others.

Beckett refers to the importance of listening to the voices and experiences of children and that 'Nowhere is this more needed than in respect of siblings. Children and young people have much to tell us about the importance of brothers and sisters in their lives' (Beckett 2018, 2021). However, listening to a child's wishes and feelings should not automatically result in those wishes being instigated. The child's often paradoxical wishes and feelings about their relationships must then be put into the context of what is best for that child at the time. This then must be reviewed and re-considered regularly.

If learning from history teaches about the future, what can be learned from famous siblings in history? Mary I and Elizabeth I, Cain and Abel, Jesse and Frank James, Princes William and Harry, all of whom had or still have complex relationships with each other. From fiction, Wednesday and Pugsley Adams, like the others, would take delight in torturing and terrorising each other, but when it was needed, were fiercely protective and would agree with the Beverly Sisters, who sang 'God help the mister who comes between me and my sister!' Certainly complex, loving, and conflicted, as noted by Rosetti (1862)

'For there is no friend like a sister in calm or stormy weather.

> To cheer one on the tedious way,
> To fetch one if one goes astray,
> To life one if one totters down,
> To strengthen whilst one stands.'

And Walpole, (1847)

> 'Here lies Fred, who was alive now dead:
> Had it been his father, I had much rather;
> Had it been his brother, still better than the other,
> Had it been his sister, no one would have missed her.'

The scope of the definition of a sibling stretches imagination and challenges personal belief systems, yet this must be done if children are to be truly heard, not with just their words, but the meaning behind their words. To achieve this requires examining ourselves, our belief structures, and our prejudices. As Landreth (2002) states 'Take stock of who you are and the impact you will have on the child.'

Rosemary loved her sister Fern in Fowler's book (2014), 'We Are All Completely Beside Ourselves,' and describes her love for her:

> She was my twin my fun-house mirror, my whirlwind other half. It is important to note that I was also all those things to her, I would like to say that, like Lowell, I loved her as a sister, but she was the only sister that I ever had, so I can't be sure, it's an experiment with no control.

Who can say who is or who is not someone's sibling if that 'other' provides the connection, context, support, challenge that may be the kingpin to identity, belonging, survival, or purpose in a family or other context? To know the relationship between Rosemary and Fern, you will need to read the book. It may surprise you.

The model and BBC Radio 2 host Sara Cox in her memoir shared that she was the youngest of five siblings, but six if you include the line 'I had some brilliant times with Gus, he was my best friend and annoying sibling rolled into one slightly roly-poly pony' (2019).

Bruce Perry in his book 'The boy who was raised as a dog,' describes a case example of a child with just that experience. It is always striking, though not surprising, how children and adults alike can tell us that this was normal, whatever their experience was. 16-year-old Martina normalised her experience of sexual abuse as simply how families showed love. When incubated in an experience and knowing no other, adaptation is the only option. How would Justin in Perry's book see his fellow caged dogs other than perhaps as his brothers or sisters? Many children are closer to a family pet than to their siblings, parents, or connected others. A pet may be their only source of unconditional empathic love; the pet is often a fellow victim of violence or neglect in the home and may be experienced as a much-loved ally. Concern about the pet left behind is often one of the reasons why families escaping violence return home (Akhtar 2019).

Akhtar writes about her experience of living in the midst of sexual assault, family and urban violence and territorial warfare,

> As soon as Sylvester and I met we took to each other like pups from the same litter. There was hide and seek in our grandparents' apartment where I always hid, and Sylvester was 'it.' Sylvester would always find me barking with excitement. We tried hiding one of my sisters, but Sylvester never cared to find her. There were secret times when I sat on a boulder in Narnia with Sylvester in my arms and shed the tears, I hid from everyone else. As we sat in the woods nothing ever needed to be said between us. Girl and dog both crying. It was as though somehow he knew. Sylvester nurtured me in ways no one else could.
>
> (Akhtar 2019)

Would a placement team find a foster home for Aysha and Sylvester? Or Aysha and her sister leaving Sylvester at home with the perpetrator? And if the latter, the impact this would have on Aysha's ability to settle in her new environment. Jo Carroll (1998), a social work trained play therapist, developed a creative psychometric that is affectionately referred to as 'Carroll's Islands.' This tool, when used mindfully, can allow insights into children's lives, beliefs, experiences, and connections.

Case Example: Emma

Emma was placed with her adoptive parents, their 13-year-old birth child Rebekah and their adopted son, Jacob aged 8, when she was 5. She rejected Jacob and was ambivalent towards both Rebekah and her adoptive parents. She spent most of her time with the family dog and cat, who she also treated with ambivalence, but fastidiously; unlike her brother and sister, she named them as her siblings.

Case Example: Lana

Lana, aged 16, was separated from her birth sibling when removed from her birth family at the age of 10. She spent the next four years in a residential unit before being moved to a foster placement, where she developed a relationship with the family dog and was seen to relate to it with a sense of sibling rivalry.

Case Example: Tinn

Tinn, a boy aged 10 lived with his mother, 12-year-old sister, and their stepfather. Tinn was perpetually angry with his sister and only referred to her with expletives, in the same manner he referred to his birth father. Tinn spoke most often about his grandfather's dog, and when seen at home, he kept the dog with him. So why do some children identify so strongly with animals? The answers should always be first raised as hypotheses.

When exploring the definitions of types of siblings, even those definitions do not fully explain why a child sees a given person as a sibling or not. Play therapy in practice can illustrate this: when a child chooses a symbol (figure), perhaps a panther. It may be because the child wants a panther, it may be because what is actually wanted is a cheetah, but there isn't one available, it may be that the panther is mistaken for a cheetah, it may be what is needed is a great big cat or may have read or seen the Jungle Book and needs the character values of Baghera. In the same way, there will be multiple levels as to why a child may see a sibling in a certain way which may require further exploration, clarification, and understanding.

Another example when using an eco-map to assess relationships in a family to establish which sibling should/could be placed with whom could reduce anxiety and resistance in the child by creating a metaphor. One might be to ask the child to choose an animal for each of their family members, then ask about their characteristics as the animal rather than the individual. It would be important not to make assumptions but to reflect on and listen to what is said and perhaps later look at similarities and differences between each individual and the chosen animal.

Case Example

A 7-year-old boy was referred for an anger management assessment. He described his 14-year-old brother as a butterfly, his 6-year-old sister as an ant and himself as a gorilla. His explanation, whilst surprising, was insightful and helpful in deciding who should be placed with whom if they could not be placed together. A butterfly was very easily broken and had to be handled with care or he might die, an ant was always underestimated because of its size, yet it was evil and nasty, its bite full of formic acid. The gorilla always loved his family and would fight to protect it. It is also of note the gender he attributed to the animals. The earlier decision made to place the teenager separately, if a foster home for all three could not be found, was changed as a result.

There is no doubt there are many positives to be gained from having siblings who will practise sharing, negotiating, conflict resolution, and, importantly, how it is possible to love someone but not actually like them. There are also many negatives and paradoxes in sibling relationships such as:

Feeling second best or not loved at all.
Watching a parent demonstrate their ability to love one child but not another.
Witness affectionate but non-reciprocated behaviour with a sibling,
Be isolated in, or excluded from, a sibling group.
Be expected to care about and for a sibling with whom there is nothing in common but with whom they have to live.
Be in conflict with receiving a limited amount of available love.
Feel anger towards them because their coping strategies are not the same as your own and/or exacerbate a situation when staying quiet was safer.
To experience favouritism, inequity, or scapegoating.

The research on whether siblings are better off living together or apart is just as conflicted and paradoxical as the sibling relationship itself. Much of it, carried out from the 1980s through to the 2010s, predates the wider knowledge of the impact of trauma on the physiology and psychology of relationships. Researchers often quote siblings describing how much they missed each other, inferring that outcomes would have been better had they remained together, without considering that pre-care relationships were imbued with conflict, challenge, terror, loss, and competition. These dynamics can create trauma bonds, not the kind of 'missing' that follows a healthy, loving internalised attachment with each other. It is the natural harking back for a dream which could be true, when reality is altered, rose-tinted glasses are put on, or the creation of an opaque version of the relationship when gripped with aloneness, grief, loss, despair, and alienation.

It is easy to find texts and references on age-appropriate attachment behaviours but almost impossible to find anything comparable on separation behaviours. Consider the six and eight-year-old siblings who cry inconsolably on separation from their family or each other at the end of contact only to stop just as immediately when distracted. Or those who say goodbye without looking back, or who sob intermittently for hours. Which, if any of these reactions represent age-appropriate attachment or separation behaviours that would inform decision-making about placement together or apart? Or the eight-year-old who cries daily for his six-year-old brother, only for contact to dissolve into competition over trainers, toys, gifts, their foster carer's attention, and then into fighting, despite repeated attempts at redirection.

Any well-informed, up-to-date assessment must start from a hypothesis which is neither for nor against togetherness or separation and neither for nor against contact. An assessment needs not to be just a narrative, but is a well-informed, up-to-date analysis with conclusions, recommendations, and timescales for review. It needs to name the resources needed, not just resources that are available.

Part III
Evidence and Ethics
Research, Law, and Policy

Chapter 6

The Myth and the Measure
What Research Really Tells Us

Wilkinson and Bowyer (2017) summarise the challenge clearly:

> Research has its limitations and bodies of evidence change over time. Decision makers need access to information that is comprehensive and regularly updated; this review offers a picture at that time. Secondly, the application of research evidence in making decisions in relation to individual cases requires learning and development support and relies on those informing the decision making to have an in-depth understanding of the individual child, their family and wider context. There are no generic answers that research can provide that can be applied in a wholesale way across the specific case circumstances of individual children, young people and families. Much can be learned from the aggregated evidence that research provides, but that evidence only gains meaning when it is applied, with analytical rigour and critical thinking, to each individual situation. Thirdly, whilst this review is intended to be useful to decision makers in Local Authorities and within the Judiciary, it is recognised that colleagues working in different parts of the system will have their own professional perspectives and areas of specialist expertise.

Unfortunately, much of the available evidence is more than ten years old, predating the focus sharply shifting to keeping children at home, within their families, or extended families. This resulted in the harm continuing sometimes for years before Care Proceedings were initiated. Such practice paid little heed to the research showing outcomes for children depended on how long they had lived in an abusive or unsafe environment. This way of working was influenced by the increasing body of research outlining the poor outcomes for children leaving the care system. This required need to keep families/siblings together, the pressure of high caseloads and the reduced time available, impaired the ability of social workers to understand and pay attention to nuanced needs and use their analytical skills and judgement to assess the negative or positive impact on each individual child in a family (Rushton 2003). At the same time, research on the consequences of physical and psychological harm on children's development from toxic stress or trauma was growing, for example, research on ACES (Fellitti et al. 1998).

DOI: 10.4324/9781003724797-9

ACEs, when unbuffered by ameliorating positive influences, create dangerous levels of stress that derail healthy brain development, resulting in long-term effects on emotional regulation, relationships, learning, behaviour, and health. Neurobiological research indicates that 'toxic stress' (defined as prolonged activation of stress response systems in the absence of protective relationships) associated with ACEs alters brain development vulnerability to future stress, heightens the risk of health-harming behaviours, and mental and physical illness (McEwan 2015, Couper and Mackie 2016). Positively, the old saying, 'You can't teach an old dog new tricks,' applies only to dogs, not to humans. The human brain retains its plasticity and potential for change throughout the life span, offering real hope for recovery from harm. The belief, 'I can't change,' often means 'Change is something I am not doing.' Understanding that change is something to be feared because it is too risky, pain-filled, difficult, or lonesome also enables the necessary questions to be asked without shame or blame: 'What makes you believe that?' 'What would happen if change was possible?'

Further, research rarely identifies outcomes for individual children (Wilkinson et al. 2017). Children in care proceedings are all individuals with specific social, racial, cultural, familial, and genetic characteristics. All of them form their identity within some form of family relationship and experience traumatic relationships in their own unique way, creating specific vulnerabilities. This legion of factors results in children having differing susceptibilities and resiliencies, so the outcomes vary between children, even within the same family. Research on groups and outcomes can inform decisions, but cannot predict an individual child's future. What is crucial is knowing what builds resilience in each sibling and applying that knowledge when planning placements and contact to secure the best possible outcomes (Putnam 1997).

What Is Known about Ordinarily Developing Siblings?

A number of texts support the proposition that sibling relationships are a significant factor in the emotional development and resilience of children (Bank and Kahn 1997, Dunn and Kendrick 1982, Dunn 2002, Herrick and Piccus 2005, Kosonen 1996, Wojciak et al. 2018).

Howe, Recchia, and Kinsley (2023) site four major characteristics of developmentally expected sibling relationships:

1. That they are emotionally charged, defined by, 'Strong uninhibited emotions of a positive, negative and sometimes ambivalent quality' (Dunn 2002, 2015, Howe et al. 2022, Volling et al. 2025).
2. Often characterised by intimacy, the amount of time they spend together in early years creates knowledge of each other that enables opportunities to support (Kramer et al. 2019), play (Howe et al. 2005, Howe et al. 2015 and Leach et al. 2022) be humorous (Pain et al. 2019, 2021) fight (Volling et al. 2025, Buist et al. 2013, Dirks et al. 2019, Howe et al. 2002, Perlman et al. 2007, Recchia 2009 and Ross et al. 1994) and understand each other's thoughts and

feelings (Hou et al. 2022, Leach et al. 2017, Paine et al. 2021, Recchia et al. 2008 and Tan et al. 2022).
3. Sibling relationships are 'Characterised by large individual differences in the quality of children's relations with one another,' (Dunn 2002, 2015, Howe et al. 2022 and Kramer et al. 2019).
4. That, 'The age difference between siblings often makes issues of power and control' (Abuhatoum et al. 2020, Abuhatoum et al. 2013, Campione-Barr 2017, Della Porta et al. 2019, Della Porta et al. 2022, Della Porta et al. 2012), sibling rivalry and jealousy (Kolak and Volling 2011 and Volling et al. 2010), but also room for teaching each other (Abuhatoum et al. 2016, Howe et al. 2016, Howe et al. 2012 and Klein et al. 2002), a source of help (Dunn 2002, 2015, Kramer et al. 2019, Klein et al. 2002 and White et al. 2014), caregiving interactions (Kramer et al. 2014 and Kramer et al. 2019) and pro-social behaviour (White 2014, Tavassoli et al. 2020, Tavassoli et al. 2019, Tavassoli et al. 2023).

In addition, these authors also describe the siblings' perspective of perceived differential parental treatment, an issue that compounds the relationship of siblings who have experienced developmental trauma (Kramer et al. 2019, Meunier et al. 2012, Richmond 2005, and Volling 1992).

What is known about the impact on siblings who have *not* experienced toxic stress or developmental trauma before being placed together or apart elsewhere is surprisingly limited. Most evidence comes from interviews with evacuated children (Andersson et al. 2019, Summers 2011) when more than two million children in Britain were sent away from their family home during wartime, a time of fear, uncertainty, and violence. These mass movements in times of war, with the addition of widely varying family backgrounds, do not easily translate into separations as a result of developmental trauma. In otherwise healthy family systems, such accounts were often described as distressing at the time but followed by recovery when children were placed in nurturing environments, particularly when carers facilitated sibling contact or reunification. In these cases, grief and anxiety were typically mitigated by stable attachment histories and sensitive caregiving in the new placement. Other insights have come from practitioners' recollections of separations from siblings or parents, whether brief or prolonged, and what explanations were given or not. The impact on each individual is just that, entirely individual and unique.

Instead, reliance is placed on research about children who have not experienced ACEs, asking what enabled happy, trauma-free children to recover from the grief of loss. Bowlby (1969) wrote, 'Children resolve losses just as favourably as an adult when':

1. The child has enjoyed a reasonably secure relationship with his parents before the loss.
2. He receives prompts and accurate information about what has happened and is allowed to ask all sorts of questions and have them answered as honestly as possible.

3. He participates in the family grieving, including funeral rites.
4. He has the comforting presence of a parent or adult he trusts and can rely upon in a continuing relationship.

These findings cannot be easily applied to children with a history of developmental trauma. The protective buffers which support ordinarily developing children—secure early attachments, consistent parenting, and a coherent narrative about identity—are seldom present in children who come into care. While it is helpful to understand normative sibling development as a benchmark, decisions about togetherness or separation must be rooted in the lived, embodied experience of each child, not in idealised models of how siblings should feel or function.

A number of authors comment on the protective qualities of sibling relationships.

- Influences emotional development (Kolawole 2025, Sellars et al. 2024, Pike & Oliver 2017).
- Emotional support: A consistent emotional outlet (Kolawole 2025).
- Social learning: Teach empathy, conflict resolution and enhance emotional regulation (Kolawole 2025, Dunn 2002).
- Resilience development: Increases resilience through managing stress and adversity (Kolawole 2025, Wojciak et al. 2018).
- Influence positive well-being (Sellars et al. 2024).
- Cognitive development shared activities build social competence (Kolawole 2025, Cicirelli 1995).

But also recognise that they can equally be challenging.

- Prevalence of sibling victimisation (Sellars et al. 2024).
- Sibling rivalry leading to chronic stress, anxiety, low self-worth and reduced regulation (Kolawole 2025).
- Normalisation of sibling victimisation as harmless rivalry despite levels of violence and links to severe outcomes including, depression, anxiety, self-harm, and suicidal intent (Sellars et al. 2024, Dantchev et al. 2019).
- Unlike peer-to-peer violence, siblings often have an inability to escape, which compounds the psychological impact (Sellars et al. 2024).
- Increase in long-term mental health risks with a dose risk, with more frequent victimisation increasing internalising and externalising presentations (Sellars et al. 2024, Toseeb & Wolke 2022, Caspi 2012).
- Sibling abuse (Kolawole 2025, Sellars et al. 2024).
- Insecure sibling attachments (Kolawole 2025).
- Conflict escalation (Kolawole 2025).
- Social cultural norms downplay sibling aggression (Khan and Rogers 2015).

Practice with children who experienced ACEs must then ensure:

Point 1: a matched placement where a secure relationship can be established and maintained.
Point 2: prompt and accurate information provided within the child's timescale and for that information to be given to the child and their carer with time and encouragement to ask questions.
Point 3: the need to grieve the loss of family, siblings, friends, toys, pets et al is accepted; support and understanding, not criticism, for the grief-informed behaviours which follow in placement.
Point 4: time is allocated to the social worker to enable these to be offered to the child and/or the carers.
Point 5: perhaps an Agency issue; there is no change of social worker or team at critical times of change, transition, and grief.

Although Jewitt (1982) wrote about the impact of loss and separation on children without ACEs, her work offers much to learn about 'normal' grief reactions. These insights help professionals to understand and respond to grief reactions and behaviours in placements rather than misreading them as pathological consequences of trauma. To summarise, in her writing she identifies the following four 'normal' reactions and behaviours to loss and separation, which are summarised with trauma-informed considerations.

Phase 1: Early grief. Shock and numbing mixed with panic. The body's readiness for action following the alarming loss is seen in flight, fight, freeze, increased arousal, dry mouth, toileting problems, difficulty in letting one's guard down and hence difficulties sleeping and relaxing. Behaviour often mimics the diagnostic criteria for ADD/ADHD. Alongside this, there is denial and disbelief seen in refusal to believe the lost parent/sibling is not available, will cry to see, or conversely deny their existence.

Phase 2: Acute grief and despair. Regressed behaviour, eating too little or too much, restless, aimless, agitated searching for, or preoccupation with thoughts about the lost person, compulsion to speak to, at the same time when reviewing previously spent time together, ignoring anything not positive. Any negative is irrelevant. Increased feeling of waiting for something to happen and a direction of attention to places where the 'lost' person is likely to be found. Feelings of sadness, anger, guilt, and shame inform behaviour and take precedence over other feelings. Adults are tempted to say, 'It's not your fault.' An unhelpful rescuing response which is not intrinsically helpful. School work becomes disorganised, remembering and following instructions is difficult, much easier to lose oneself in books or play station.

Phase 3: Integration of loss and grief or encumbered by losses when these have been or become too many. Grief and loss can also be recycled or delayed on anniversaries, when coping with other usual developmental losses such as a change of school/teacher, innocence, friends, parent remarrying, or the arrival of a new baby. Also, when Proceedings, Guardianship or Adoption are finalised, it brings the loss of hope for reunion.

Phase 4: Grief and loss surface or resurface during recovery from trauma, where children become aware of what is going on around them when, as a result of their stress responses becoming less triggered, they become more able to access their higher cortex. This progress produces the somewhat ironical paradox that the child's increased ability to notice what is going on around them leads to noticing for the first time how different they are, especially in school in relation to their educational difficulties or attainments in comparison with their peers. This can then cause regressed behaviour. This presents the double bind: to suffer trauma compromises learning ability, but the recovery from trauma increases learning capacity, causing a wave of loss for the person the child could have been to hit home. Again, this can cause regression to those previous trauma-related behaviours.

To these four reactions must be added:

Phase 5: Knowledge about disorganised attachment and trauma bonds.

Moreover, Bowlby writes, 'When the effort to restore the bond is not successful sooner or later the effort wanes. But usually, it does not cease. On the contrary, evidence shows that, at perhaps increasingly long intervals, the effort to restore the bond is renewed: the pangs of grief and perhaps the urge to search are then experienced afresh.'

(Bowlby volume 111 p 42)

Research also identifies developmental differences between siblings but again in a trauma-free population of children. It is useful to consider these 'normal' reactions when looking at the behaviours, thoughts, and feelings of children removed from parents or siblings again to note whether none, some of all of these are normal or pathological.

One Charity website reviews normal grief reactions in siblings where a baby has died as a result of being shaken as if they were ACE-free children, without considering the likelihood of the death happening in an ACE-free environment. They divide reactions into age groups, summarised as follows:

Children aged between three and six often do not initially respond to hearing that someone has died. This leaves many parents concerned when their child has no immediate reaction or visible grief. It is important to understand that children at this age do not think death is permanent. Children in this age group do not comprehend the concept of death. A person is gone, then they are there. In cartoons, television shows, and movies, children see characters 'die' and then come back to life constantly. Having viewed 'death' countless times, it's not surprising that children believe it is a temporary condition.

Children aged between six and nine begin to grasp the concept of death. They start to understand that the person will never come back because he or she is dead, and 'dead' begins to take on a definite meaning but can be confused by adults saying the deceased has, 'Gone away,' 'Left us,' 'Been lost,' 'Passed on,' or 'Gone to sleep.' This leads to confusion and anger and inhibits grief. Children at this age grasp the permanence of death but may feel removed from the experience. Interest in the vivid, morbid details may be stronger as they attempt to understand what has happened. This is not morbid or unnatural; it is just part of their process. They also become concerned about practical issues, like how this will affect them and their day-to-day routines. They may start asking who is going to take them to the places the person who died used to take them. They try to find ways to break the loss into smaller parts to allow them to process it, which may seem uncaring, selfish, or attention-seeking. This age group is ready for more information, but remember that this is a crucial time of development. A 'tween' has one foot in childhood and one in adolescence. Even without grief and loss, this developmental stage is both an exciting and scary place to be for some children.

Children aged between 9 and 12 may have already begun to develop an understanding of the irreversible nature of death. Curiosity about details might be stronger at this age level. As they process the death, fears may arise, making clear conversations and support critically important. Guidelines for this age group are similar to those of children aged three to six. Lots of questions will be asked but not a lot of detail is needed. Children will ask if they want to know more.

Teenagers lean on their friends more than family as they grieve. This is developmentally normal and should not be discouraged. Teens need support in ways that are most meaningful and 'accessible' to them. Friends can provide that. Hormonal changes and mood swings might be intensified during grief. Education about the normal reactions to grief can help. Children in this age group need to know they are not going crazy and can trust the way their minds, bodies, and emotions are reacting. Often, teenagers feel a loss of control, and regaining it, even in a small way, is important. Normal teenage activities resume once the teen is ready to re-engage in them. They may be ready right away and use them as a coping mechanism, or it may take some time. Grieving takes a lot of energy. Be encouraging and let them know you love them and will support them always. Let teenagers know that you are there to listen whenever they would like to talk—today and forever. Side-by-side conversations are more acceptable than face to face.

Making decisions about siblings living together or not is full of complex paradoxes for individual children, for siblings, adults, carers, and professionals. Resolving these paradoxes is not easy and leaves decision makers with anxieties that could be described as separation anxiety mirroring the siblings' experiences and feelings. Perhaps this is why there is a search for a simple answer rather than face the complexity of so many paradoxes.

The reasons for the feeling of 'separation anxiety' become clearer and clearer. Practitioners too need time, reflective supervision, research-informed guidance and energy to consider all the implications and consequences of this important aspect when planning for children, their siblings and those who care for them to enable crucial decisions and recommendations to be made.

Chapter 7

Law and Paradox

Policy, Courts, and Sibling Futures

Macduff's statement in Macbeth (1606), 'Confusion now has made his masterpiece,' could just as well describe the current legislation and guidance.

> The Law Commission's review that led to the reforms introduced by the Children Act 1989, proposed a modification of the paramountcy rule whereby, 'The interests of the child whose future happens to be in issue in the proceedings before the court should not in principle prevail over those of other children likely to be affected by the decision. Hence their welfare should also be taken into consideration.'
>
> (The Law Commission 1988: para 3.13)

What follows includes a number of 'shoulds' which in trauma-informed practice would replace with 'coulds' and 'ifs' to generate ideas and solutions:

The 1989 Children Act (s 22 c) cites 'Local Authorities should place a child with siblings where practicable and provided that it is in the best interest of each child.' It would seem that one condition, *practicable*, absolves or overrides the other, *best interest*. If a placement for the siblings cannot be practically found, then there is no need to assess the best interest of each child, or having assessed the best interest of each child, every effort should be made to find the correct placement but only if practicable with the 'no delay' principle in mind. What is regularly heard is there is a shortage of placements for all children with siblings, or without siblings, and matching the child to placement, while it should be considered and attempted, rarely happens (Saunders and Selwyn 2010). What then follows this 'non-match,' as commented on previously, is focusing on placement stability, every effort being made to sustain a clearly wrong placement with no concurrent planning/assessment of the children's developing or changing needs and no search made for the correct placement.

'The decision to separate permanently siblings who have lived or are currently living together should, in our view, be treated with the same seriousness as the decision to separate children permanently from their parents' (Lord and Borthwick 2008, p. 21).

'Siblings with existing bonds should in principle not be separated by placements in alternative care unless there is a clear risk of abuse or other justification in the best interests of the child. In any case, every effort should be made to enable siblings to maintain contact with each other, unless this is against their wishes and feelings.'
(United Nations General Assembly, Resolution: 64/142 2009)

Further in 2016, the UN Committee on the Rights of the Child, in its report on the United Kingdom, noted its concern about 'Siblings being separated from each without proper reason,' and reiterated that wherever possible alternative care placements should 'facilitate contact with siblings' (UNCRC 2016: 52(d), 53(c)). One of the problems that practitioners face is the use of language without any clear definition. The starting principle of 'Siblings with existing bonds' is a complex statement. Siblings can have bonds that lead to either secure or insecure bonds or even trauma bonds, all of which can appear, no matter how positive or skewed, to seem strong and therefore seemingly positive, where in fact they may be far from that position.

These are not definitive requirements to keep siblings together. There are more 'shoulds' in other Guidelines and some Case Law (Guidelines for the Alternative Care of Children 2010, para 17). The legislation attempts to be clear that where possible every effort should be made to keep siblings together. For sentimental reasons, there is a wish and determination to keep siblings together. Difficult histories, violent interactions, and skewed attachments make an assessment necessary, and practical difficulties should not be used as an excuse.

As a result, it becomes easier for someone with a personal view that siblings need not be kept together to emphasise other factors as more important and support separation, and conversely for someone determined to keep siblings together to find research to support their view. Both positions risk skewing decisions, lead to delay, the selection of an inappropriate foster home, or the choice of a least-worst option. The need for an enhanced assessment of, and provision of ongoing support to both potential carers and the sibling group is therefore crucial to avoid or minimise the impact of personal bias and their repercussions.

Too often, placement disruptions follow situations such as where a carer bonds with one sibling and not the other, an immediate liking of one child prompts acceptance of a whole 'sibling package,' where sibling rivalry is beyond 'normal' or totally absent, where there is a request to move one sibling who is actively harming the other sibling or the foster carer's child or pet. In addition, there are the recurring themes where arranging contact is a practical and emotional nightmare and therefore is not arranged, or arranged without purposeful planning, causing major emotional and practical disruptions or termination.

The Children and Young Persons Act 2008 (8) notes the Local Authority must ensure that the placement is such that (a) it allows C to live near C's home, (b) it does not disrupt C's education or training, (c) if C has a sibling for whom the Local Authority are also providing accommodation, it enables C and the sibling to live together, (d) if C is disabled, the accommodation provided is suitable to C's particular needs. The word '*ensures*' suggests this is always the right thing to do when it may not be. The better word '*enables*' puts the onus of responsibility onto ascertaining what is the right thing to do. Thus, changing the word '*ensure*' to '*enable*' in reference to siblings living together allows the Local Authority to not use, '*where reasonably practicable*,' but 'following an in-depth assessment the conclusion is ...'

Another starting strong, but then drifting. Legislation in 2011 relates to the Right to Family Life and the Right to Freedom from Fear in the United Nations Convention on the Rights of the Child (UNCRC), a legally binding international agreement setting out the civil, political, economic, social, and cultural rights of every child, regardless of their race, religion, or abilities. The European Court of Human Rights recognised the Right to a Family Life and the need to preserve ties with the family in Neulinger and Shuruk v Switzerland (App No 41615/07 (2011) 1 FLR 122 but then added another should: 'This should happen when it was clearly in the child's interests to ensure its development in a sound environment,' concluding that parents cannot be entitled under Article 8 of the European Convention on Human Rights to have their children live with them when, 'Such measures taken would harm the child's health and development.'

More recently, the Children and Social Work Act 2017 introduced Corporate Parenting Principles, which are intended to change Local Authority culture so that all staff and departments consider the impact of their work on children and young people for whom the Local Authority is the corporate parent, as well as on those young people under 25 who were previously in the care of a Local Authority. The Corporate Parenting Principles state that English Local Authorities, including County, District, Borough, and Combined Authorities must 'Have regard to the need to take certain actions in their work for children in care and care leavers.' These are in Section 1:

a. *to act in the best interests, and promote the physical and mental health and well-being, of those children and young people.*
b. *to encourage those children and young people to express their views, wishes and feelings.*
c. *to take into account the views, wishes and feelings of those children and young people.*
d. *to help those children and young people gain access to, and make the best use of, services provided by the Local Authority and its relevant partners.*
e. *to promote high aspirations, and seek to secure the best outcomes, for those children and young people.*
f. *for those children and young people to be safe, and for stability in their home lives, relationships and education or work.*
g. *to prepare those children and young people for adulthood and independent living.*

Section 8 extends the definition of the permanence provisions in the Children Act 1989 so that it includes kinship care, adoption, and other types of long-term care. The courts will be required to consider the impact on the child concerned of any harm they have or are likely to have suffered, their current and future needs, and the way in which the long-term plan for the child's upbringing would meet those current and future needs.

There is also guidance from the SCIE (Social Care Institute for Excellence) (Wilson 2004). Their recommendations in the interests of good practice are clear and certainly a basis for good practice, but with no reference to trauma-informed decision-making and the practice implications involved, then or since 2005, are perhaps somewhat out of date. It is noted on their website that a further paper from Sinclair is awaited. Nonetheless, points 4 and 8 are especially useful. They suggest Local Authorities must:

1. Ensure that all decisions taken about sibling care, placement and contact (including recommendations below) includes siblings who may be adopted, those who share one birth parent, and stepbrothers and stepsisters.
2. Ensure contact orders made by a court are followed, and place siblings together unless assessments and the wishes of the child or young person suggest otherwise.
3. Ensure a placement strategy is in place that addresses any shortage of foster carers or suitable residential placements to meet the needs of sibling groups, for example through:
Recruiting foster families specifically for sibling groups.
    - Commissioning homes for small family groups.
    - Meeting the additional financial and housing needs of foster carers to enable siblings to be placed together.
4. Where a looked-after child or young person has a brother or sister in care, identify a placement that allows siblings to live together unless there is clear evidence that this would not be in their best interests, or the child or young person is unhappy with the arrangement.
5. Ensure this approach applies equally to siblings of multiple heritage.
6. Ensure siblings have the same social worker, wherever possible and practical.
7. Establish a clear communication and liaison plan where siblings have different social workers.
8. Where decisions are made to separate sibling family groups:
Record clearly and explain sensitively to the child or young person the reasons for separation.
    - Make robust plans for ongoing sibling contact according to the wishes of the child or young person.
    - Ensure social workers coordinate any ongoing contact desired by the child or young person, arranging appropriate supervision where necessary and supporting foster or residential carers.
    - Review a separation decision if the circumstances of a sibling change.

9. Provide additional support and resources that help the co-placement of siblings to prevent disruption and possible end of a placement for any child or young person in a sibling family group.
10. Where siblings live or are placed in different Local Authority areas ensure that arrangements are in place for their Independent Reviewing Officers or social workers to liaise on their needs, ensuring ongoing contact and any possibility of future co-placement are regularly considered from the perspective and wishes of each sibling.

Changes in policy making and practice to keep families together at home resulted in children continuing to live with parents and siblings in profoundly life-impacting trauma for years until the damage done is so significant that the children coming into care do not require what was once called 'parenting plus' but need skilled therapeutic parenting in placements which also require additional support, for both the carers and the children, from external trauma-informed services. Unfortunately, these are scarce, poorly funded, and often unavailable, such as CAMHS, Psychologists, and Independent Therapy Services.

Rowe and Lambert (1975) wrote about interviews with children in care who expressed their sadness at the loss of or had little knowledge about siblings, which further impacted on place-together practice. It would be very unlikely that this level of loss would be heard today. Instead, what is heard is about the impact of children continuing to live with a sibling whose coping strategies and behaviours cause continuous significant trauma within placements, schools, and disruption in both situations where the support provided was what was available rather than assessed need. The shortage of resources, pressure of work, the feeling and need to be seen to be doing something, add to the practice of 'sign posting' internally or externally, making this a too easy option. What also follows are repeated assessments, or support offered would, at worst, be non-informed and, at best, poorly informed about the impact of early trauma and ongoing trauma on behaviours and coping strategies needed then and now when siblings live together.

Further damage is done to already damaged, perhaps fragile, or conflicted sibling relationships where siblings have been separated and contact is arranged, which has no clear purpose or without assessing what content is needed, the skills of the supervisor are needed to repair and (re)build sibling relationships, resulting in placement breakdown, causing more harm.

Many authors (Sinclair 2005, Jackson and Martin 1998, Minnis and Devine 2001, Sinclair et al. 2003, Ward 1995) have written about the significant negative impact on children of placement disruption. Meakings et al. (2017) comment somewhat tentatively and unusually on the possible significant harm of placements continuing. Three research studies evaluated specific interventions in the USA, which could be useful in improving sibling relationships (Linares et al. 2015, Kothari et al. 2017, and Waid and Wojciak 2017). These studies however were limited and all commented on the lack of research on sibling relationships and helpful interventions.

The lack of research in this area seems to be a common theme which must lead to questioning how there can be guidance on such a complex and important area if research is not continually updating the information on its efficacy or challenging its robustness or accuracy? Selwyn et al. (2014) demonstrated a comparison of placement disruptions over a five-year period between Residence Orders, Special Guardianship Orders, and Adoption Orders, Post Adoption Orders, and whilst this gave a clear insight into the differences, it leaves questions about the outcomes prior to these Orders and the implications for siblings placed together in foster care or children's homes. This area is so vast with so many variables that it would require a national, joined-up and coherent approach to addressing the research gaps. Wilkinson and Bowyer (2017) citing Wade et al. (2014) found 'making Special Guardianship Orders quickly, before relationships have been properly tested may carry some future risk of disruption,' but went on to state that there was no evidence to support this at present. If there is a dearth of clear data around disruption for individually placed children due to the number of variables, how much more complex it becomes to consider siblings and sibling groups.

Monk and McVarish (2018) tried and concluded, 'There is no requirement to conduct a sibling assessment (sometimes referred to as a "together or apart" assessment) nor any binding guidance as to how it should be undertaken' and

> There is a lack of clarity in law and practice about when and how sibling relationships should be formally assessed. While sibling assessments appear to be more common, there is no standard format. Concerns exist about the impact of time and resource limitations and that sometimes assessments function as evidence of decision making rather than a tool for better decision making.

Their report also concluded that, 'There is no consistent national method for assessing sibling relationships currently embedded in social worker training or in practice.' There is a relative silence about siblings in the other disciplines, or indeed any chapters specifically about siblings in any practitioner or academic child, family, social work, or law, or in the much-used and OFSTED-approved Signs of Safety texts, with limited and sometimes no references to them in their indices.

One Judge tried to address the concern when highlighting the different expectations about contact,

> In care cases, you know, children will see siblings and see parents once a month, four times a year, yet if it was a private law case, it will be once a fortnight and you will not tell me there is a difference. I cannot figure out what the difference is. You ask that question of a social worker in a witness box, or a Guardian, they look at you as if you are mad and they chuck out stability, security, undermining placement. And with Mum and Dad that would be different, why? Tell me. So I do not know. I do not get it.
>
> (Monk and McVarish 2018)

In conclusion, the legislation appears to be clear and straightforward but then weakens with provisos. This is something which might actually be praised rather than criticised given the confused, outdated research on the impact of having a sibling and whether living with one is a good idea or not. This means if a view, whether personally or professionally well-informed, that siblings should be together or apart, legislation can be found to support that view. The need therefore for thorough and detailed assessment of the individuals in a sibling group, the dynamics of that group, their individual and group therapeutic needs, and just as detailed an assessment of foster carers and adopters who would care for a sibling group is of paramount importance if further harm is to be avoided rather than consequential. The written and verbal evidence made available to a court will perhaps then answer the Judge's needs to understand difference and, 'Get it.

Part IV

Trauma and Development
Body, Brain, and Behaviour

Chapter 8

Incubated in Terror or Held in Mind?
Attachment, Regulation, and Developmental Trauma

There are many theoretical models for understanding child development. These include psychoanalytic theories, cognitive development, learning, biological models, social, developmental psychopathology, and genetics. What is unhelpful is to have an either/or approach. People are complex integrated beings where all these theories can, to an extent, coexist. For clarity, the focus will be psychoanalytic, with its attachment theory, psychopathology, and developmental trauma, but from a staunchly person-centred perspective. Other theories will be interjected.

Common statements made include, 'We know about attachment,' 'We are a trauma informed school,' and 'We are trained in…' These statements may all be true, but what they convey in reality can vary widely. They rarely indicate a shared understanding of the topic or the terms, nor do they necessarily reflect an appreciation of the impact of trauma or what the implications of this are for each individual child.

This chapter sets out some understanding of these issues, not for them to be a definitive guide to what is right or wrong, but to create clarity in the use of these terms so that this text can provide a coherent and consistent approach.

Historically, at least within social care, it seemed that the advances in understanding attachment came firstly in Bowlby's seminal work in 1958. The impact of trauma appears to have been slower to understand or define, with good reason. Perhaps surprising when Charcot in the 1890s explored the origin of the mental health condition known as 'Hysteria' and argued that it manifested as a result of psychological trauma (Nijenhuis 2015).

Attachment, the state that is cultivated as a result of 'good-enough' parenting, is a process in child development which results in the child developing an attachment strategy. This is then given the term secure, or tends towards insecure avoidant, or tends towards ambivalent, all of which can be within 'average,' 'expected,' or 'normal' parameters. All are dependent on the type of care-giving and care-receiving the child experienced. Developmental Trauma, on the other hand, falls into developmental psychopathology, the label given to the study of what happens when a child's expected development goes off kilter, the impact of this is clarified further by understanding the consequences of the different types of trauma: types 1, 2, 3, and 4.

DOI: 10.4324/9781003724797-12

Klaus and Kennell (1976) describe attachments as, 'An affectionate bond between two individuals that endures through space and time and serves to join them emotionally.' It is a process that relies on the responses of primarily two individuals, the mother and her child. Primarily, because whilst the partner, where involved, will be an important and influencing factor in the child's developing attachment style, only the mother has carried the child in utero for nine months. The positive and negative qualities of these months are still often neglected and not commented on in assessments.

As described previously, Maslow's Hierarchy of needs is identified as the foundation of successful child development, but is it really the starting point? He starts with all the things that a system needs to survive. The need to belong and be loved does not appear until the third tier, after order and limits, yet the first thing a newborn baby does is cry to stimulate and achieve re-connection before settling on recontact with the mother. It may be some time before the infant becomes hungry. Connection is the keystone in attachment. If using the 'wall' exercise, where would the 'connection' brick be put?

To avoid repetition, a number of presumptions will be presented:

- A bond is an emotional glue that forms and sustains a connection between one person and another. It involves a set of behaviours (in good enough parenting) that will help lend to an emotional connection/attachment. It is the process of forming an attachment.
- An attachment is the nature and quality of the actual relationship (e.g. secure or insecure attachments).
- Attachment capabilities refer to an individual's capacity to form and maintain an emotional relationship. This is a two-way concept. It must include the parent's ability to give (and therefore their attachment history and experience are fundamental) and the child's ability to receive needs to match in a relatively harmonious manner.

Howe et al. (1999) describe the timings in the attachment process in the following way:

0–2 months	Pre-attachment: Indiscriminating social responsiveness.
3–6 months	Attachment in the making: Discriminating social responsiveness.
7–36 months	Clear attachment: Active initiative in proximity and contact.
36+	Goal-corrected partnership.

The first attachment made is biological; the fertilised egg to the wall of the womb and the biological formation of the foetus are followed by the social process of attachment in relationships. These processes are separate but are intrinsically interconnected, and therefore it is not always helpful to separate them (Gerhardt 2004). Music states, 'It (the foetus) is profoundly influenced by its milieu' (2011, p. 14). Therefore, Howe's timings need to include other factors:

9–0 months Pre-disposition:	Environment influenced
0–2 months Pre-attachment:	Arousal range formation
3–6 months Attachment development:	Discriminating social responsiveness
6–36 months Attachment style:	Active use of strategy
36–48 months Attachment wiring:	Deepening and transferring

Pre-disposition—Conception to Birth

The children of Hannah and Devon. Each time Hannah discovered she was pregnant, the news was received by both parents-to-be and their network as a celebration and a blessing. The couple remained financially secure and supported. They ceased any moderate drinking. They undertook and maintained their balanced diet. They had all the anti-natal support offered with each child to ensure they were well-informed in case there was new information over the period of time that they had their children. They continued their lives with each foetus in mind. Arguably, the children all presented with similar thresholds for dealing with daily stress because their in-utero experiences were all so similar. They were incubated in bliss.

Tia was not a wished-for child. Originally destined for termination, which was only avoided by the murder of her mother's then partner, this unfortunately did not stop her experience of being incubated in drugs and further violence. Reports stated that Tia's birth parents were, from a young age, involved in criminal activity and drug misuse, including heroin, cocaine, and diazepam, continuing throughout the pregnancy. Their relationship was described as violent and chaotic.

Domestic violence, an enduring feature of their relationship, is associated with: 'Hypertension during pregnancy and intrauterine growth retardation' (Arcos et al. 2001). 'It causes stress in the mother, and stress in the mother causes higher risk of foetal suffering, increased risk of prematurity, higher frequency of growth inhibition and lower gestational weight' (Rauchfuss and Gauger 2003).

Stress results in higher cortisol production. A high level of cortisol in the mother is associated with high levels of cortisol in the foetus, which causes increased foetal activity, lower capacity for habituation, and higher reactivity in the baby. Tia was just as impacted by her mother's distress and rage, leading to higher cortisol levels, as she was by the maternal use of drugs.

> There is clear evidence for foetal and newborn sentience, the ability to interact with the environment. Newborns and foetuses in utero have been shown capable of classical habituation and conditioning. The foetus is as capable of experiencing negative impact and distress as a newborn.
>
> Scaer (2014)

'As self-concerned with both social existence and goal direction' (Nijenhuis (2015), Is, 'Impacted by external relationships' (Zoia et al. 2007), and 'Biologically as a result of the placenta's deficits in its inability to being able to filter all of the substances consumed or created by the mother from smoking and alcohol' (Williams and Ross 2007), to 'drugs and medication' (Bhide 2009, El Marroun et al. 2014) to, 'an unhealthy diet' (Monk et al. 2013), and 'Cortisol as a stress outcome' (Entringer et al. 2011). This is all summed up nicely in Perry's paper 'Incubated in Terror' (1997). Scaer in 2014, concludes, 'The assumption that infants in all stages of development do not experience pain, do not register arousal with threat, and do not process a response to traumatic stress is clearly outdated and invalid,' which would mean until 2014, that was current thinking.

> The mother-foetus relationship is more akin to a tug-or-war with the foetus being able at times to have as much influence over the mother's biology as the mother can have over the foetus. Further, the mother's state of mind during pregnancy is key and can predict an infant's behaviours a year or more after birth.
>
> Music (2011)

Pre-attachment—0–2 Months

Hannah and Devon's children continued to be loved, despite their growing family. Their competing needs, from the order of their birth bringing the rivaling needs that a larger family brings, were juggled. Their outlook remained ever optimistic despite the usual trials of life testing their resources and resilience in the same way we all face challenges. The parents became the barometer of the children's ability to regulate as Gerhardt states, 'In the early months of life, the organism(baby) is establishing (or deepening) just what the normal range of arousal is, establishing the set point which its systems will attempt to maintain' (2004). The child therefore is reliant on her/his parents to regulate their arousal in either excitement or distress because both can lead to the infant exiting their window of tolerance that at their birth, even in an ordinarily developing infant is 'Pillbox' thin. As described earlier, this social or interactive regulation by the parents, but particularly the mother is to 'maintain the child's arousal within the moderate range that is high enough to maintain interactions…but not too intense as to cause distress and avoidance' (Schore 1994). This is achieved utilising the attachment encouraging behaviours.

From the outset, Tia's system had been put into overdrive and/or underdrive as a result of the in-utero drugs she received. Following birth, this drug dependency had to be equally pharma-therapeutically managed as did the high cortisol levels she experienced as a result of the environment her mother lived in. Her lack of human interaction in those early weeks, coupled with her inability to tolerate touch, may have been the source of her developing a fierce self-reliance and an inability to tolerate proximity-promoting behaviours, forming developmental classical conditioning and habituation.

Attachment Development 3–6 Months

Hannah and Devon remained consistent in their approach to life and childcare. They worked, which was sometimes consuming for Hannah, taking her away from her children (rupture), but she always acknowledged it and made it up to them with her love-filled time (repair). As stated previously, perfection is not a healthy state. Children need to face some purposeful, age-appropriate adversity to grow, learn, and survive. It is these (little) ruptures that help us do the most important childcare task—and that is the repair.

Even in her first six months, Tia's mother, a sex worker, consistently abandoned her. Leaving her alone whilst she worked, leaving her vulnerable to the vagaries of those around her who did not understand or care much about what was good or not for this infant or her needs. This experience would have mirrored her experience of coming into the world: being on her own. She will have cried as all babies can do when distressed. Prolonged and uncomforted crying is the breeding ground for mood disorders, hyperactivity, conduct disorders, depression, and anxiety. Cortisol is not just released during stress responses to abuse or danger but also by separation or abandonment. Cortisol, constantly produced and then released in sensitive areas of the brain without assuagement, becomes toxic. Eventually, however, she stopped crying, stopped 'calling' for her mother. 'By not crying or outwardly expressing their feelings, they are often able to partially gratify at least one of their attachment needs, that of remaining physically close to a parent' (Freedman 2018). Max, baby Tia's six-year-old brother, who had already experienced the absence of his mother, survived through his own tenacity after the death of his father, and knew his sister's survival rested on his shoulders. His pseudo-parentified life's purpose was now to keep his sister alive.

Attachment Style 6–36 Months

Hannah and Devon's children met each new relationship, relatives, and family friends with the expected level of relational security versus separation anxiety. The family developed a secure and stable base as a result of reliability and consistency creating the foundation, that sense of safety allowing their children to grow in confidence, to achieve, and become resilient individuals. They were on varying degrees of the continuum, secure in their attachment style.

Despite her start in life, Tia continued to live with her mother for the first two years of her life, sometimes being cared for in an insufficient way by her six-year-old brother, who, whilst attempting to meet his sister's needs, also had aggressive tendencies towards her. She was neglected, left home alone, received physical injuries, and given her mother's high-risk work, was likely, at the very least, to have been exposed to her mother's sexual activity. How she presented during this time is not known. On entering foster care at the age of two, she was described as having 'A good attachment with her carer,' an outcome, given her experiences of no stable person in her life, that was simply not possible. More consistent with her history were the observations of significant developmental 'lags,' 'anger regulation' issues, and described simultaneously as being 'wary of strangers, and being indiscriminate with no stranger awareness.' Tia, a highly anxious child, swung from extremely controlling behaviours to desperate clinginess.

Tia did not have a secure attachment system and neither did her brother. Despite Tia's concerning behaviours in the reports on Tia's responses to her foster carers and then her adopters, she was repeatedly described by social workers and foster carers as having 'a good attachment to her carer,' 'a strong bond to her brother,' and that she was 'forming a healthy attachment to her carers.' Yet Tia was closest and the most relaxed with her cat.

She was seen to present with dual insecure attachment strategies, both ambivalent and avoidant. Where both avoidant and ambivalent themes are present, a disorganised attachment pattern emerges.

> Disorganised behaviours are considered to be indicative of an experience of stress and anxiety which the child cannot resolve because the parent is at the same time the source of fright as well as the only potential haven of safety. In the face of this paradoxical situation, the organized strategy is expected to fall apart.
>
> (Van Ijzendoorn 1999)

Disorganised children develop aggressive self-reliance and controlling behaviours; they deny internal views of themselves as helpless and vulnerable or in need of comfort, which raises the likelihood of misusing power and control to avoid these needs, which raises anxiety and dysregulation. Their internal working model becomes the template for how these 'disorganised' children see relationships, especially those where there is caregiving and care-receiving. This template cannot be replaced immediately; it is a process. What is usually observed is the development of a healthier alternative—a veneer over the original template. As the child learns to adapt to experiences with new parents or carers over time, adaptations become familiar or procedural and the old template will begin to diminish. This can explain why periodically, when stress, transition, anniversary, season change, or anything 'out of the window' reminds them of their parents' parenting style, the child reverts or regresses to an old tried and experienced as useful strategy.

Attachment Wiring 36–48 Months

Hannah and Devon's children were provided with multiple opportunities to deepen their experiences of human relationships: meeting up with relatives, grandparents, family friends; organised and regular, spontaneous, and unique pre-school activities. They engaged with professionals: midwives, health visitors, GPs and nurses, dentists, opticians, and other specialists as required. Every time the children met people who responded in a similarly accepting and nurturing manner, it deepened their outlook and developed their internal working model that essentially the world was a good place. When they were faced with adversity, where the people they met were frightening, gruff, and disinterested, their parents were there to make the repair and reassure them. They survived the adversity and developed their resilience. As these experiences continued, their newborn fragmented selves integrated so that by the time the children went to school aged four, they were ready to face the world, in so much as any four-year-old child can face the world. The notion of when it is okay for a child to start school in the United Kingdom is not child-led; effectively, it is not even parent-led, a notion that is for many children a decision that lacks coherency with their needs. Imagine then what it is like for a child who has faced a traumatic start to life or indeed is living in that trauma, either actually in reality or psychologically, in the here and now.

Tia was one such child and her needs, as so often is the case, differed from those of her brother. She needed connection and could not accept it; her brother's raison d'être was to care for his sister. He became ferociously protective when people tried to meet Tia's needs. Whether he was protective of Tia or protective of his believed purpose of existence, or both, neither or something else can only be hypothesised. The older he became, the more restrictions he placed on Tia and the more violent he became. Tia would not let her brother or anyone else care for her because care came to equal fear. She could not trust her primary caregiver, her mother, to look after her because her mother was simultaneously frightened and frightening.

> With a [frightened/frightening] caregiver, infants are caught in a relational trap: their defence systems motivate them to flee from the caregiver, while at the same time their attachment system motivates them, under the commanding influence of separation fear, to strive for achieving comforting proximity to her or him.
> (Liotti 2011)

She could not trust her birth father. He was a frightening man. She could not trust her brother because he could not prevent the danger. He did try when there was danger and when there was nurture, because for him they ultimately equated and were intimately intertwined. Her brother was as frightening as those around her. She became self-reliant, but like her brother, in an insufficient way. In her foster placements, she kept everyone at bay.

She was both nocturnally and diurnally encopretic and seemed not to notice or be affected by its impact on those around her either at home, later at school, or in the community. She refused to eat anywhere except in her bedroom alone, controlled her bedtimes, presented with 'ADHD-like' behaviours, as 'dyspraxic,' 'dyslexic,' and with 'sensory processing' symptoms. When her anger and rage were not present, she was overtly dissociative. When she was finally adopted aged four her task was clear: to survive she must divide and conquer internally and externally.

The process of our attachment formation demonstrates how it is linked to both child development and psychopathology. The parameters of a secure attachment relationship may include elements of insecurity within those parameters and child psychopathology, whereby the developmental trauma experienced is either the cause of an insecure or disorganised attachment pattern or heavily influenced by it. Therefore, it is unhelpful to separate attachment styles from developmental or complex trauma. These experiences also impact our character strategies (Fenichel 1945, Reich 1933, Kurtz 1990). Ogden (2006) identified the following nine character strategies that can shape our presentation to the world. Whilst Ogden identifies character formation in some attachment styles and not in others, she acknowledges that they are all formed in our early years. The asterisked ages are prescribed by her; the others are based on professional observations.

Character Type Age of development
Sensitive-Withdrawn 0–12 months*
Sensitive-Emotional 0–12 months*
Dependent-Endearing 18–36 months*
Expressive-Clinging 18–60 months
Charming-Manipulative 18–60 months
Burdened-Enduring 24–60 months*
Tough-Generous 36–60 months
Industrious-Over focused 36–60 months
Self-Reliant—Realisation 36 months

The earlier the experience makes it more likely the child will develop a dependency on a single strategy or default to a strategy for security. These strategies are on a continuum and are more defined when there is adversity in the formative years when the child learns that to get their needs met, one or more of these strategies are more helpful than others. Easy identification of one over others may be an indicator of how fragmented versus integrated a person may be. If someone is truly integrated, they can roll with the blows presented by the whims of life experiences and perhaps do not need to default to a single manner or character strategy but can remain, as Schwartz describes, as our 'real' or 'core' selves or '9 C.' How many people are truly their 'real' or 'core' self, 'B' or 'secure' in their attachment style all the time, and who remains this way when under stress? Everyone has a window of tolerance of individual width enabling stress to be managed, but beyond which makes them dependent on fewer but heightened strategies or into crisis or burnout.

Case Example: Becky and Tom

Becky was dismissive of and oppositional towards her carers; she ignored boundaries, limits, rules, or expectations, was verbally abusive, lacked self-care with poor personal hygiene, and targeted her brother, continually tormenting and goading him. Her attachment style tended towards ambivalence as a result of unpredictability in her care-receiving experience from her birth parents. She was quick to anger and quick to reject but always kept trying. She never knew how her birth mother would react and transferred/projected this expectation to all other relationships: an enduring and ongoing internal confusion. It would be easy to describe this as Becky not knowing how other people would react, and therefore she did not know any other way to be around people but to describe it like this would be shaming and blaming her for something she had not and could not learn or integrate and was therefore not her fault. Better to say she had to manage her life with a 'not knowing how other people would react' and therefore a 'not knowing of how she should be.' Unfortunately, her strategy could break down further under stress and become disorganised where no workable strategy existed. She would seem to be self-reliant in her character strategy because she believed she could rely on no one else. For her, this was true.

This is not just about the children but all those people connected to them to understand how they relate to each other. Cicely kept the placement going whilst concurrently constantly talking about Becky's shortcomings. She lacked empathy or perhaps only kept on keeping on as a result of a sense of duty, perhaps the shame of stopping and ending the placement was harder for her to do than continuing or perhaps out of sentimentality. She could not talk about her past, just stating that it was lovely in the similar way she spoke about Tom and Becky's placement. She did not want to overtly acknowledge the challenges she faced historically or in the present. Her keeping on, keeping on was hard work. Her shoulders rounded as though she carried a burden, one of her presenting character strategies, burdened enduring. She talked, a non-stop stream of persistent negativity; she would cry but could not emote and couldn't see the paradox in her complaint that Becky would not stop talking. Cicely talked emotion, but it was as though it did not come from the inside. She presented with both sensitive-emotional and expressive clinging traits, suggesting that she continued to be affected by unprocessed early childhood care-receiving deficits or trauma, but was not yet ready, able, or aware enough to acknowledge them to herself, let alone anyone else. As long as she, indeed practitioners have, unprocessed childhood experiences, there will be a continual risk of being triggered by people or events. Developmentally traumatised children are experts in identifying and targeting weak links, our Achilles' heels, and with the accuracy of an Exocet missile, hit that target or push that button. If anyone is not aware of internal vulnerability, their responses are likely to be less that of 9 'C' and indeed could be devastating if meeting like-with-like relationship making or communication. Cicely met Becky with hostility, contempt, irritation, and dislike, but met Tom with understanding.

Tom kept himself to himself. He did not approach Becky or his carers. He internalised his feelings. Tom was not ok. He had internalised his experiences, so was less likely to trigger his female foster carer, but he triggered his sister, who constantly targeted him. He also had to endure watching his sister being treated differently. He managed this by withdrawing further.

It is often the externalising child who is referred to therapy. Their behaviour is obvious and is a problem to those around them. It is often the behaviour used to describe or refer to them. The referrer often says, 'There is something wrong with this child.' Rarely does a referrer say, 'What must have happened to this child?' or, 'This child is so angry and violent. They must be hurting so much inside.' Repeatedly heard is their behaviour is the problem rather than the answer to their problems. When the referrer is asked about the externalising child's sibling/s, so often the response is, 'Oh, they are fine.' It must be made clear that the same environment, where two children are living, will not produce one child who is ok; they may seem ok, but will not be ok. A child who internalises experiences will have feelings that are equal to the energy of their externalising sibling. When one child is tearing radiators off the walls, questions must be asked: 'What must it be like internally for this child who is not tearing radiators from the walls? And for their sibling?' Where one child is scapegoated, beaten, neglected, or raped and the other is not does not lead to the 'cared-for' child being ok. As witness to their siblings's treatment, they too had and have to survive this skewed relational pattern and develop their own required character strategies.

Any intervention, from initial assessment to planning to provision, begins and continues the process of change and healing. It must be trauma-informed without any shame or blame but with empathic curiosity, not wishy-washy, but with tenacity and time. Therapeutic responses to developmental trauma need to take account of the whole family, system, or context to create the change required and to create and sustain longevity in that change.

Chapter 9

Brains under Siege
How Trauma Shapes Development and Behaviour

The impact on the child's developing brain and the behavioural responses that follow is crucial knowledge for sibling assessments. The speed with which the advancement of knowledge in this area from research and studies grows means some of the information can become outdated and redundant quite quickly. If being used in a court report or dissertation, checking current validity will therefore be necessary.

This chapter **should** be thousands of words long … woops, this chapter **could** be thousands of words long **if** ….

In this, as in so many ways, the change in one word evokes a different intellectual and visceral response.

Every sibling group **should** have an assessment informed by the impact of trauma and neurobiology. Every sibling group **could** have an assessment informed by the impact of trauma and neurobiology **if**….

Every sibling group **will** have an assessment informed by the impact of trauma and neurobiology **when**….

Too many words, too much knowledge, too many changes and advances challenge thinking, time available, and resources. Identifying the crucial components to include brings the question, Will there ever be enough? to mind. At the same time, it energises and maintains curiosity to learn more, develop skills, and encouragement to deal with the emotional and practical skills to deal with bumps, challenges, and beliefs. Having a parent does not provide parenting; having a brain does not provide the skills to heal hurt brains. Both require compassion, consistency, reliability, theoretical knowledge, and the will to provide an empathic living relationship.

The advent of functioning Magnetic Resonance Imaging (fMRI) scans has enabled researchers and neurobiologists to view and determine differences in brain function in response to everyday non-traumatic events and how this differs from its response to stressful and/or traumatic events. It is currently thought that the brain has more than 2 million miles of neuronal fibres and each of the 20 billion neurons is connected to an average of 10,000 other neurons; this makes for an incredibly complex network of trillions of synapses, yet it is 75–80% water, the rest split between fat and protein. It makes up 2% of our body weight but uses 20% of our

DOI: 10.4324/9781003724797-13

energy; in babies, this is 65%. Most of its growth happens in the first two years. It is 95% of its growth by age 10 but not fully wired until the mid-20s—perhaps we should consider and take into account that teenage 'thinking' may continue until then. It burns 400 calories of energy every day at the same rate, no matter how hard you are thinking or not thinking at all.

Care is needed to determine the difference between stress and trauma, and in just the same way, to be clear about the difference between being anxious and anxiety, a want and a need, selfish and self-care aware, manipulativeand trying hard to have unmet needs recognised or met, attention seeking and attachment seeking. All of the former words have a negative connotation but on reframing from a trauma perspective the latter words are more appropriate. Doing this helps explain why one child in a family experiencing the same negative parenting within their home, or later goes to the same contact would find it stressful and another find it traumatic (Siegel 2002, 2012), Putnam (1997), Lanius (2013), Hughes (2017) Chapman (2014), Haines (2018), Howes (2014).

It is also not unusual for the child who internaises their distress to be described as 'stressed' or 'resilient,' leading to the misconception that the child was less affected by what was done or not done because their behaviour is not perceived to be upset enough. This could be because their experience was stressful and not traumatic (Cairns 2002) or was traumatic, but internalised and therefore impacted less on those around the child. Had it been externalised, more attention would be drawn to that child and the question asked, 'What is wrong with that child?' sometimes followed by a diagnosis because the behaviours overlap the diagnostic criteria and medication prescribed. But the cause of the behaviour remains unaddressed because the questions, 'What is happening to or what has been done to this child?' have not been asked or had been asked and the answers not accepted or ignored. Another explanation could be that the child had an external resource, a teacher, friend, friend's mum, or even a pet, who was able to buffer the impact or soothe the child after the event, reducing the impact and 'sowing the seeds' of resilience.

Siegel (2002, 2012) explains the difference between stress and trauma in a mammal's ability to tolerate the potential stress of any situation using what he calls the 'window of tolerance.' Whilst 'in the window' stress is tolerated and managed; for example, high levels of excitement, fear, or sadness are managed 'in the window.' Intolerable distress, however, is 'out of the window' and results in one of two possible strategies: (i) hypo/shutting down, mimicking depression or ADD (Attention Deficit Disorder), or (ii) hyper/frantic responses, mimicking ADHD (Attention Deficit Hyperactivity Disorder); and sometimes, when behaviour alternates between the two, mimicking the diagnostic criteria for Bi-polar or Borderline or Unstable Personality Disorder or Conduct Disorder.

Babies can only tolerate a limited amount of stress before becoming distressed Siegel (2002). As long ago as 1997, Perry wrote about the impact of a mother experiencing trauma on her baby's developing brain in utero, inferring the baby would be born with a narrower window of tolerance than a baby whose mother had a happy, relaxed trimester. While 'in the window,' the baby/toddler/adult manages what is happening and is able afterwards to developmentally reflect on this whilst still able to manage any distress caused by this reflection. Mentalisation and consistent, loving, empathic responses to the baby's needs enable the window to widen. The growing child can then tolerate more stress, developing resilience before becoming distressed or traumatised. Putnam (1997) assists our thinking about resilience, identifying 13 variables which can increase or decrease the width of this window:

1. The detailed nature of the child's attachment to his or her parents.
2. The age and developmental level of the child at its onset.
3. Its duration and frequency.
4. Whether different forms of abuse coexist.
5. The relationship of the child to the abuser(s).
6. The type and severity of the abusive acts.
7. The existence of multiple abusers.
8. The degree of physical violence and aggression used.
9. The age and gender of the offender.
10. The existence of peer or adult supports.
11. Whether or not the child has been able to tell.
12. The parental reaction to the disclosure.
13. The 'institutional' impact: how agencies responded positively or negatively.

This last point adds a further level of trauma as identified by Summit in 1983 but is still experienced by children and adults today, explaining why allegations are retracted, silence is kept, and wishes that nothing had been said continue, because what has happened after disclosure is experienced as more painful and chaotic than the harm being investigated or assessed (Summit 1983, Howes 2014).

Types of trauma: Before explaining the difference in brain function, it is important to understand the basic difference between Type 1, Type 2 (Terr 1991, 1992, James, 1994), Type 3 (Solomon and Heide 1999), and Type 4 trauma (Howes 2014).

Type 1 trauma: Refers to a one-off, sudden, and unexpected event, often later described as an accident. There is appropriate self-blame and guilt, alongside recognition that the perpetrator or circumstance was to blame, but also understanding the event was not planned, for example a car crash or a natural disaster. When the victim says, 'it was my fault this happened' it may be acceptable, but not always advisable, to reply, 'it was not your fault,' and later enable them to apportion appropriately. Some literature also classifies rape as a Type 1 trauma but only when this is a one-off, randomly selected stranger rape with no relational dependency. This distinction is crucial, or it would be classified as Type 2. Even in a one-off situation, the victim may still blame themselves especially when the perpetrator has not been caught.

One survivor explained,

I need to believe this was my fault to feel to believe I can prevent it happening again. By making it my fault I can choose to do something differently. I can choose when to go out, what to wear, how to walk. I could not leave the house if I thought there was nothing I could do to stop this from happening to me again.

With Type 1, there may be symptoms of acute traumatic stress, but these are short-term and do not usually lead to post-traumatic stress disorder.

Type 2 trauma: Refers to events which are planned and repeated, and therefore cannot be described as accidental. They generate overwhelming self-blame and shame. Shame differs from guilt by the level of self-blame experienced. The belief resulting from guilt is, 'that was a terrible thing that I did.' The belief emanating from shame is 'I am terrible.' Type 2 trauma includes all forms of child abuse and inter-personal violence. When harm occurs within a relationship, the victim often protects the perpetrator from blame in order to preserve their own attachment and dependency needs (Herman 1992). This heightens self-blame. When the victim says, 'It was my fault this happened' the response, 'It was not your fault,' causes the victim to experience confusion, distress, and significant empathic disruption or withdrawal. The automatic reply, 'It's not your fault' may create confusion, distress, and empathic rupture. A more helpful response is to acknowledge the belief, gently explore it,

'Where did that idea of fault come from?' 'how long it has been present?' 'who else makes you feel that way?' and 'what might it be like to consider even briefly, it was not their fault?'

The need for self-blame is a major coping strategy for both Type 1 and Type 2 trauma. Saying, 'it was not your fault' does not resolve this belief. Instead, understand and empathically connect with the belief and understand its function.

One person recalled her mother waiting behind the back door with a walking stick ready to hit her if she was more than a minute late home from school. Her mother told her that lateness was a sign of rudeness and rudeness was a sin. Her Bible said spare the rod and spoil the child, so she must be punished. No matter how hard she tried, she could not make it home on time. She told herself, and others, that it was her fault for not running fast enough or missing the first bus. But what if she dawdled because she was reluctant to go home? Would that make it her fault? She had never considered that her mother's refusal to let her wear a watch, despite being 14, coupled with a 5-mile journey and a 30-minute bus ride, made punctuality almost impossible. It was unthinkable, whilst dependent on her, to see her mother as violent or cruelly misquoting her Bible. It was safer to blame herself, believe the punishment was for her own good, and cling to the belief that if she hurried enough, she could avoid the stick.

Type 3 trauma: Refers to ongoing trauma where the victim's emotional and dependency needs are exploited to meet the perpetrator's needs with little or no concern for the impact of those needs on the victim. Sexual exploitation is a clear example. Here the trauma bond from Type 2 is used to manipulate the victim into doing things which would not otherwise be agreed to and are deeply shaming. Trafficking provides another example where the victim's physical survival is the primary risk, and this dependence is exploited by the trafficker to ensure payment and compliance. Later, fear of discovery is manipulated, replacing emotional dependency on the exploiter.

It is not unusual for a Type 1 trauma to occur when there is already a Type 2 or 3 occurring or indeed is in the past and memory of the event has been dissociated. The response to the Type 1 is then described as ridiculous, unnecessary, over the top and age inappropriate in the circumstances. For example, a foster child's scraped knee results in tears and distress which then increases exponentially and dramatically when the bottle of TCP is opened. The child is also responding to dissociated memories of events, triggered by the smell of the TCP, in the past when their natural reaction to the sting of TCP resulted in them being smacked by their mother and shamed by their father calling them a 'cry-baby,' then being stood in the corner facing the wall to help them 'toughen-up.'

Type 4 trauma: Arises from the behaviour and interventions of the very agencies victims, parents, or carers turn to for help. Thresholds set too high or waiting lists too long often mean repeated assessments, first being asked what was done, then what it did to them, perhaps even asking what was missing. Each opens up painful wounds, only then to be told the agency is not the correct one to help them. They may be placed on a waiting list to be 're-assessed' every three months with the same questionnaire or referred to other agencies with similar intake methods. The victim experiences this as another trauma, feeling they have failed to meet the agency's needs and, as victims often do, then blame themselves for the rejection or delay. Serious case reviews and National Enquiries from the 1970 and currently in 2026 into historical allegations of abuse repeatedly identify this avoidable harm and yet it continues today. Agencies could reduce the impact of Type 4 trauma by reviewing their referral and intake procedures, to reduce if not eliminate this secondary form of trauma.

The ability to deal with any experience is not just age dependent but is influenced by previous life experiences, both traumatic and non-traumatic events. When a child has empathic support, a secure, reliable attachment figure, a return to safety, resolution, reparation, processing, and an understanding of why something happened, this response then helps remove the 'trauma' from the experience and allows a greater chance of recovery.

Case example: A child who is accidentally lost by a parent while shopping but is hugged by the parent when found, and the parent apologises.

Whilst shopping in a packed shop, a child is seen as confused and, with increasing levels of terror, is looking around for a lost parent. Just before they lose control, an adult intervenes and says, 'Oh dear, has your mummy lost you?' The child half smiles but then assesses this adult as potentially helpful, decides yes, and holds their hand, answering the question, 'yes.' The child is then asked, 'shall we try and find your mummy?' Again, a nod and a, 'yes.' 'I wonder how we can find her. Shall we shout out her name?' The nod is not quite so clear. His brow furrows and lips tighten. The adult notices, wonders if shouting is allowed in his world, and takes responsibility for shouting and says, 'I'll shout. What is your mummy called?' The child's predictable answer is 'mummy.' The child is then asked, 'What does daddy call your mummy?' Thankfully, the answer is her name. This is then shouted out after a count of 3. Immediately, the child's dad appears, lifts his child, hugs them, pats their back, and apologises for losing them. The child begins to reassure dad by patting dad's back in return. Both recover quickly, make sense of what happened, their trust in each other and their attachment to each other is deepened, and the event—while painful at the time—is no longer a trauma. This settled emotional state, with the resolved neuro-biological consequences, informs the child's behaviour and relationships in the future. This reciprocal interaction results in this being a Type 1 trauma.

Alternatively, a child who is lost by a parent while shopping is smacked when found, blamed for being lost and for upsetting the parent, and still has to make sense of what has happened. The child cannot blame their parent, who has given the message that this was their fault. The child would, if they did blame their parent, experience the distress of recognising they have an unreasonable parent who is also abandoning, unavailable when needed, frightening, and who also lies. But the child knows this already because this is not the first or last time this has or will happen. This example of fear without resolution is noted as one of the causes of a disorganised attachment—Type 2 trauma (Main and Hesse 1992, Cloitre et al. 2009, Shemmings and Shemmings 2011). In their teenage years, the child frequently stays out late, meets friends in the local park, and begins experimenting with alcohol and drugs. The young person is noticed, targeted, and groomed by a gang master who involves them in sexual exploitation and county lines activities—type 3 trauma.

The importance of assessing parent/child to observe who is meeting whose needs and who is exploiting those needs to meet their own needs is recognised. More importantly, it also needs to be included when assessing sibling relationships.

Consider the initial contact observation of a sibling group with mum. The siblings are boys aged ten and four, and girls aged nine and two. The ten and nine-year-olds are placed together, as are the four and two-year-olds who are now in their second week of short-term placements. Their greetings are brief. The ten-year-old plays on his Xbox alone, ignoring everyone. The nine-year-old plays with her younger siblings for about ten minutes then focuses on the two-year-old, shunning and teasing the four-year-old by taking his favourite toy until she grows bored, sighs, and moves over to look out of the window. The four-year-old then interacts with the two-year-old, tempting her to play with him, cuddling her, and holding her close. As he did so, he constantly brought what he was doing clearly into mum's line of sight to seek and gain her approval for his kindness to his sister.

When she stopped responding to answer a question from the nine-year-old, he ran to his mum, punched her in the stomach before pulling up her top and attempting to suckle. She let him suckle, smoothing his head as he did so. The two-year-old then competed for this attention. Neither of the older children paid any attention to this behaviour.

The Brain

It is also important to know the various parts of the brain and their functions. Knowing this can be extremely useful for helping children, adults, and others find explanations, not excuses for responses, beliefs, and behaviours.

The human brain is divided into two hemispheres—right and left, connected by the corpus callosum. The corpus callosum begins to develop at the end of the first year and is significantly developed by the age of two. It continues to mature past the age of ten but is not fully myelinated until the thirties. An underdeveloped corpus callosum inhibits communication and rapid movement between the left and right hemispheres, which can result in staying more on one side than the other.

> Early abusive memories are stored in the right hemisphere outside of conscious awareness. These traumatic memories are in an imagistic form along with the survival behaviour employed at the time of, and as a result of, the abuse. Further, because the cortical hemispheres contain two different types of representational processes and separable, dissociable memory systems this allows for the fact that early emotional learning of the right hemisphere, especially of stressful, threatening experiences can be unknown to the left hemisphere but the required survival behaviour can still be used at any time, later in life, when required.
>
> Schore (2003)

Case example: A baby has a limited repertoire of movements or actions it can take to avoid or deal with something which causes them acute distress, something traumatic. One baby aged six weeks was observed with her foster carer maintaining eye contact and mouthing to mirror the movements in her foster carer's face. In contact, it was noticed she fixed her eyes on her mother's and then moved her head to one side away from the overly penetrating gaze of her mother, not just once but several times. At this age, she could not 'say' why she needed to do this, whether it was the smell of her mother or the intensity of her mother's gaze, but either way she could not manage the intensity and did what she could—moved her head away, then shut her eyes, appearing to be asleep. Her mother stepped away and sat chatting to the contact worker about the makeup and nail varnish they were both using. A baby has a limited repertoire of movements or actions they can take to avoid or deal with something which causes them acute distress, something traumatic.

Later, at age six months, she was observed to reach her arms out to her mother. When her mother did not respond, she then began to fidget and then cry loudly. Her hyper-responses demonstrate the baby's way of managing her distress as a result of her mother being physically present but emotionally unavailable (see Still Face

Experiment). She then 'crashed' (hypo-arousal) and fell asleep for the remaining two hours of her contact, using her hypo-response to try another way to manage and effectively escape from her distress. At 9 and 12 months, the child continued to use versions of these strategies, which are adaptations of the 8 'F' stress responses.

The difference in her behaviour with her foster carer was noted only when an assessor observed the child in both contact and foster home scenarios. In her foster home, she was responsive and alert, smiling and engaged, easily soothed, and more importantly, awake to enjoy her world.

The right hemisphere is mainly responsible for insight, imagination, art, awareness, attachment, control of the left side of the body, hearing music/melody, and pattern recognition. It is therefore responsible for the more abstract aspects of thinking and memory. The left hemisphere is mainly responsible for reasoning, problem solving, control of the right side of the body, spoken and written language, mathematics, and science. It is therefore responsible for the more concrete aspects of thinking and memory.

Research done on the human brain has found that following injury one hemisphere can take on the other's tasks and importantly recover neuron loss and create new pathways in a way that had not been seen in experiments done with animals where damage done to a developing brain was permanent (Doidge 2007, Begley 2009). In other words, change and recovery from trauma are always possible. This has also practically revolutionised the treatment of stroke and brain injury, ensuring less impairment and therefore a better prognosis and recovery. Exercises to stimulate the brain's recovery are needed to facilitate the setting up of new neural pathways around the damaged area. Jackie Ashley (Andrew Marr's wife) writes about the boring repetitive nature of these exercises but the necessity of doing them to ensure Marr's recovery from his stroke (The Guardian August 1 2013).

The F Responses

Increased levels of any physical or emotional feelings cause the neo-cortex (initially necessary to solve a problem) to go offline. The sub-cortex then comes online and when still no solution is found, the limbic system operates with feelings, scripts, internal working models, or state-dependent memories of other times and places when the same range of feelings were present, and the solutions that worked then are used rather than a thinking response to the situation now. The body responds now to these feelings from then, as it did then, activating one or more of the ten F's on a sliding scale from a little to maximum activity, but always the correct amount to ensure physical and emotional survival.

The five Fs in a hyper response (sympathetic nervous system operating) are:

- Flight response: fidgeting feet, legs and/or fingers, actual running away, daydreaming, or dissociating when physical escape is not possible.
- Fight response: clenched fists, tight shoulders, chin out, increased level of breathing, and determined thoughts such as 'I will solve this problem, it will not get the better of me.'

- Feed response: the stomach tries to produce the necessary energy to enable the other Fs, often seen as a hand placed over the stomach, looking sick, tight throat, shallow breathing, and thoughts or statements such as 'I have butterflies in my stomach,' 'I have a gut reaction to this.'
- 'Fuck' sexual response: hand over genital area, crossed legs, squirming, need for the loo, and flushed skin. For victims of sexual assault, this can be very shaming and confusing. It can also be manipulated by the perpetrator to persuade or infer the child or adult is ready for or wanting sex. This link between high levels of physical or emotional arousal is also seen in violent situations such as domestic abuse and war. Perhaps this can be explained as necessary for the survival of our species, in that if fear and violence inhibited sexual behaviour, the human race would have died out in evolutionary times or during war and conflict: a primordial need to affirm not having been vanquished from existence.
- Freeze response: rigid muscle tone, eyes wide, shallow slow breath—no thoughts or words, speechless with terror, unable to understand language, hyper alert to tone of voice, and immobilised defences. Later a significant level of self-blame is felt and expressed when there is no understanding that shouting out or screaming was impossible because Broca's and Wernicke's areas are 'switched off' when in this state of freeze and indeed fuck and flop. An important consequence of this response is to note that it is the tone of voice heard that becomes a much more reliable indicator of intent rather than the words being used (Perry et al. 1995).

The two Fs in a hypo response (para-sympathetic nervous system operating) are:

- Flop response: muscles relaxed, not tense as in 'freeze,' often with the accompanying words, 'I was never any good,' 'it's my fault this happened.' This is the body's way of protecting itself from both physical and emotional injury; indeed, it ensures survival.
- Fart response: noticed with actual farting or urgent need for the toilet. This sphincteric response to fear is noted in statements such as 'scare the shit out of someone,' being 'shit scared.'

Three further Fs have entered frequent parlance in trauma training scenarios.

- Flock: a natural attachment response. This is commonly seen in toddlers when they separate from their primary caregiver exploring their surroundings, only to go running/toddling back to that safe person when a new or unknown person enters the room. This is seeking safety at a time when there is an unknown risk—but the higher cortex is online enough for the child to assess risk and be able to find their caregiver and make their way back to the safe place. This suggests that the level of stress/trauma has not switched off the capacity to process in the way the others do.

- Fawn: the 'chameleonesque' response that relates to the process of people-pleasing to avoid conflict, trying to placate a perceived threat. This relies on the social engagement system to be online where it is essentially 'off' in the other examples. Whilst this is a strategy, it fits more with a survival part of self, rather than a lower brain survival response.
- Fellowship/friendship: is the trauma-free experience of smiling, opening eyes wider, dilating pupils, sitting forward and being in relationship.

Dissociation

Dissociate and disassociate are often used interchangeably. Dissociate comes from Latin, and disassociate, coming from Old French, is not referring to a trauma responsean important distinction.

Arguably, disassociation could be seen in some situations where there is a conscious decision not to associate rather than the unconscious lifesaving dissociation. An example might be someone who has to manage an experience of going to the dentist for a procedure. The person consciously not associating enables them to stay in control with awareness of all that was happening, but without focusing on the procedure—not unlike highway hypnosis.

There is general agreement that the hypothesis that humans are born dissociated is correct and all forms of abuse, particularly inconsistency and emotional neglect, impact the ability to associate, and the likelihood of a diagnosis of a dissociative or other disorder in children or adults therefore increases (Barach 1991, Liotti 1992, Main and Hesse 1991, 1992, Putnam 1997). Loving, empathic, attuned, and consistent parenting enables the developmental task of association, usually achieved around age four. Mentalisation enables the association of feelings in the tummy being hunger, or pain or needing physical connection (Fonagy et al. 2004, Hart 2008). Emotions and body, body and needs are associated. The 'window' expands. A sense of self and being integrated develops.

It is imperative that anyone working with children or adults who have experienced any type of trauma knows about, understands and can explain dissociation. This also changes interventions in mental health services from a medical model to a trauma model.

Dissociation is an unconscious coping strategy used when a situation physically or emotionally overwhelms age-appropriate coping mechanisms. It enables aspects of an experience which are intolerably painful or life threatening, i.e. 'out of the window' to be dissociated or split off. This enables coping at the time and/or on later reflection. Especially useful when the perpetrator who is or was responsible is still depended upon to meet care and attachment needs. The level of dissociation needed is on a continuum, recognised in the DSM diagnostic criteria, from highway hypnosis, depersonalisation, derealisation, fugue states, dissociative amnesia, dissociative disorder not otherwise specified (DDNOS), and dissociative identity disorder (DID).

Normally, during the calm period after the traumatic event, the child/adult, when feeling calm and safe enough, associates the different aspects split off. If there is no period of calm, or if another traumatic event occurs before the first event is processed, where the environment or relationships are persistently traumatic, the dissociated aspects cannot be associated; hence the continuum. This impacts everyday life, being able to make appropriate attachments and do 'joined up thinking,' all vital for a sense of self, self-worth, self-safety, planning ahead, learning from experience, physical, and future mental health. The amount of dissociation needed and used is consistent with the amount of trauma experienced (Putnam 1997, Weiland, 2011, Silberg 2012, Chapman, 2014). Measuring the level of dissociation being used then becomes an important part of any assessment, especially when it has enabled comments like, 'I'm ok,' 'It only happened once,' self-blame, and hope.

Two ways of understanding how dissociation works were usefully written by Braun (1988) and Levine (2010).

BASK model—Bennett Braun SIBAM model—Peter Levine

B = BEHAVIOUR	S = SOMA/SENSATION
A = AFFECT	I = IMAGE
S = SENSATION	B = BEHAVIOUR
K = KNOWLEDGE	A = AFFECT
	M = MEANING

Aspects of an event when in 'the window' can be slotted into either BASK or SIBAM. Actions, thoughts, body feelings, and emotions fit together and are congruent with each other, processed and resolved. Trauma, dissociation, high arousal, double binds, double thinking and 'out of the window' cause incongruence and one or more of the components to split off or be dissociated to ensure emotional and physical survival at the time and until processed. Common phrases used to describe the consequences of using dissociation are: 'I was beside myself with terror,' 'I was in bits,' 'I had to pull myself together,' 'I was not myself,' 'I did things I just can't do,' 'time and space went all peculiar,' 'I could not stop shaking.' Van der Hart also invites thinking and learning about structural dissociation and its consequences from chronic trauma (Van der Hart et al. 2006). Shaking is needed to discharge the toxic chemical soup released in the body. Advice given without understanding the neurobiology behind it is, 'Pull yourself together and give yourself a good shake.'

Case Examples of the Use Made of Dissociation in Type 1 Trauma

A mother whose son ran into the road and was knocked down by a car. He was trapped underneath it, screaming. The mother dropped her shopping, put her hands under the back bumper, and lifted the car off her son. It took three police officers to lift and move the car from where she had put it to allow the traffic past the accident.

Another mother was driving with her two children in the back of the car. A drunk driver crashed into the car, causing damage to the front and driver's side. She explained later that her concern was the car could catch fire, so her priority was getting her children out. She could not open her door, climbed across the consul, exited through the passenger door, lifted her four-year-old, sat her out of danger on a low wall, returned to the car, lifted her eight-month-old and a book, and sat with the baby on her knee, her arm around her four-year-old, insisting she read the book whilst the resulting chaos continued with her noticing. The four-year-old, talking about what happened later, described it as having been created for her entertainment: the arrival of the police, ambulance, fire brigade and air ambulance, annoyingly interrupted by her mum continuing to insist she read a book she had already read; then, by her mum going to sleep, she missed the best bit—the ride in the really, really fast ambulance, so fast she was sliding in her seat. Her mother's injuries were life threatening and included major fractures to her sternum and ribs, disabling her from coughing, sneezing, or lifting anything for months afterwards without re-experiencing the horrific pain which should have rendered her unconscious had she not dissociated at the time.

For both women, dissociation enabled them to do what they needed to do by dissociating the A, S, and K, ensuring the survival of their children and, in the second example, herself. It is not unusual to hear or read reports of people being able to walk, talk, and behave normally whilst doing something in trauma situations they would never be able to do in non-trauma situations. When the trauma ends, and it is safe physically and emotionally to do so, association occurs.

The young man who survived the sinking of the Estonia ferry in the Baltic Sea. Every other person in the life raft he was in died from hypothermia before being rescued. His campaign and lobbying of ferry companies to change the procedures needed were documented in a television programme. Whilst travelling, he chatted with the cameraman about the incident. He was asked if he had nightmares. He replied,

> Not so often now but I do understand why these happened, what I cannot understand, and I don't know, is why I am not able to remember is what the child I was holding, and trying to keep warm but died before being rescued, looked like.

The cameraman asked, 'Have you thought of writing to her parents to ask for a photograph?' His numbed, frozen silence followed by the words, 'That might be a good idea,' had the therapist shouting at the television, 'Don't do it.' It's dissociation his brain needed, and still needs to 'not know.' Dissociating the K, to protect him from the pain of knowing until he was able to deal with that pain. What followed was the therapist's connection to the use of photographs in therapeutic work with children in Life Story Work, or creating Timelines with adults to help in seeing the child they were when the harm was done.

'I don't know,' or 'I don't remember.' Trauma-informed understanding changes these answers to, 'What I did and am doing to cope is 'not know,' or 'not remember,' and 'not doing joined up thinking about the many overwhelming aspects to give me some feeling of being in control and not dissociating or disintegrating.'

Putnam's Child Dissociative Checklist is a helpful screening tool to measure the amount of dissociation a child is continuing to use, especially when deciding whether or not a child is ready to do Life Story Work to meet the child's needs or is recommended following discussion in a Looked After Child Review to meet the requirements of OFSTED rather than the child.

In response to Type 2 trauma, a ten-year-old girl, who was later found to meet the diagnostic criteria for dissociative identity disorder, was referred for therapy. Her parents had divorced two years earlier. Court-ordered contact meant she had to see her father every other weekend and half of her holidays. Her father was part of a paedophile group. Her behaviour, development, or learning raised no suspicions until just after her father told her he was returning to court to increase contact. She was observed by children putting the plugs in the sinks in the school toilets to flood them. When asked why she had done this, she denied it; indeed, she seemed to be telling the truth. The confused teacher invited her mother to the school to discuss what could be done, not about the flooding but about her denial. They stopped about 20 minutes into their conversation, both wondering if they were talking about the same child. Their experience of the child was so different; at home she was obsessed with ponies, something her teacher remained unaware of.

The contact application led to interviews being conducted with all concerned. The interviewer asked the child, both parents and the teacher to complete standardised psychometric tests. Only the one completed by the child indicated her clinical level of dissociation, which likely met the diagnostic criteria for dissociative identity disorder. This was correct. Each adult only knew about, and was in a relationship with, one of her identities. This led to further investigations resulting in dad's arrest, imprisonment, and the cessation of contact. In therapy, the child explained that when with her dad and the other people were doing sex stuff with her, she would 'go into the field next door and play with the ponies.' When she returned home, and her mum asked her what she had done at the weekend her answer was, 'Played with the ponies.'

She could talk to her mum about ponies, not sex. She could not talk to her teacher about either. Three different identities were needed to keep this secret: not talk about, keep going to school, and her mum and grandfather alive. Her much-loved grandmother had died suddenly, leaving her mother and grandfather bereft. Grandfather was often heard to say, 'I'm so upset I could die. I don't know how I can go on living without her.' which always drew mum's response: 'Oh, dad if anything happened to you, I'd be so upset I don't know how I could go on,' empathically supporting the grandfather but providing her dad with the perfect silencing threat: 'If you tell they will be so upset they will die.'

Keeping secrets inhibits or prevents processing of, and making sense of, what just happened when to do so would lead to fear of silencing threats containing an element of truth coming true, that what happened had to have been planned and was therefore not an accident, of going mad, loss or disruption of needed/hoped-for attachment. This is especially so when the perpetrator causing harm or failing to protect is someone the child, or indeed the adult, had or still has an innate need for attachment and safety.

Type 3 trauma is seen in young women being sexually exploited. Their use of dissociation, when measured, was always elevated, often at clinical levels. Their levels of dissociation at a clinical level are consistent with their need to separate body and mind whilst maintaining highly dependent but disorganised attachment or trauma bond with those exploiting them.

One of the consequences of relational trauma is the need to hide the impact that any trigger has on the ability to think, listen, or stay present. It takes a great deal of energy to mask or hide the impact, a fairly constant intrusive response to what would to other people be a normal everyday event. People who are close by will often fail to notice, but interestingly dogs, in their responding to subtle changes, can be a source of immediate comfort and reconnection with the here and now and a useful pointer to parent, carer, or therapist.

One young adult explained,

> I worked out that if I thought through this event logically and sequentially, I would realise one of my parents planned to hurt me and the other failed to protect me. This was and is too painful and too risky to know so it is better to stop trying to work out or make sense of what just happened. It is better to blame myself for what just happened. My parents also told me this, so it must be correct.

This way of coping, useful at the time, had consequences seen later in out-of-time, age-inappropriate coping behaviours, continually saying everything was her fault and self-harm and a very conflictual or intense relationship with her sibling. These behaviours, mimicking diagnostic criteria, resulted in the diagnosis of the 'negative' mental health disorder of ADD/ADHD, conduct disorder, borderline, and unstable personality disorder.

Perry (1995) describes, 'When emotional states become behavioural traits.' Negative or positive attachment also affects how shame, fear of abandonment, trust, control, loss, and anger are managed with positive approved behaviour or with negative behaviour which brings a blaming response. Processing ensures the 'toxic soup' released in response to trauma is discharged and therefore has no continuing impact on physical and psychological well-being (Sapolsky 2000, Sunderland 2007, Schore 2003, Levine 1997, and van der Kolk 1996, ACE. study).

Worldwide research being carried out on brain function, neurobiology, and behaviour is phenomenal. One of the most renowned, leading researchers interviewed for a television programme said that what was known about the brain was the equivalent of a centimetre square in the centre of a flip chart sized sheet of paper. His comment related to 'normal' brain function and only briefly related to the impact of trauma and stress on brain function. It will therefore be important to keep up to date with this research to further inform and ensure decisions made about the impact of trauma on children's and adults' short, medium, and long term physical and psychological well-being, especially when we are assessing siblings' lives and their future relationships with each other, are not based on anecdotal beliefs, out of date research, OFSTED requirements, ill-informed government policies, or to meet the needs of one person in a system, but on well honed, up to date research and its informed implications.

Chapter 10

Bound by Fear

How Trauma Hijacks Attachment

A trauma bond is in the same category as a disorganised attachment (Schore 2003). So called because it disrupts thinking and floods the body with a chemical soup to manage the situation. It is easy to understand how this works when someone who is loved and trusted to be safe walks into the room and without thinking there is a smile and turning towards or even sometimes walking towards that person; it is instinctive. There is a feeling of happiness. Bodies produce feel-good chemicals to enhance this feeling: oxytocin, dopamine, and a little cortisol (Yahuda 2017). Defences are lowered. The core is open to receive the loving and tender care expected.

Alternatively, when the person who enters is frightening, cannot be trusted, or their response is unpredictable, the body responds differently. Eyes scan the room, checking for escape routes before refocusing on the risk. The body releases adrenaline, noradrenaline, cortisol, and natural opiates, readying the system for flight, fight, or freeze; the 'F' system is activated. The body is caught between two systems. Should it welcome or defend? Raise defences, so no love can get in. Lower, and pain may follow. This uncertainty disorganises thinking, and neither mind nor body can tolerate this confusion. The only option to survive physically or emotionally is often through dissociation.

Survival is made possible by the belief that this person, despite the harm they cause, is essential for meeting the innate needs of attachment, safety, and survival. If we do as we are told, we will please them. Obedience ensures survival. Children implicitly know what has happened before will happen again. They learn that the harm is not the adult's fault, but their own. Crying means they need to be stronger, and not crying means they can cope with more harm.

These core beliefs form and sustain the trauma bond. Changing these beliefs is challenging. They are reinforced not only by experience but by threats which always contain an element of truth. This partial truth reinforces the system's belief. This fear, combined with helplessness and hopelessness, keeps children out of their window of tolerance, dissociated, unable to think logically, and unable to challenge the lie within their beliefs.

DOI: 10.4324/9781003724797-14

When the incident ends and there is space for reflection, any small challenge to these beliefs feels dangerous. This results in reactivation of the trauma-driven survival system and the reinforcing of the trauma bond (see Table 10.1).

Briere's abuse/trauma dichotomy helps in understanding how the need to believe the true bit of threats used reinforces this bond (Briere 1995). What follows is a paraphrase. Where he only uses the word parent but, in this context, it is useful to replace or additionally use the words partner, carer, or sibling:

I am being hurt, emotionally or physically, by my parent or other adult or sibling whom I love, care for, and trust deeply. Based on how I think about the world thus far, this injury can only be due to one of two things: either I am bad, or my parent is bad. But I am being told by other adults, either at home or at school, that parents are always right, and always do things for my own good (any alternative is simply too frightening to grasp or consider). So, when parents occasionally hurt me, it is for my own good, because I have been bad. This is what I am told is the punishment I deserve. Therefore, it must be my fault that I am being hurt, just as they say. This must be the punishment I deserve. Therefore, I am as bad as whatever is done to me. The punishment must fit the crime: anything else suggests they are bad, which I have rejected because they are doing things for my own good because I depend upon them to love me. I have felt loved sometimes. But I have seen them be loving to someone else. I am bad because I have been hurt. I have been hurt because I am bad. But I am hurt quite often, and or quite deeply. Therefore, I must be very bad. This is also beautifully articulated in R.D. Laing's poem, Knots (1970).

John McCarthy (2015) wrote about the 'trauma bond' he developed with Brian Keenan during their five year captivity as hostages in Beirut. When guards removed Brian from the room they shated, John's memories of previous similar removals reminded him Brian would be tortured. This evoked deeply paradoxical feelings: he wanted Brian to return, because being alone was unbearable, but dreaded seeing

Table 10.1 Comparison between the developmentally driven and the trauma-driven processes

Secure Attachment	Trauma Bond
• Person is needed for survival	• Person is needed for survival
• Love	• Terror
• Takes time	• Instantaneous
• Reciprocal and caring	• Domination and fear
• Association/mentalisation/curiosity	• Dissociation/confusion/passivity
• Proximity = safety	• Proximity = fear/alarm
• Separate and independent person	• Not separate - extension of other
• Self-mastery	• Mastery by others
• Empathy to needs of others	• Attunement to other's needs
• Autonomy and individuation	• Obedience
• Separation is managed	• Separation intensifies bond

him again, because he would then be confronted with Brian's pain and his own helplessness in the face of it. He felt useless, angry and responsible for not stopping it. To ensure this conflicts did not happen again, and give himself a sense of control over his situation, when he heard the guard approaching he would antagonise the guard to make sure it was him and not Brian who was tortured. He explained to Parkinson thanked him for his kindness. He explained this was not kindness but survival (BBC archives of Parkinson Interviews).

What neither John nor Brian understood for a long time was the extraordinary intensity of the 'missing' felt when they were finally released. This confusion is echoed in the accounts of others: victims of violence, those who have witnessed harm to loved ones, survivors of torture, children separated from siblings, or those who live in families defined by fear.

A trauma bond, by its nature, challenges perception of the state of the relationships between the perpetrator and those affected. How often does a family member say they are happy or OK? Dissociation enables then to present as compliant, organised or maybe achieving academically, to wear a smile that tells the world, 'All is good here.'

It is easy not to be curious about these relationships, especially when under pressure to overlook that a trauma bond has formed in response to fear and violence. The relationship may appear wanted; the person is missed, needed, or appears closest to the very individual who does the most harm.

Case Example: Fabian

Fabian, aged 12, lived with his father. His father was unemployed and spent his time running a children's football club, volunteering at youth activity centres and youth clubs. Fabian was referred for therapy as a result of concerns about his low affect and 'low level but repeated sexualised behaviours.' Fabian was brought to therapy by his father, who was effusive, confident, presented appropriately, and relaxed. Fabian and his father were observed to be always close in proximity but never touched. Fabian was restricted in his play and spent his time drawing or making penises, from simple line drawings to a six-foot model. He was stuck, regardless of the intervention, reflection, or experiment. His play would not progress. Whilst being stuck can be a sign of the complexity or depth of the issue, it can also be a sign that the child believes their environment is not safe, or that the child is not safe, or both. A trawl of the files found that his father had multiple allegations of a sexual nature made against him by children over a long period of time, but none had been founded. The commissioners of the therapy would not believe that Fabian was at risk because his father was actively bringing him to therapy and Fabian went everywhere with his father. One way of looking at this relationship phenomenon is using the 'Duck test,' Reiland (2002).

The Duck Test is described as an experiment to understand the impact of abuse on children. Ducks, like people, develop bonds between mother and young. The purpose was to test how that bond would be affected by abuse. The control group was a real mother duck and her ducklings. For the experimental group, a mechanical duck was used. This mechanical duck was set at intervals to peck the ducklings—a painful peck, one a real duck would not give. The groups were varied. Each group was pecked with a different level of frequency.

The ducklings were observed to grow and bond with their mother. Over time, the ducklings in the control group would waddle along behind their mother, but as they grew, there would be more distance between them. They would wander and explore. The purpose of a secure foundation is to allow the young to feel secure enough in their attachment to explore. The ducklings with the pecking mechanical mother, though, followed much more closely. The group that 'bonded' and followed most closely was the one that had been pecked repeatedly with the greatest frequency. The more the ducklings were pecked and abused, the more closely they followed. This was what was happening between Fabian and his father.

Torturers are recruited and trained in countries where torture is part of the criminal justice system. In different countries, similar techniques are used without international training events. The torturer's behaviour and the developing coping strategies and alliances that occur in the victims of torture are what happens in families and sibling groups experiencing or witnessing violence, scapegoating, objectification, and depersonalisation (Galston 1998).

Case Example: Jordan

Jordan was four when his mother met her new partner while visiting her ex in prison. On his release, he contacted her, and she agreed to meet him. She was struck by how different he seemed from her ex. With tears in his eyes, he told her he had been convicted of sexual offences against his teenage daughters. He insisted he was innocent, but he said he pleaded guilty immediately to spare them the ordeal of the interviews, medical examinations, and attending court. He said he could endure prison if it meant his children could stay with their mother. She compared this to her ex, who continued to deny his offences despite the mounting evidence against him, forcing the girls to testify. He demanded she choose between him and her daughters. In choosing him, she lost her daughters, who then refused contact with their mother. Her anger focussed on the social worker, who did not force them to see her but continued to forward their letters to their father in prison.

She was thankful that over the next three years she found this new partner was adept at controlling Jordan's tantrums and violent outbursts. He even accompanied her to the appointment where Jordan was diagnosed with ADD/ADHD and prescribed Ritalin. He was interested in what she wore, how her hair was cut and would phone her at least three and sometimes six times a day to tell her he loved her, ask what she was doing, and ask if she missed him. It was not his fault that sometimes he would lose his temper and hit her when she forgot something he had asked her to do or had not wiped up the drips from the coffee machine proving she had used it despite being told it was only for his use and not hers. She smiled when she recalled how he would be so sorry and lovely after he hit her, and the sex always had an extra quality following one of these rows.

When asked where Jordan was during these increasingly frequent and escalating rows, she looked confused, then recalled times when she had tried to stop her partner from giving Jordan a hiding when he had forgotten to take his pills, or had won when playing on the PS4, or did not do as he was told immediately, or mentioned his sisters or dad, and the time when she had beaten Jordan herself to show she was not taking Jordan's side in an argument between them. This, she thought, was the time he was most angry with Jordan because when Jordan had jumped on his back to stop him kicking her, his back was bruised, and Jordan needed to be kept off school for three days as a punishment.

On the day Jordan returned to school, he was changing for PE when his teacher noticed some bruising on his back. Jordan immediately said it was his fault and that he could not remember what had happened. An out-of-hours social worker visited that evening. Jordan was sent upstairs to his bedroom so that the adults could talk, but sat on the top stair to listen. When he heard goodbyes being said and the front door opening, he jumped but misstepped and bumped down the stairs on his back. His stepfather immediately asked him if he was all right, was kind and gave him a hug. He then told the social worker that Jordan was such a clumsy child, always running when he should walk and frequently falling down the stairs. When asked if he agreed with this, Jordan knew this was the truth but not the whole truth and telling the whole truth would make things worse at home for his mum who was nodding her head and had that please do not argue look. After all, it was his fault. He was always being told at home and school how clumsy he was and he did fall down the stairs because he should have done as he was told and been in his bedroom. When asked he said he loved his mum and stepdad very much, even more than they loved him.

Jordan stayed at home for another three months until his mother was admitted to hospital with a punctured lung from fractured ribs. Mother was unclear about whether Jordan or her partner had caused the injury. If only she could get things right and not always be in a muddle, neither would need to get angry with her.

The Trauma Bond in Practice

It is easy to find many texts and references on age-appropriate attachment behaviours but difficult, if not impossible, to find anything comparable on age-appropriate separation behaviours.

- Watching six- and eight-year-old siblings cry inconsolably immediately on separation from their family or each other at the end of contact, only for this to stop just as immediately when distracted by someone or something.
- Paradoxically, six- and eight-year-old siblings who say goodbye without looking back.

- The eight-year-old, who cries and says many times a day how much he misses his six-year-old brother and wants to see him, when contact is arranged for the first five minutes competes with him over named trainers, toys, gifts, their foster carer's car, and then fights physically with him for the rest of the contact despite several interventions from the contact supervisor to try to distract them into nice play with each other.
- The mother who repeatedly leaves her children in the family home to live with her parents, then returns to live with her violent, alcohol/drug-abusing partner, and then cries when asked about the impact this has on her children, saying she knows this because of the terrible impact it has on her.
- The father who cries about how much he misses his children but cannot join in any programmes offered by the social worker or drug team to deal with his addictions or violence.

When considering these situations as examples of trauma bonds between individuals, it is also important to recognise the likelihood of trauma bonds with alcohol, drugs, or violence. Addressing such bonds requires far more empathic, relationship-based work. Attending Drug and Alcohol services, or anger management courses to answer questions and provide urine tests is not enough. Nor is simply placing siblings together or apart, or increasing contact, unless this work is purposeful and includes interventions aimed at building healthy, safe relationships.

It is also not helpful when there is a trauma bond and a child or adult says, 'It's my fault this happened to me,' to respond with 'It's not your fault,' or a similar phrase. Although the intent may be well-meaning, such reassurance has little or no value. The victim may still need to believe in their own culpability to preserve a dependent relationship, maintain hope, feel some sense of control, or absolve the perpetrator. That belief is a coping strategy when they cannot change the behaviour of the perpetrator or the situation they are in. Rather than contradict it, the belief should be accepted (Unconditional Positive Regard) and held with mindful curiosity. Instead, whilst emotionally regulating and helping the person stay in their window of tolerance, ask gently, 'How long have you thought that? Has there ever been a time you did not believe it? Has anyone else told you that?' Timing, of when to ask questions, when to stop, and when to revisit or follow up, must be undertaken with care. The process is at the rhythm of the individual's process; it is mindful. Telling someone, 'It's not your fault,' can be experienced as disbelief, blame or shaming. It invalidates the trust placed in sharing and reinforces the sense that they have got something wrong again. The victim feels blamed for choosing the wrong person to tell, confirming another strategy used by perpetrators to silence victims, 'If you tell you will not be believed.' Whilst the intention may be to ease victim distress, reduce self-blame or reduce the feeling of helplessness the listener experiences, it can instead reinforce the trauma bond and the perpetrator's messages.

It is not safe to internalise a trauma bond or disorganised attachment in the way a secure attachment would be; therefore, separation and loss cannot be managed in a developmentally appropriate way. The developmental task of internalising a secure attachment is therefore incomplete. The terror of being out of sight, and therefore out of mind, remains. This raises the philosophical question: who am I if I do not exist in the mind of another? Instead, separation intensifies this bond, which can be mistaken by both victim and practitioners as 'missing the other.' The ongoing need for a secure attachment remains in conflict with high levels of anxiety and arousal, linked to feelings of helplessness and hopelessness.

This helps explain the difference between emotional neglect by omission and emotional abuse by commission. As one 15-year-old put it:

> My mum calling me names or treating me in a terrible way was better than her not remembering I was there at all. It wasn't even that I was forgotten; it was that I wasn't important enough to be remembered. If it's my fault, maybe I can do something. If it's not my fault, there's nothing I can do, but I can't survive without some connection. So, I keep trying to be noticed. She doesn't notice when I'm good, so I try being annoying and bad. That's why I wasn't lovable, because I was bad.

In such situations, self-blame becomes a deeply entrenched survival belief. Saying 'it's not your fault' will not create change. Until someone both knows and feels they 'exist in the mind of another,' these beliefs, the trauma bond and the behaviours that flow from them, will persist.

'Our brains will continue to take in new information and construct new realities as long as our bodies fe*el* safe. But if we become fixated on the trauma, then our ability to take in new information is lost, and we continue to construct and re-construct the old realities' Van der Kolk (1996) For a child, siblings, or an adult now living in safety, that new environment, because it is so different from the unsafe one they knew, may not feel safe at all, compromising or halting change. Only when it feels safe enough can curiosity emerge and new ways of being be explored. This dynamic is worth considering not only in work with children but also in the parallel relationship between practitioner and supervisor.

Trauma bonds also need to be considered when planning contact, particularly between siblings. The purpose and content of contact must be clear to avoid undermining progress. It is equally important to remember that the capacity for change remains throughout the lifespan (Doige 2007, Begley 2009, Bryson 2019). The use of fMRI scans has shown that believing change is impossible is just that, a belief, not a fact. Change is always possible when feeling safe. Difficult, if not impossible, to feel safe whilst still finding ways to survive amid terror, chaos, or instability of living with a sibling or carer who is not safe. Feeling safe is not only useful but essential for change to occur. It is helpful, then, to reframe statements that recognise the belief into much-needed survival strategies, such as, 'I can't change,' to, 'Not changing is what I am doing because it is not safe to change.' Similarly, 'I don't remember,' can be translated to, 'Not remembering is what I have to do,' and,

'I don't care,' to, 'Not caring is what I have to do.' In the same way, 'I am not lovable,' may mean, 'I am not lovable, so it cannot be my mother's fault she does not love me.' Hearing these statements as survival strategies invites curiosity. What happened to embed this belief so deeply, and what is needed to help this child or adult remember, to care, and believe they are lovable? Lack of this transforming curiosity contributes to many placements disrupting and often siblings being split up or moved.

Case Example: Siblings Lacey Aged Four and Eleanor Aged Two

The question was asked, 'Which child would have the greatest chance of recovery?' Perhaps it is better to wonder whose strategy was most likely to achieve having their needs met. In this situation, the answer has to be neither whilst the children remained living together. Just their presence, their coexistence keeps their experience of trauma alive. They are living in a trauma bond with each other as a result of their shared experience of violence, from one frightening and the other a frightened caregiver who whilst the focus of the violence was depressed and unavailable. Neither caregiver was able to meet the children's needs and from this the children developed their own complex sibling relationship with its paradoxical but effective strategies for survival.

Yes, they were removed from this dangerous situation, but it was forgotten that the dangerous situation had not been removed from them. The foster carers were exhausted. Despite being very experienced, very well trained and supported carers, they were close to disruption. They shared their experience of having cared for all age groups from disorganised latency-aged children to disaffected angry teenagers to infants with multiple needs but had never been faced with such demanding violent young children. While they described the children to the therapist, it was clear they were still struggling to believe such young girls could have such an impact on them. The first home visit to meet the girls found them playing in the garden. In the first minute of watching through the window, they hit each other, and when Lacey was pushed over by Eleanor and hit her head, she simply got up and started playing. Eleanor, however, came in and told her foster carer that Lacey had fallen over. This pattern of violence and/or control was repeated every time the children were seen together.

This was not just a problem for the foster carers. It was also a problem for the social work agency. The agency knew these foster carers were experienced and that the children's relationship was problematic but would not accept that the children's unhealthy relationship was a trauma bond and kept throwing services at the family rather than face the unpalatable truth that this placement was not going to work for both children; indeed, no placement was going to work for both children together.

A trauma bond results from living with the increased attunement needed to determine the perpetrator's wishes and feelings. This drive to be safer and more lovable often leads to a reduction, or even loss of empathy in both victims and perpetrators, whether adults or children. Children are born with an innate ability to attune. Empathy is learned through experiencing empathic, age-appropriate purposeful mis-attunement that is brief and tolerable, where the stress caused is resolved while the child remains within their unique window of tolerance (Schore 2010, Hughes 2012). Immediate empathic re-attunement and reconciliation recalibrates the amygdala, the brain's 'smoke detector,' and teaches the child empathy, how their thoughts or behaviour affect others.

Attunement without empathy primarily allows a perpetrator to meet their own needs by exploiting the needs of their victim. Empathy enables anyone who could exploit another to consider the other's needs first and then choose whether or not to behave in a particular way.

17-year-old Jenny had been sexually exploited by her father since age six. None of the siblings knew he treated them all in the same way and he created a trauma bond with each. Jenny believed he cared for her more than he cared for her siblings, making her feel special; but she didn't know they all felt the same way, creating a chasm between them. She recalled him as being empathic, but he used this behaviour to sexually exploit and manipulate her and her siblings to meet his own needs, giving no consideration to the harm he did to her or her siblings physically and psychologically. Alongside this, he deliberately damaged her relationship with her mother, increasing her need for relationship and dependence on him. When she treated her mother with the same contempt he did, he would smile at her with approval, deepening their alliance, her dependence on him, and the trauma bond, which made separation from him painful. Practitioners hearing this pain as 'missing' arranged contact to help ease that pain. However, this would only further increase her dependence on him and not resolve the pain. Contact with her siblings would remain tense and unsatisfactory until all parties were supported to understand their father's behaviours and their trauma bonds ameliorated.

Chapter 11

The Quiet Parts Loud
Children's Voices in Sibling Decisions

Cicirelli (1995) writes, 'The sibling relationship is one of the most enduring an individual may have over the course of their lifetime.'

Dunn (2007), 'It tends to last longer than other key relationships, such as those with parents and partners and typically, children spend more time in interactions with siblings than with close others.'

Kosonen (1996) and Herrick and Piccus (2005), 'It has long been argued that children who grow up apart from siblings, and who lack contact or knowledge about them, may be deprived of support afforded by the sibling relationship in adult life.'

Rachel, aged 12,

> I didn't know I had a brother until I was eleven. He was in a different Dr Barnardo's to me. I was disabled and he wasn't so we could not live together they said. It was my social worker who was still a student told me about him. We might meet one day.

Kate, aged 32,

> I always thought my siblings needed me and I had to protect them and love them because I was oldest. My mum had seven children with five different dads. When I was seven, we three were taken into care. One was adopted. My sister and I to foster care but the foster carer did not like me, so I was moved. My mum then had four more children. Two were adopted but two stayed at home with her. The first and last time we all got together was for her funeral. I thought we would keep in touch. Funny thing was I was pleased we didn't. I didn't even like them. None was like me at all.

Jo, aged 25,

> I couldn't believe it when I met my sister for the first time when I was 25 and she was 20. We were adopted separately because we were taken into care five years apart as babies. She looked like me and spoke like me even although I grew up

DOI: 10.4324/9781003724797-15

in Liverpool and she was in Kent. We liked the same food and films and had called our eldest with the same name. We have so much to talk about and find out about each other.

Anne, aged 14,

I have to wear nail varnish all the time because my hands and my brother's hands are identical in shape. When I look at my hands, I see his hands and feel him touching me. I shake. His hands make me feel sick to my stomach. Nail varnish means when I look at my hands, they are my hands and not his. I'm not allowed to wear nail varnish in school and get suspended when I do.

Mags, aged 15,

Mum and Dad were part of a paedophile group. My brother was the only person who I had sex with who never hurt me. We took comfort from each other and would cuddle to fall asleep. When they (social workers) found out they put us in different foster homes, and we were not allowed to see each other. My therapist helped me get my head round why we needed each other and why this included sex. He never had any therapy. We can't meet up now because when he looks at me, he remembers and drinks to forget. He has tried to commit suicide a couple of times. He needs help.

Tony, aged 11,

I have 3 brothers. George, I love, Hayden I don't like and Jay is ok. I don't know why contact has to be with us all three. I can sit and talk or play a game with George. Hayden and Jay just want to play fight and when they do Julie (contact supervisor) tells them to stop and play a game with us. They just wreck the game. I don't like her (Julie) either.

Karen, aged 16,

I was four when my sister and I were adopted. The harm we experienced in our adoptive family was terrible but we had each other and without each other it would have been so much worse.

The first three quotes from researchers cover a 30-year span. The remainder are from children and adults over the same timespan, inviting careful thinking, not to make assumptions about what and who is listened to when working with siblings, to reflect on the initial response to the children's statements and then compare these with the trauma-informed, 'no blame, no shame,' enquiring responses noted at the end of this chapter.

Children need to feel a sense of belonging to people who matter to them and to whom they matter. It has been suggested that 'The provision of security and comfort once ascribed mainly to parental figures may also be a role that siblings can fulfil when children experience stress caused by life events' (Gass et al. 2007). This is true except for when it is not. When either a trauma bond exists or the 'may' in the sentence is ignored, it results in over-optimism or connection to false positives. Children who are cared for by those who are also the source of their distress find it particularly difficult to organise an attachment strategy that increases feelings of safety and reduces feelings of upset. Under those conditions, escape/distancing and approach/seeking love behaviours are simultaneously activated (Main and Solomon 1990). This becomes problematic for siblings when they become focused on their own survival needs, which can then leave a sibling vulnerable or feel compelled to sacrifice their safety for the well-being of their sibling, compete or give up, all of which can negatively impact the quality of the sibling relationship.

Attachments with siblings are of secondary and supplementary importance in children's development. To be able to make a healthy sibling relationship, first of all, requires a secure attachment with an adult. This can be clearly seen in the case of Hannah and David. This secure base ensured that an older sibling did not feel threatened by a new arrival because each knew there was enough love to go around. The children entered the world feeling loved, and the eldest children did not feel displaced but became an important cog in a bigger wheel. Where the adult's ability to extend their love is limited, siblings can be competitive for, and sabotaging of, any closeness each has with that adult. This competitive state is clearly seen between Eleanor and her sister Lacey. Their relationship/attachment with their parents followed into their similar pattern of aggression and challenge with each other. This then has a negative impact on both children because their focus was on rivalry rather than sharing.

It is imperative to consider the impact on children of witnessing a sibling being hurt or neglected. Pete, aged 11, shared,

> Mum would say we have to have a family meeting. She would go on and on about how James smelled terrible and made her feel sick when he was near her. She really hated him. What did I do? I'd put on my headphones and play on my phone. Then I didn't notice if he cried or not. I don't care if he did or not.

He was suspended from school for being rude, disrespectful to teachers, and laughing when given a detention.

Whilst hard to acknowledge, where there is harm being done to a child in a family, the other children could have been asked, encouraged, expected, or forced to join in or mete out harm to that sibling. Saying no may not have been an option or, where it was an option, a choice not free from threat of being ostracised, scapegoated, or alienated in similar ways. The adult may have offered, 'You do it or I will do it,' a choice which significantly complicates the sibling relationship both ways. It is easy to understand why being able to have empathy towards others becomes too painful and difficult, leading to coping behaviours which look like selfishness or self-absorption often mistakenly diagnosed as a range of conduct disorders in childhood and adulthood: oppositional defiant, narcissistic, borderline or emotionally unstable disorders and perhaps even Autistic Spectrum Condition, ADD/ADHD.

Attachment to the perpetrator is a key component of a trauma bond, described previously, and is needed to ensure survival. The phrase, 'If you can't beat them join them,' is an example of how normalised this behaviour is. This also complicates the relationship with the victim's sibling, who is then blamed for what is seen as their non-compliance, or in their alliance with another victim, or who is competitive for approval from the perpetrator. This behaviour is also demonstrated when people are chameleon-esque. As they move from person to person or relationship to relationship, they morph to become closer in style/hairstyle, accent, pronunciation, tone, volume, interests, etc., largely for security and safety. Threat, to and from another, changes when not standing out or looking different. This hides the fear which results from the lack of a core sense of self.

'Impaired self-reference,' seen when the child (initially) utilises emotional avoidance to manage painful internal states and to

> detect and survive interpersonal dangers and/or abandonment. These are adaptive strategies where the child lived in a somewhat maladaptive environment. Over time these strategies reduce access to internal states and identity functions and the adult becomes less or unaware of their own needs or entitlements.
>
> Briere (1995, 2011)

This behaviour starts out as an understandable, adaptive survival strategy in a maladaptive trauma-filled environment. But what he does not mention is that these same strategies are later seen as inappropriate, annoying maladaptive strategies in an adaptive caring environment. This is what trauma 'does' and what is then 'done' to survive and cope. This impact, when seen in siblings, can be mistaken for closeness and results in the making of some potentially life-changing/damaging assumptions about their relationships. Because they 'look' ok together, the question do they 'feel' ok together is not asked.

Thirteen-year-old Tom boarded at public school (UK private education provision). He attended having moved from his preparatory school where he also boarded from age eight. He was assessed as educationally below average to failing. He had few friends but appeared to get on with most of his peers. What was not considered and therefore not seen was his ability to take on the characteristics of those he spoke to and that where he morphed the most was in relation to those who bullied him the most. Tom's behaviour alienated him from his older sister, who complained she never knew who he was going to be.

The need for relationship, and the chameleon-like survival behaviours, can also be exploited by a perpetrator as a way of silencing or stopping a child from reporting harm being done. Using the threat, 'If you tell you will be in trouble,' or 'We will be in trouble,' or even, 'I will be in trouble' but concluding 'It will be your fault,' are powerful statements. Having manipulated a child into joining in harmful behaviour, these threats will work well to ensure compliance, silence and even a feeling of closeness or specialness. When the child expresses fear of talking or reluctance to tell by saying, 'I will be in trouble,' or, 'He said I would be in trouble if I tell,' could also indicate this has happened. Just as it would be inappropriate to respond to a child or adult victim who says, 'It's my fault,' by telling them it was not his fault, it would not be helpful to assure this victim and perpetrator child he will not be in trouble but to ask and explore the reason for that fear.

A threat will only work where the child believes there is an element of truth in the threat. A threat that is obviously a lie or is developmentally out of date is very unlikely to be believed.

When Joe was four, his father, who was sexually abusing him, told him there was a man in the moon who was always there even when the moon could not be seen. The man in the moon would see if Joe told anyone about the abuse and tell him. This worked when he was four. However, when aged seven, he worked out there was no Santa Claus and therefore no man in the moon, which enabled him to smash his moon-shaped bedside light used to reinforce his belief and allowed him to tell.

To threaten a securely attached child that her mother or other parent will not love her or would leave her if she tells would never work because she would know nothing would stop her mother or the other parent loving her or result in leaving her. It would work if their relationship was not secure or had been damaged deliberately to distance the child from the other parent. Another threat, 'If you tell, your mother will be upset,' will also work if that is true. If a harmed child has participated in the harming of a sibling or another child, the threat of being in trouble would also work.

Another common experience or consequence for siblings is anger with the sibling who is being harmed for not preventing the harm or for antagonising the perpetrator. This is similar to the child who is angry with her mother for the violence done to her and/or her mother harming or not stopping the harm being done to the child. Common ways of staying safe and coping include resistance, arguing, passivity, or compliance. When a child who has worked out that compliance is the best way to stay safe then witnesses a sibling being resistant and arguing with the perpetrator, which results in harm being done to their sibling, the child blames and is angry with the sibling, not the perpetrator.

The child's consequent feeling of helplessness can add to the angry feeling. The sibling is also blamed for causing that painful feeling too. Whether at home, in the same placement or placed separately, this anger has to be held inside, or it spills out in placement and/or contact, potentially impacting both siblings. It is very helpful when hearing about children having anger management issues to think about the anger being the answer to the problem and not the problem. From this trauma perspective, their anger is already being very well managed. It is the other feelings that are overwhelming and need an answer other than anger.

Alex, aged nine, regularly smashed his toys and, when able, his brother's too. Pictures and ornaments would be torn down. His brother lived in fear and was always seeking protection from first his mother, then, when in care, from his foster carer. Anger management was recommended. A support worker in the school offered to do this because she had been on an anger management course. The foster carer was asked to participate in the sessions so that she could see and learn how to apply those strategies herself. In the first session, Alex was asked to rip one sheet of newspaper, then two together, then three, until he could no longer tear them. The carer was then asked to hold the two opposite ends of the same increasing number of sheets of newspaper whilst the support worker held the other two, and Alex was invited to punch a hole in them. This he did until he was not able to, at which point the session ended. On the way home, Alex stepped off the pavement without looking. The carer instinctively grabbed his wrist to protect him. With all the force he had already practised, he punched the carer in the face, causing significant injury and resulting in the placement disruption for both brothers so that they could stay together. In conversation with the support worker afterwards, she was asked how she had assessed Alex's ability to use empathy, one of the key components needed to manage anger. She said she knew he had empathy and didn't need to assess this because on one occasion, when she was getting something out of the filing cabinet, Alex had accidentally shut the drawer, trapping her fingers. She had wrongly experienced his immediate sorry as empathy and not as a learned strategy to avoid being told off. The brothers were later placed in separate foster homes for their own protection and that of those around them. Contact was arranged.

Contact is not the place for therapeutically working on a troubled sibling relationship. Sibling contact requires the same detailed level of thinking and planning that is necessary when planning parent and child contact. This is crucial if children are not to be traumatised or re-traumatised by ill-planned or unplanned contact with a sibling. If it is not well planned, then any possible positive long-term relationship between the siblings can be sabotaged. Trauma-informed observation of contact is required to observe sibling behaviours with each other as part of a sibling assessment.

Case Example

Clive, ten, and his two brothers Ben, eight, and Kayden, six, were taken into care because of physical abuse by both parents. The case papers noted that Clive was a sad lad who had taken responsibility for the care of his youngest sibling by making sure he was fed and hidden from what was happening at home. When he was first removed from home, Clive was placed with foster carers under an agreed interim order, later a full care order.

His brothers were placed with a maternal aunt and her family under an agreed interim order, later a full residence order. Their mother committed suicide at the end of the proceedings. Their father received a lengthy prison sentence. Maintaining the relationship between the boys was noted as being, 'Very important.'

The carers were encouraged to arrange this between themselves as often as possible and agreed to do so. The case papers made no note of any assessment of the relationship between the brothers. Contact was stopped after three sessions because of the chaos and disruption in placement and school before, during and after contact. No contact was arranged to allow the placements to stabilise. Later, when Clive accessed his care records to establish the loss of contact with his brothers, records agreed the 'Very important' words were more to do with sentiment and that the 'proper assessment' of sibling contact was never completed.

Putnam (1997) at the National Institute of Mental Health in the US considered the issue of resilience, as did Cairns (2002), and how the impact of what was done to a child differs with each sibling. They concluded: 'To date, investigators have largely considered each type of abuse and its severity in isolation, rather than examining these variables as interactive factors.' The 13 variables they identified are summarised as follows:

- the detailed nature of the child's attachment to their parents,
- the age and developmental level of the child at the onset of abuse,
- its duration and frequency,
- whether different forms of abuse co-exist,
- the relationship of the child to the abuser(s),
- the type and severity of the abusive acts,
- the existence of multiple abusers,
- the degree of physical violence and aggression used,
- the age and gender of the offender,
- the existence of peer or adult supports,
- whether or not the child has been able to tell,
- the parental reaction to the disclosure, and
- the 'institutional' response.

The existence of peer or adult supports who clearly gave the child the message that the child was ok but what was happening to them was not, even when intervention to stop the harm was not possible, is one of the consistent factors identified in many research studies on resilience. Obtaining information about all of these variables on the siblings and anyone else who is being considered for contact is necessary to ensure any contact, on balance, does 'more good' and less harm. Reflecting on these variables can result in new insights and learning when siblings placed together experienced this as positive, despite continuing to experience significant harm in placement, for example, Karen and her sister mentioned earlier. Karen's answer, 'We had each other,' needed to be explored further with the questions,

'What was it about having each other? What were the variables?' to avoid this example becoming another mantra used to inform decision-making about other siblings in their home county.

The seen, heard and hidden in sibling relationships are just as, if not more, difficult to assess as child/parent relationships. Collusion with or reinforcing trauma bonds needs to be avoided and cognitive distortions/thinking errors needed to manage complex, paradoxical feelings must also be identified. More importantly, having been identified they must be worked on to ensure a less damaging and hopefully positive relationship between the siblings and consequently with other people in the future.

Trauma-Informed Responses to the Sibling's Quotes at the Beginning of the Chapter

The purpose of the responses is not to gain answers to the questions held by the social worker/therapist/interviewer but to enable the respondent the space to explore the meaning behind their comments, their limiting or deeply held beliefs and to face the pain of their hurt, grief, loss and pain in a manner that lets them know they are held and safe to explore their oft confusing, unstable and abusive histories. The responses here are not an exhaustive list but demonstrate how much information and clarification can be gained from very little information.

The purpose of the communication and the role of the interviewer will have a direct bearing on which responses fit. The ABE-trained social worker establishing whether harm has been experienced will choose a different line to the social worker seeking wishes and feelings to the therapist opening the door to provide the opportunity to go deeper into the pain of loss and hurt. Context here is key, and so not all responses will fit every purpose.

Best is not to ask questions, or as can be seen to limit them. Questions suggest that the motive is only to establish information and that it is the responses that are important and not the person. Helpful words and phrases include:

- 'It seems like': Provides an element of doubt that allows the respondent to correct the interviewer/listener.
- 'It's almost as though': Allows exploration without leading. Enables clarification whilst providing the respondent with the opportunity to easily correct anything that doesn't fit their world view.
- 'Ah ha': Demonstrates listening.
- Reflect feelings to validate them.
- 'I wonder' is technically a cheat. It allows a question to be asked without it being a direct question but creates expansion whilst still enabling a choice not to expand.
- 'I wasn't there when…' This allows the respondent to know that the listener only knows what the respondent has said. They can then choose to fill in the gaps or not.

- 'Maybe.' At the start of a sentence allows exploration.
- 'Huh.' Allows doubt to be expressed and invites space for a response, a clarification, or a correction.

Rachel, aged 12,

> I didn't know I had a brother until I was eleven. He was in a different Dr Barnardo's to me. I was disabled and he wasn't so we could not live together they said. It was my social worker who was still a student told me about him. We might meet one day.

Rachel's possible needs

Gaps in family history.
That she was separated from her sibling.
That she did not know why they were separated.
She may have felt their disability was blamed for the separation and perhaps it was her fault.
That she didn't quite believe what they were saying.
That it was a professional who told her, but there was something significant about it being a student.
Does she want to meet her sibling, is she ambivalent, wistful or full of loss?

Helpful responses

Reflect the feeling or incongruence to the feeling.
'There was so much you didn't know about your family.'
'It's almost as though you felt blamed for being separated from your brother because of your disability.'
'It seems relevant that you were told about your brother by a student social worker' (maybe because they hadn't been told by a qualified social worker previously, or that they had a good relationship with the student, perhaps they had put in more time to research her life or that maybe the telling had been a mistake).
'It seems like you still don't know if you will ever meet your brother.'
'I wonder what it might be like if you did meet him' (would allow possible scenarios to be considered).

Kate, aged 32,

> I always thought my siblings needed me and I had to protect them and love them because I was oldest. My mum had seven children with five different dads. When I was seven, we three were taken into care. One was adopted. My sister and I to foster care but the foster carer did not like me, so I was moved. My mum

then had four more children. Two were adopted but two stayed at home with her. The first and last time we all got together was for her funeral. I thought we would keep in touch. Funny thing was I was pleased we didn't. I didn't even like them. None was like me at all.

Kate's possible needs

Her belief about her responsibilities as a carer then.
Doubt about her past experiences now.
The importance of the makeup of her family and its size and complexity.
The importance of her age when she was removed.
The fact that she felt 'taken' (but we don't know if this was too soon, wrong or too late, or that it was different for the following four siblings).
Mum had four more children after they were taken (did she feel she was simply replaced?).
Three siblings were adopted, two stayed at home, her sister had a single foster placement, but Kate had more than one foster placement. The differences may seem unfair, lack equality or make her feel different in some way.
If she was responsible for protecting them and loving them and yet they were taken and had such different placements, will she feel like she succeeded or not? If not, what does that mean for her?
How will she feel that two managed to stay at home?
The irony of only meeting her estranged siblings at the time of her mother's death only reinforces the loss.
That she had expectations that the joint loss of their mother might be a conduit of change (but couldn't see or accept the complicated nature of the mother's relationship and variety of paternity will leave all seven siblings with very different feelings).
That she had conflicted feelings about her siblings.
It is easier not to like them, even though she didn't know them.
She experienced no sense of family identity.
Perhaps she felt different or alienated.
She seems to hold a pessimistic outlook in relation to reunification or helplessness.

Helpful responses

'You always thought the care of your siblings was your job, it seems like you have a different view now.'
'Even though you were the oldest, you were still only little/a child.' 'You really believed it was your job.'
'Every child deserves to be looked after by their parent rather than have to look after their brother/sister/s.'
'It sounds like your mum struggled to cope when she had three children, even with all your help.'

'It sounds like things changed when you were seven and you lost your siblings.'
'I wonder whose job it was to look after your sister when you went into foster care?'
'The foster carer didn't like you huh? And then you had to move.'
'I wonder what life was like after you were moved away from your sister?'
'Thing's didn't change when you left, your mum had more children, I wonder what you felt/thought about that?'
'Two stayed at home. I don't know if that was OK or not?'
'Three brothers and sisters were adopted, one stayed put in foster care, and two stayed at home and you had so much change.'
'Your mother's funeral was a goodbye and not just to your mum.'
'You thought things would be different between you and your siblings.'
'You say it's funny, but there is no laughter.'
'Real pleased you didn't all keep in touch; I wonder what had happened if you had.'
'It's easier not to like them.'
'You can't see yourself in your siblings, so different.'
'I wonder what it would take for things to be or feel differently?'

Jo, aged 25,

> I couldn't believe it when I met my sister for the first time when I was 25 and she was 20. We were adopted separately because we were taken into care five years apart as babies. She looked like me and spoke like me even although I grew up in Liverpool and she was in Kent. We liked the same food and films and had called our eldest with the same name. We have so much to talk about and find out about each other.

Jo's possible needs

Jo was surprised when she met her sister. It was as though she didn't expect it to happen.
She could talk about facts but keeps feelings at bay.
The age difference was significant to her and maybe how she holds the rationale of the siblings' separation as justifiable.
There is an information gap that creates an incongruent 'gap.' Jo was five when her sister was born, but they were taken into care as babies. A five-year-old is little but isn't a baby. So how she viewed herself and her sister needs to be borne in mind, or that she was removed as a baby and then her sister was removed as a baby, which then leads to her unasked question, why didn't my adoptive parents adopt my sister, could they have, etc.?
Jo saw similarities in the way they looked, suggesting identity and belonging were important. Whilst both areas mentioned, one in the Northwest and one in the Southeast, can be accent-less, the difference between Scouse and the Medway

valley accents is notable if they are not. However, she could be referring to lilt, prosody, volume, inflection, or mannerisms, etc.

She seemed to find comfort in the fact that they had similar tastes, and they shared many similarities around identity.

Jo seemed to find a sense of hope in the future, but one has to wonder if she is over-idealising or over-optimistic about the relationship.

Helpful responses

'Real surprised' (the Americanism can be off-putting for some but the shortening of really allows for the emphasis to be on the feeling. Just saying this allows the feeling of being heard as well as reorientation back onto the feeling to check the 'fit' of the word).

'I don't know the circumstances of you meeting your sister' (allows the person to know the gaps in your knowledge whilst not leading them somewhere that they do not wish to go).

'Your ages seem important' (this allows Jo to explore the loss of her childhood sibling relationship).

'Really thinking about meeting her as an adult' (allows her to explore not meeting as a child).

'Letting me know there was no contact in your childhood' (presents the loss directly within what was not said in what she said).

'Not only separated but placed so far apart' (the distance between the siblings is a metaphor in itself. It also raises the question: would things have been different if they had been placed in the same area?).

'So many similarities, but I wonder about the differences' (allows exploration of diversity, difference, individuality, and still be able to be connected).

'It's like you can see a sense of future, I wonder how your sister sees it' (allows the possibility of empathy; can she see the world from her sister's perspective).

'I wonder who makes the most contact' (directly addresses who is the driver in the relationship).

Anne, aged 14,

I have to wear nail varnish all the time because my hands and my brother's hands are identical in shape. When I look at my hands, I see his hands and feel him touching me. I shake. His hands make me feel sick to my stomach. Nail varnish means when I look at my hands, they are my hands and not his. I'm not allowed to wear nail varnish in school and get suspended when I do.

Anne's possible needs

To be separate from her brother.
To see herself as different from her brother.

To have her own identity.
To feel safe.
To feel understood, validated and supported.

Helpful responses

'There is a reason for wearing nail varnish that seems different to your peers' (being seen helps feeling understood).

'Just because many 14-year-old's want to wear nail varnish, doesn't mean they all wear it for the same reason' (focusses on the difference).

'You have no choice' (focusses on the statement that she has no alternative, this act is crucial for her well-being).

'You cannot see the difference between your hands and those of your brother' (shows Anne she has been heard).

'You need your hands to look different from your brother's hands' (focusses on the need).

'Your hands remind you of his hands, even your hands don't feel safe' (when your own body is the trigger).

'His hands remind you of when you were not safe' (keeps the trauma in the safety of vagueness).

'His hands remind you of the touching you did not want or could not stop' (moves toward direct understanding).

'I wasn't there when your brother was touching you, but it seems that touching wasn't good' (allows Anne to know that you only know part of the story and she can expand or not).

'There are all types of touching; caring and supportive, good, bad, uncomfortable, hurtful, physical and violent or physical and sexual, I don't know what type of touching it was because I wasn't there.' (Sets the parameters of knowledge and allows space for the respondent to clarify or not).

'The sight of his hand makes you sick and when you feel that sickness where in your body does that start?' (establishes the body is having a reaction and helps Anne stay in that feeling).

'And when the sickness comes is there an image, or a memory, or a feeling, or a sensation or a thought that goes with that' (expands the feeling and explores the feeling as stemming from an event, experience, or trigger).

'You have found a way of making your hands your own' (enables Anne to show that she has agency and separation from her brother).

'Even though you have found a way of being ok, others don't understand you and worse, punish you for trying to feel ok so you can attend school' (lets Anne know that you hear her, that other's don't, and that she is working so hard to find a way to keep on keeping on).

'It's almost as though school cannot see the pain you are going through' (acknowledges that she isn't being understood).

'And the last thing you want to do is to tell the school what your brother did' (names the Catch 22, the paradoxical situation she is in).

'Maybe all you want is to have one part of your life (school) where you can feel differently' (seeing the world from Anne's perspective).

'And then you get punished, when you have found a way of managing to attend school' (highlights the injustice of her predicament).

'You were hurt, and now you are being hurt for being hurt' (empathy).

'I wonder what your brother sees when he looks at his hands' (allows Anne to be curious about her brother).

'I wonder if your brother is ever suspended from school' (gives the potential of exploring the differences between the victimised and the victimiser, the reactive versus the proactive, the acting out and the acted on).

'You didn't have a safe relationship with your brother' (acknowledges the missed experience that she should have had.'

Mags, aged 15,

> Mum and Dad were part of a paedophile group. My brother was the only person who I had sex with who never hurt me. We took comfort from each other and would cuddle to fall asleep. When they (social workers) found out they put us in different foster homes, and we were not allowed to see each other. My therapist helped me get my head round why we needed each other and why this included sex. He never had any therapy. We can't meet up now because when he looks at me, he remembers and drinks to forget. He has tried to commit suicide a couple of times. He needs help.

Mags's possible needs

She wasn't safe.
She didn't have the opportunity of a safe family.
Sex and love are skewed.
Trust is anathema.
Sex can feel safe, even when it is wrong.
Enmeshed relationships.
Being taken from the familiar.
Separation and loss.
Lack of consistency in the family and outside of the family.
Cognitive understanding versus emotional understanding.
Future contact.
Seeing the impact of abuse.

Helpful responses

'There was no safety in your family' (allows Mags the opportunity to see the world through another's eyes.
'You know you were not safe now, I don't know if that's how you felt then' (allows Mags to see change or to be challenged about how life is or was.
'You know now that your parents were different from other parent's, I wonder if you knew that then' (moves the here and now to the there and then whilst staying in the here and now).
'There were so many people who could have hurt you' (responding to the fact Mags was able to share that the people around her parents were also not safe).
'I wonder how your parent's showed love' (allows the potential of the response being sex).
'I wonder what sex means' (allows the potential of the response to be love).
'I wasn't there when you were growing up, so I don't know what it would have been like for you' (allows Mags to choose the aspect of her experience she wants to avoid or explore).
'It's almost as though sex with your brother was safer than any other relationship' (noticing the difference of sex in this relationship).
'You had no choice of where or with whom you were to live' (acknowledges the same lack of agency being 'rescued' as when she was at home. Adults hold the power).
'It's almost as though you had no power' (allows Mags's space to explore agency).
'You could see that sex with your brother felt so different from sex with anyone else' (allowing Mags to know that no matter how taboo. It is safe to explore these issues, and to be heard).
'It seems like you didn't even have the opportunity to have a sex free relationship' (acknowledging the loss whilst leaving doubt and space to be corrected).
'It sounds like the relationship with your brother brought comfort to you both when there was no one else' (acknowledges how the children had to look after themselves).
'When you were placed in foster care, it's as though you lost the only source of comfort you had' (acknowledges loss).
'I don't know how old you were when you moved into foster care, and I don't know how that felt.' (Statements rather than questions allow the child to know the parameters of your knowledge and they can fill in the gaps or not).
'And when you were not allowed to see your brother, I wonder what happened next' (allows exploration of subsequent behaviour).
'I don't know what reasons you were given for not being able to see your brother' (fills in gaps).
'Someone "switched on sex" before you were developmentally ready, I wonder what happened when you moved into foster care because "switching off sex" is harder' (Acknowledging that prematurely sexualised children have lasting consequences).

'I wonder what it was like when you moved to a place where adults didn't have sex with children, and they didn't allow children to have sex with children?' (acknowledging that she may have strong feelings about this).

'You had therapy, but your brother didn't, that doesn't seem equitable or fair' (acknowledging difference).

'Your brother can't bear to recall what your relationship was based on, that must be so hard' (allows the feeling and the impact to be talked about).

'You lost the relationship you could have had with your brother, then lost your brother and now you can see your brother, you can't because it was too painful for him' (the awfulness of her situation is witnessed).

'And now your brother finds it too overwhelming to live' (at the extreme end of this may be that his guilt about what he did to Mags may lead to; when he sees her or thinks about her, he wants to die. This is a huge potential burden to carry).

'You know he needs help, but it's almost as though you can't help him get that help he needs' (the lack of power she has for meeting her brother's needs).

Tony, aged 11,

> I have 3 brothers. George, I love, Hayden I don't like and Jay is ok. I don't know why contact has to be with all three. I can sit and talk or play a game with George. Hayden and Jay just want to play fight and when they do Julie (contact supervisor) tells them to stop and play a game with us. They just wreck the game. I don't like her (Julie) either.

Tony's possible needs

To explore his relationships.
To understand the reason for his feelings.
His capacity to influence contact.
His level of agency.
To understand the differences in sibling relationships.
His feelings towards the contact supervisor.

Helpful responses

'Letting me know you have brothers, seem like they are on your mind' (concrete response opening up to discussion and emotion).

'Three very different feelings toward your three brothers' (letting him know he is heard and that those feelings are not judged).

'I've never met George. I wonder what it is about George that is likeable' (opening the door for exploration).

'I've never met Hayden. I wonder what it is about Hayden that is not so likeable' (opening the door for exploration).

'I've never met Jay. I wonder what it is about Jay that makes him "just" OK' (opening the door for exploration).
'I wonder what it would be like if you saw George on his own' (future projecting possibilities not promises).
'I wonder what it would be like if you saw Jay on his own' (future projecting possibilities not promises).
'I wonder what it would be like if you saw Hayden on his own' (future projecting possibilities not promises).
'Seems like you and George can talk and play together, that seems safe' (to play you have to feel safe, but doubt is still inserted).
'I don't know but it seems like something happens to Hayden and Jay when they see each other' (exploring the trigger).
'Sometimes playfighting doesn't feel like play. I wonder what it reminds you, or them of' (acknowledging the apparent trigger).
'I wonder what George thinks of Hayden' (all sibling variables can be explored in this manner as it enables children to show their capacity for empathic reflection and thought).
'I wonder why George and Hayden don't fight' (again all variables of all behaviours can be examined).
'I wonder why you don't like Julie' (gives opportunity to explore)
'You may not like Julie because she is stopping Hayden and Jay from playing, or that she is interrupting your game with George if they have to come and play with you, or that she can't see that you don't like Hayden, or doesn't care that you don't like Hayden, or doesn't care that Hayden may ruin your game or something else' (this is called a menu and allows the child to explore a range of possibilities if they would otherwise be too restricted and the final phrase diminishes the likelihood of the child picking the last thing you say. It reduces the risk of leading which offering one suggestion may induce).
'Maybe there are other reasons for not liking Julie. Maybe you think it's her fault you have to see your brothers in the way you do' (gives the message it's ok to explore feelings).
'Maybe Julie reminds you of someone else' (explores the possibility that she may be a trigger).

Part V

Hearing the Child
Listening, Validating, and Understanding

Chapter 12

Between Truth and Survival
Forensic Neutrality, Therapeutic Empathy, and the Discipline of Hypotheses

This is a forensic and therapeutic consideration. When is it safe to believe or not believe any allegations of harm done currently or historically? Another question frequently asked is whether or not children or adults lie when talking about or disclosing their experiences? The correct answer is: Of course they do. They will tell you, 'Nothing happened.' 'It only happened once.' 'It doesn't matter.' 'It won't happen again.' 'It was an accident,' 'Nobody knows.' 'I'm the only one this has happened to.' ' I love my mum, and she loves me.' These statements are repeatedly made, even when it is clear from their behaviour that something has happened, there is medical evidence, or it has been witnessed by a sibling or another adult. Of course, this raises another question, 'What would be the purpose of this lie?' Answering this question about these paradoxical statements is especially complicated where the allegation involves harm done by someone who is or was relied upon to be protective, safe, and nurturing and often appears to be when interviewed.

The aim is to listen to what is being alleged without bias about 'true' or 'untrue' and to take what is being said seriously, form hypotheses about what was said and why it was said before thinking about the necessary questions to conduct a thorough investigation or conclude an assessment. 'Hypothesising, asking many, many questions is important before coming to any conclusion' (Mandel et al.1995). Lord Clyde in his summary into what happened in Orkney also commented on the necessity of hypothesising to avoid jumping to conclusions. A singular hypothesis is a decision, i.e. the mind is made up about something without exploring other possibilities. The following two examples demonstrate different levels of complexity.

Case Example

The social worker on duty had a call from a teacher concerned about a child in her class. The children have news jotters with half the page blank for a drawing and half with lines for writing about their drawing. Six-year-old Katy had drawn two faces, a child and a man with their eyes closed and what looked like a finger in front of their lips. Below she had written, 'Daddy and I with our eyes closed. We have a secret.' The teacher had asked Katy to tell her who was not to know about the secret. Katy had replied saying, 'Mummy.' The teacher then asked Katy to tell her about the secret. Katy replied saying, 'Mummy and grandma went out last night. Daddy was looking after me. We had a bath, and daddy did something really rude. We made a promise not to tell mummy.' At this point, the teacher stopped the conversation and, concerned that something did not sound right about this, called the social worker for advice. The teacher had recalled her Safeguarding Training, where the advice was not to question a child in case the wrong questions sabotaged an investigation/likely prosecution later. These hypotheses followed: Katy was making this up. Katy was a child who lied or exaggerated. This was something sexually concerning, a game, or something else; therefore, a safeguarding issue.

Each of these hypotheses required lots of questions to be asked, the answers found, then ruling in or ruling out each hypothesis before a decision could be made about what action was needed. The teacher was confidently able to say that Katy was a happy but quiet little girl who presented with no problems in class or playtime. She could not recall any incident where Katy had lied or exaggerated when telling a story or giving an account of something she had done. It was agreed that nothing further could be done until someone found out what the 'really rude' behaviour was. The teacher agreed she would ask Katy. If it was something sexual, she would not ask any more questions about the incident but would not stop Katy from saying anything she wanted, thank Katy for telling her and record everything both of them had said. A decision could then be made about what action, if any, was needed.

Katy gave the teacher a detailed account of the bath times she shared with her dad and that last night was the first time he had farted in the bath, causing several bubbles in the bath water, making them both laugh. A farting game followed. Daddy asked her not to tell mummy and to make this their secret. Case closed or one further hypothesis to be followed up? Was this the start of a grooming process, the keeping of secrets from mummy, which would lead to the need for more questions and answers to rule out this further hypothesis?

A more complex example: 15-year-old Amber whose new social worker stopped her therapy following their first meeting.

Amber had been incubated in drugs and violence. Her first month was spent in a special care baby unit (SCBU) where she received treatment for withdrawal from heroin and cocaine, both a result of her mother's addiction. She screamed when touched by nurses.

No hypothesis was developed at this point, not even 'what might be making her scream?' Instead, the nurses worked with their conclusion that the level of pain she was experiencing was extreme and was exacerbated by touch, so Amber spent the majority of her time in hospital without direct loving physical human contact. In her foster placement, at three months old, she could not bear to be picked up but equally could not bear to be put down. This paradox led to her displaying high levels of control in early life that continued into adoption when she was 18 months old. In her adoptive family, she presented as pseudo-independent, self-reliant albeit in an insufficient way, oppositional, defiant, and controlling. She was desperate for connection, but connection held a psychic memory of pain. She had developed a 'nourishment barrier.'

> Then, there are people who commit to the lonely path of doing it all themselves. They don't expect any consistent support. They don't expect any real help from the outside. They don't expect nourishment. They have the view of the world as an empty place, where you can't count on anybody. When you offer nourishment, they reject it. They see something wrong with it. They won't take it in. As a result, they are never satisfied. They avoid taking in nourishment or even finding it in the world, because they do not want to deal with the possibility of loss. The state of getting what you want is anxiety producing. Having the thing so wanted leaves one vulnerable to losing it again. They're not good at taking in what's available.
>
> (Kurtz 1990)

Amber's inability to connect led to her having an enduring internal crisis of wanting and needing the very thing that she could not tolerate—human contact. Amber subconsciously developed her own answers, then found strategies to meet some of those needs. Initially, this was in risk-taking behaviours and conflict. By eleven, she was running away, and in doing so, she had her parents, social workers, police and others frantically searching for her. She felt seen but not held or contained. Her strategies did not result in what she craved: emotional connection and belonging.

In order to understand Amber, it is necessary to hypothesise about the connections between impacts on her from pre-birth, the reasons for beliefs and behaviours, and what help she needs. About the baby in utero where everything for the baby is contained and 'on-tap': Temperature is regulated, no thirst, hunger, defecation, urination, or breathing, all managed via the placenta and umbilical cord. In addition, the environment provides subdued lighting, muffled sounds, a perfect ecosystem in a safe family protected from harm. Then, as a baby faced with three levels of trauma in the birthing process; stage 1, outgrew the space available, resulting in constriction and reduced space to move, the resultant greater physical connection may have led to increased discomfort and not knowing what if it gets tighter. Stage 2 when contractions started. The mother felt these. They ranged from uncomfortable to extremely painful as the contractions gathered momentum. What then for the baby as the contractions came in waves and hit the child to expel them down that even tighter birth canal? Then stage 3, born into the pain of the world, bright light, loud noises, change in temperature, rough textures and handling, gasping for breath into previously unused lungs, umbilical cord severed, and a tranche of physical feelings, hunger, thirst, need to defecate and urinate followed. Then maybe contact regained with mother or not. Amber, like any baby, needed reconnection to the familiar smell and sense of mother.

> Birth is the greatest challenge to human survival…the newborn must have the skills to regulate autonomic processes (breathe, feed, digest, thermoregulate)

and to communicate autonomic state needs to caregivers (cry)…even with healthy full-term newborns, there is great concern by health care professionals and parents about an infant's physiological regulation competency in negotiating this complex transition.

(Porges 2011).

Think of the loggerhead turtles (Caretta Caretta) on Zakinthos. Their journey starts at hatching and then digging out of the deep sand nest and making that long and perilous journey down to the sea, with their brothers and sisters but very much a journey on their own. When arriving in the sea, they are faced with the tide and currents and a myriad of dangers. The greatest dangers are not the birds and sea creatures but humans. The holidaymaker who says, 'Oh hon, you are really struggling,' then full of compassion and kindness picks up the newly hatched turtles and takes them out to sea where they promptly drown. The hatchlings need to make that perilous journey to develop their strength and expand their lungs to survive in the new environment. In other words, they had to face adversity to build resilience. Understanding what is helpful and what is harmful is not always obvious, straightforward, and sometimes counterintuitive.

Amber had no connection to her birth mother, and the first experience she had, after the normal trauma of birth and disconnection, was a disconnection from her drug supply. She remained disconnected when she was taken to the SCBU, isolated and away from her mother, where she was given different drugs to manage her withdrawal, to manage her pain, and no touch.

The intervening years between her arrival in placement and pre-adolescence were a constant struggle for Amber's adopters to provide the connection or containment she so required but could not accept. They loved her unconditionally, but Amber gave nothing back. Activating the hypothesis that more boundaries were needed resulted in her kicking against them. Reason was treason. Amber's inability to connect to her higher cortex led to an inability to hear her parents' pleas. Tighter boundaries led to increased rebellion and flight. Consequences were experienced as oppression that led to increased non-compliance. As the parents' parenting toolkit diminished, they were left increasingly with escalating punishments that did nothing but drive them all further apart.

Even before she entered adolescence and puberty, she was searching further afield, becoming even more vulnerable. She met up with other disaffected youth, with whom she could not physically connect, and so started her initial exploration into drinking and taking drugs that allowed her to connect whilst her inhibitions reduced. The sexual connection that resulted was way more than the physical connection she sought. Perhaps she thought the physical connection would achieve the emotional connection or that because she could not connect physically, this made the emotional unachievable other than superficially in the moment. Hence the drugs, subconsciously familiar and stupefying, gave her a sense of physical connection but without the emotional connection she unknowingly was desperately seeking. This led, unsurprisingly, to her being recruited by her peers into sexual exploitation and the development of a cycle of increasingly dangerous behaviours. The outcome was her reception into care for her own safety and a placement in a residential unit where there was even less likelihood of developing the secure and consistent relationship she needed.

Amber did not want to come to therapy. For Amber, nothing was wrong; she could not or would not see the dangers around her, and like many children and young people with developmental trauma, she was not in a position to see or conceptualise the pros and cons of undertaking or not undertaking therapy. Despite saying she did not want to come to therapy, she arrived with her support workers, complained for sure, but came and continued to come for 18 months. A career opportunity arose for her social worker, who left and was subsequently replaced. In her first meeting, the new social worker listened to Amber and stopped the therapy. The irony of this timescale replicating her move into adoption was not missed by the therapist. This action was based on the social worker following the mantra 'believe the child,' without hypothesising whether or not in this instance this informed good practice.

Good practice, serious case reviews and case precedent advise to neither believe nor disbelieve what the child is saying but to take it seriously, hypothesise, work out what questions need answers, then follow the usual rules and procedures below before making decisions.

1. See the child directly. This mantra resulted from so many times the child was not seen, one of the findings in the tragedies where seeing the child had been missed by professionals. Although Amber was seen, no account was taken of her in context, in time and space. This was the first meeting she had with this child. Without contextual information, action was subsequently flawed. Also missing were the three stages required to build an emotional connection with her:
    I. Engagement (Crenshaw et al. 2015). This is the initial introduction. It is one way the child oftentimes has little choice in the process. The new teacher in the new school introduces herself, the social worker describes why they are involved with the family, the doctor assigned to deal with the child's injury, or the therapist introducing why they are seeing the child are all inherently power-based, and instead what is needed is creating a level playing field.
    II. Building rapport (Crenshaw et al. 2015). Rapport building is the first stage in the development of a deeper relationship but is weighted differently. Rapport can be defined as a 'harmonious, empathetic, or sympathetic relation or connection to another self,' and an 'accord or affinity, in an ecological alignment with another system' (Newberry and Stubbs, 1990, p. 14). This is a transition phase that enables a relationship to develop. It is as uncomfortably evident in a 'grooming' situation as it is in an investigative, assessment, or therapeutic

process. 'The interviewer uses the rapport period to build up trust and mutual understanding with the child and help them to relax as far as possible in the novel environment' (Achieving Best Evidence Guidance, 2001).

III. Developing a trusting connection/therapeutic alliance/relationship (Ryan and Wilson 1996, Vanfleet 2010, Nijenhuis 2015, Gill 2017). This relationship or alliance is the conduit for change between the practitioner and the client. 'In the emotional warmth of the relationship with the therapist, the client begins to experience a feeling of safety as he finds that whatever attitude he expresses is understood in almost the same way that he perceives it and is accepted' (Rogers 1951).

Within this process builds empathic attunement. Growing evidence suggests that people are connected via mirror neurones (Bryson 2019) and experience a 'felt sense' of connection. This was a problem in Amber's situation. What she experienced was that her need for connection and love was met by grooming, exploitation, and engagement in sexual activity, leaving her with a skewed belief that a need for connection is likely to be answered with harm. Then later in a foster family or therapy the same sexual expectation may be triggered. The intention to meet her needs by building a mutual empathic relationship is experienced as a threat.

2. Listen to the child. Again, this is good practice, but to understand what Amber was saying needed exploration and hypothesising about what was being said. Just because she said, 'It is boring;' did not equate to this being something she did not want to do. It was not enough to just listen to her words, but to take into account her prosody, tempo, volume, and how it was being said alongside her cognition, body language, physiological reaction, eye contact and movement, her affect/emotional content, her sensorium, and her context. Hypothesising about the meanings behind Amber saying, 'It is boring.' In other words, to not immediately believe but take seriously and hypothesise about the reasons behind the words, to consider and explore all possible avenues, no matter how unlikely.

Rather than stop her therapy, the social worker could have considered these alternative hypotheses:

a. Amber did not want to tell her how she truly felt about the intervention because they had only just met.
b. Amber's acute antennae had picked up in the social worker's tone that she was dismissive of therapy.
c. She was like other people who thought therapy was for mad, bad people.
d. She was angry that her social worker knew about her therapy and was embarrassed, ashamed or angry that this private, personal experience was known and she might not want to discuss it with her).

e. The most common hidden meaning behind, 'It's boring,' is that whatever the child is doing or experiencing is actually really very hard work. Therapy by definition is emotionally excruciatingly painful.
   f. A mixture of the above or indeed
   g. Something else that is not yet known.

Listening to children and adults for that matter, is complex, paradoxical, and is not just about what is said.

3. Believe the child. This social worker did not take what Amber said seriously and instead believed what Amber was saying, taking the comment at face value, without hypothesis, without question, without context, without analysis, and without the opportunity for further exploration. Believe the child is trying to tell you something but the words chosen to express this are not necessarily the correct ones.
4. Take action. This social worker acted. It is important to act. It is of limited value to obtain information and then do nothing with it. In other words, do not do nothing, unless, of course, doing nothing is a well-thought-out decision and the least harmful intervention. At what point should or could she act? It was not known if this decision was discussed in supervision or not, but what was known was it had not been discussed with the therapist or the Independent Reviewing Officer (IRO) or the staff in her residential unit. They were immediately informed the therapy had been stopped. Not just for Amber, but due to the complex, paradoxical nature of children's communication, particularly traumatised children's communication, it is vital that information is shared and discussed before action is taken to ensure no further harm results from, however well-intentioned but misguided actions.
5. Assess capacity. Amber was understood by the social worker to be Gillick/Fraser Competent (Gillick, 1986). This is an extremely complex matter for many traumatised children and young people. Despite the legal desire for people 'to be,' or 'not to be' competent is an oversimplification of the issue, especially in people whose trauma has caused fragmentation, disorganised attachment, and dissociation. Amber was able, under certain conditions, to hold a very clear and coherent view, but at other times she behaved in a paradoxical way that was a danger to herself and sometimes to those around her, demonstrating that if you are not Gillick/Fraser competent for most, if not all, of the time, then you cannot be Gillick/Fraser competent.
6. Consult. Finally, there was no interagency discussion. No Team Around the Child meeting and no opportunity for others, including the therapist, to provide further explanation, opinion, or process to share their knowledge of the child.

Of course, it is important that anyone being interviewed does not suspect the interviewer is disbelieving what is being said. It is not uncommon for someone to ask,

'You don't believe me, do you?' or the opposite, 'Do you believe me?' These questions often result from there being no explanation about the need for lots of questions, or the person being interviewed not wanting to believe it themselves, or from just suspicion about the unconscious or conscious doubting reactions of the interviewer. Rather than answering, 'Of course I believe you!' much better to gently and empathically answer, 'Mmm, that's interesting, I'm wondering where that thought comes from,' or 'what makes you ask that.' The interviewer then answers honestly the comments or questions which follow, whilst still maintaining the stance of neither believing nor disbelieving, until fully investigated. It is therefore important that there is no indication by tone of voice or body movement that there is belief, and even more important that there should never be any sign of disbelief. Instead, there must be an equal amount of empathic curiosity about whatever is being talked about. This will enable both participants to remain in their window of tolerance before concluding this is true or not true, believable, not believable, or indeterminable.

Any allegation that involves a loved or important adult, for example, a parent/sibling/relative/teacher/priest/other trusted adult, is made more complicated both forensically and therapeutically by the victim needing to disbelieve their memory of what happened, hope that it cannot be true or must have been an accident because the pain, distress, and consequences of it being true are globally overwhelming. Also, there is fear that threats made to ensure silence might also come true. It is easier to disbelieve what is remembered could have happened and actively try to disprove what is true to stay sane, function physically and emotionally, and stay in a dependent relationship where, if what was remembered was true, it would destroy that relationship. And, if it was actually not true, making such an allegation could have the same consequence. Threats that are used are more believable if they contain an element of truth. And of course, the unconscious use of dissociation to not remember negatives, reinforce a coping belief or disbelief, and stop any joined-up thinking makes belief and disbelief more difficult for all.

It is crucial that any investigator or therapist understands this and remains curious and open-minded, not just about an allegation being made, but also about believing (or not) something positive which is being said about the circumstances of the alleged offence. For example, a victim where the father is the alleged offender could say, 'My mum didn't know,' or 'My mum loved me very much.' Both the victim and the investigator would like this to be true, but it cannot be accepted as true. It must be taken seriously, and questions asked to determine if this is something which the victim needs to believe is true because the emotional distress of the truth that the mother knew and failed to protect is just too painful to believe. It was uncomfortable and at first shocking that when working with sex offenders to hear them say their choice of, and grooming of their partner needed even greater care than their choice of victim. Their partner, if not well chosen and managed, could report their behaviour for a number of reasons, for example: protecting the child, jealousy, anger, to split up. They knew from their own, or others sharing their experience, the partner would be praised for protecting their child with no other hypotheses raised to look for or explore if there were any other paradoxical reasons.

Case Example

Working with a six-year-old who is now living with adoptive parents who, no matter what they try, have been unable to stop her wetting the bed. The parents have been very careful not to blame or shame the child, so any medical reason is explored, resulting in using medication such as Desmo spray/tablets. From their training courses, they remember children will often use negative behaviours to gain attention, so they began by being positive, using a bell/buzzer, a star chart, and no drinks after 6 pm, all to no avail. Finally, using a paradox, another suggestion from their training, the child is asked to just change her own sheets and put them in the washing machine herself. This results in her screaming at her adoptive parents that she knew they did not love her and stomping off to her bedroom. This problem and her reaction are shared with the therapist on her first visit to meet the parents. The therapist suggested that wetting the bed may not be the problem but the child's answer to a problem, and trying to remove the answer while the problem still exists will not be successful. They hypothesise together what the problem might be; she was sexually assaulted in her birth family, and wetting the bed might be a way of feeling safe. Being smelly might be for the same reason; she is dissociative and does not recognise she needs to wee; she knows it annoys her adoptive mum, and any attention, including negative attention, is being sought.

It is agreed the therapist will have a conversation with the child in an empathically curious manner about what wetting the bed is about and what problem it could be the answer to. One of the questions asked was, 'What would happen if you did not wet the bed?' Her immediate answer, 'I would know for sure my mum did not love me.' This puzzling answer was followed up by exploring who was mum and what would a mum do if she loved you. Her answer, 'My tummy mummy loved me very much, much more than my new mum. She loved me very, very much.' 'Wow, tell me something your tummy mummy did that told you she loved you very, very much, much more than your new mum.'

> My tummy mummy knew I did not like sleeping in a wet bed. Whenever daddy sexed me, it would make the bed wet, and it didn't matter how tired my mum was she would always get up and change my sheets and hug me till I fell asleep. That's how much she loved me.

It was then clear that the attempts to stop the bedwetting would never answer the problem, and time would be needed to help her understand the complexities and paradoxes about love and relationships. If she had just been immediately told that her mum's behaviour was not loving at all but a significant failure to protect her, she would not have been able to hear this. She needed to come to that conclusion herself as a result of the love from her adopters whilst working with the therapist. The adoptive mum needed support to help her understand her responses and the confused sense of responsibility she felt about failing and not understanding quickly enough what to do and how this linked to similar feelings she had experienced in her childhood. It is not uncommon for parents, birth, adoptive, foster, or even relatives or residential support workers to acknowledge for the first time, recall, or accept their own childhood trauma has a direct result of their ability to support their own child or young person in therapy.

This way of working with gentle, empathic, in-the-window curiosity also applies when trying to obtain a child's wishes and feelings, also remembering Lady Butler-Sloss' comment that obtaining wishes and feelings need not result in meeting them, especially if they are not in the child's best interest.

Chapter 13

Conversations on the Edge

Staying within the Window of Tolerance

Interviews can often be disrupted or not achieve their goals when either or both the interviewer and the child are dysregulated. Understanding and using Siegel's Window of Tolerance (also referred to by Wilbarger and Wilbarger 1997 as 'optimal arousal zone' and Porges 2011 as 'the Poly Vagal Theory') is one of the crucial components in a successful interview. Siegel (1999) describes each individual's ability to tolerate varying degrees of stress as their unique Window of Tolerance. The capacity an individual has to tolerate or manage stress is not so much by measuring the level of stress they are experiencing, but their capacity (Window) to contain or manage it. The size of each individual's 'Window' correlates to natural resilience, temperament, innate traits, and experience of having been enabled to successfully navigate adversity. Adversity has to be experienced to build resilience. This is not at all similar to the levels of missing basic needs as described by Maslow and/or the levels of neglect when trauma is experienced. Thus, if a child has been raised in a caring and loving environment with a parent or parents who have made mistakes (adversity) such as dealing with a crying infant as though hungry (misattunement), realise their error (awareness and re-attunement) in discovering the infant has colic, make a repair (reassurance), and resolve the colic. This child is likely to develop greater resilience than the child whose parent was correct immediately.

A child whose parent(s) make unintentional mistakes and make prompt repairs is likely to develop a widening Window of Tolerance, eventually a 'Georgian' window that can contain greater levels of stress. A chil whose parent(s) make no mistakes has reduced opportunity to face (mild) adversity may only develop a 'croft' sized window. A child, whose parent(s) are preoccupied, absent, dismissive, neglectful, or abusive with the absence of repair is facing more adversity than their delicate and immature developing window can tolerate. This child is likely to develop a 'pillbox' thin window. It becomes clear the level of stress that takes the child with the croft-sized window to their maximum capacity would overwhelm the child who had a pillbox thin window but would be well within the capacities of the child with the Georgian sized window. Knowledge, and the ability to assess

DOI: 10.4324/9781003724797-18

the unique capacity of each sibling's window is a crucial component alongside Putnam's abuse trauma variables.

Differences seen between 'in' and 'out' of the window responses in individuals and organisations when either or both are experiencing stress or trauma:

In the window—anxious.	Out of the window—anxiety.
In the window—tolerable.	Out of the window—intolerable.
In the window—creative and dynamic.	Out of the window—blaming and shaming.
In the window—resilience.	Out of the window—reliance.
In the window—deepening attachment and managing separation.	Out of window—disorganised attachment or trauma bond making separation intolerable.
In the window—positive thinking/planning.	Out of the window—Catastrophising.
In the window—joined-up thinking.	Out of the window—disjointed thinking and/or dissociation.
In the window—trauma-informed.	Out of the window—inspection and targets focused.
In the window—self-aware.	Out of the window—fear for self.
In the window—conscious awareness.	Out of the window—unconscious coping strategies/solutions.
In the window—thinks of consequences.	Out of the window—now, not later, matters.

How often are practitioners or organisations asked where they are in their window, and does this change hearing about or experiencing stress or trauma?

One of the ongoing consequences of trauma is an enlarged amygdala or 'smoke detector' constantly searching for any likely 'smoke.' Its enlargement brings an extra level of sensitivity, particularly in adolescence. It is on edge, ready for action and will react immediately there is anything which could be a wisp of 'smoke' without assessing what actual risk the current 'smoke' presents. There is limited ability to manage any additional physical or emotional challenge. Every effort is focused on dealing with the feeling of threat, not assessing the level of threat or any safety which would lessen it. The solution which worked before is immediately applied because it worked the last time. Quite different to what happens while in the window where the search for safety to balance thinking and responding to an assessed threat.

The nearer someone is to the edge of their window, the more their response is informed by their feelings rather than thinking. This emotion-driven response prompts what is called state-dependent memory, i.e. the memory of a time when those feelings were prominent and the behaviour which was used, at that time, to survive or just get through the previous incident. This tried-and-tested behavioural script, or solution, informs behaviour because it worked then, rather than thinking of a more appropriate response to this 'smoke' now. Sometimes, this response is appropriate, solves the problem, and reinforces this solution, ready for immediate use the next time 'smoke' appears, but can also cause additional problems.

Case Example

The duty officer received a phone call from Hayden's mother saying that if he was excluded from his third senior school, she was going to terminate the placement. Hayden was 14. His mother was asked if she had discussed the difficulties with her supervising social worker or Hayden's social worker. Her response was, neither. The curiosity of the duty social worker was piqued by the words 'disrupt the placement' when there was neither a social worker for the child nor a supervising social worker, so rather than advise the mother on how to access the appropriate people within the education department, she asked some more questions and searched for any departmental files. It transpired Hayden was removed from home aged four and placed in foster care, the middle of five siblings removed from their parental care where there was violence, physical and emotional neglect. The children were split into three groups: the two youngest and the two oldest together, Hayden on his own. He had contact with all his siblings for about a year but none since adoption, and their cases closed. The original family case file noted that Hayden was the 'family clown with a wicked sense of humour,' who used his humour in a very skilled way, even at age four, to divert any hint of violence or anger (detected by his enlarged sensitive amygdala) in his home. This comment repeated in case records while in his foster placements, during contact with his siblings, in his current placement and his previous primary schools. His file was closed following his adoption at age six. Rather than signposting, a full assessment of his current situation was agreed. One recommendation suggested working with Hayden on his understanding of his behaviour which resulted in so much trouble at school. He said it was not fair because all he was doing was being funny. He was asked to describe a recent incident from the beginning.

He described becoming anxious and not following the teacher's instructions. He was worried the teacher would pick on him again for his daydreaming and then not understanding what had just been said. As soon as the teacher looked at him, he would crack one of his favourite jokes to make his class laugh. The teacher would then be diverted to calm the class down, and just when he was succeeding, Hayden would crack the same joke again and repeat this usually once more, resulting again in him being excluded from the class and given a detention. By doing this, he was no longer frightened of the teacher being or becoming angry with him.

In effect, what he was repeating was the tried, tested and successful solution to the same feelings he had when he was four. This was seen in his use of humour, not just any humour but the same content as his four-year-old's jokes which worked then, repeating them over and over like a four-year-old until being made to stop. An exercise using the letter V was used as a metaphor to help him understand this process and to think with the practitioner about what other solutions he could try to avoid getting into so much trouble. Hayden came up with an alternative and creative answer. As he grew more aware of the limitations of his old strategy, he was able to create a new solution which solved the immediate problem of avoiding exclusion from this school. However, the underlying problem was that his adoptive parents had never been able to bond with him, their emotional neglect incongruent with their practical care and his ability to self-regulate limited by his window of tolerance remaining narrow.

Each sibling will have their own unique ability to evaluate and tolerate the potential stress of any situation. The Window of Tolerance diagram can be used to help children explore their own capacity in a non-judgemental way. This can also be used in psycho-education when needed to evaluate physical and emotional growth, learning, curiosity, innovation, and possible misdiagnosis of ADD or ADHD when the lack of trauma-informed wondering resulted in medication. Intolerable distress, trauma, or toxic results in one of two possible strategies: (i) hypo/shutting down or (ii) hyper/frantic responses sometimes swinging between the two, mimicking the diagnostic criteria for ADD or ADHD, depression, or mania, and what follows later in adulthood—a diagnosis of bipolar or borderline or unstable personality disorder. Instead of wondering what is wrong with someone with these 'symptoms,' trauma-informed wondering is needed to find out what must have happened to this person to make these coping strategies necessary (Figure 13.1).

Siegal (1999) first described the two lines of the Window of Tolerance as being together when a baby is born, and each child's experiences widening, or not, of their unique window. More recent research on the baby's developing brain in utero suggests these lines begin to widen as the baby's brain develops during the last trimester, as long as the mum is not experiencing trauma during these last months of her pregnancy. A safe nurturing relationship with empathic attunement and mentalisation consistently meets the developing child's emotional and physical needs, to manage waiting, increasingly difficult developmental challenges, and the many stressful, daily experiences from baby to adulthood. Curiosity is encouraged, developed, and applied (Figures 13.2 and 13.3).

Emotional states at first externally regulated are then increasingly internally regulated. The adult uses purposeful, developmentally appropriate empathic attunement and developmentally appropriate empathic mis-attunement/dysregulation to safely encourage the baby/child/teenager's awareness of their own and their joint

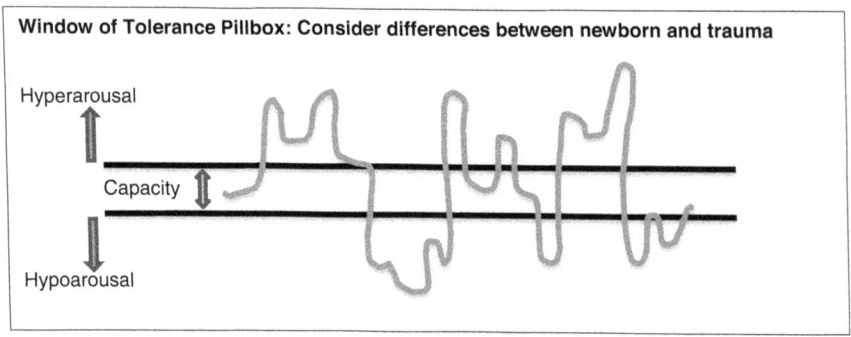

Figure 13.1 Window of Tolerance Pillbox.

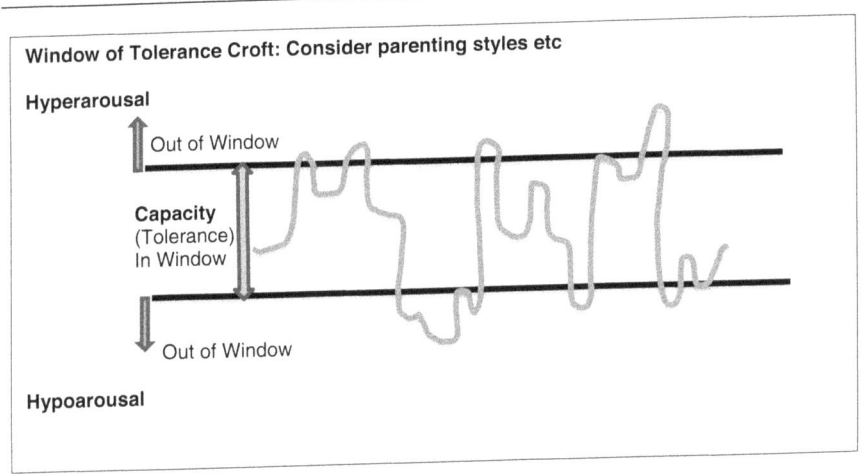

Figure 13.2 Window of Tolerance Croft.

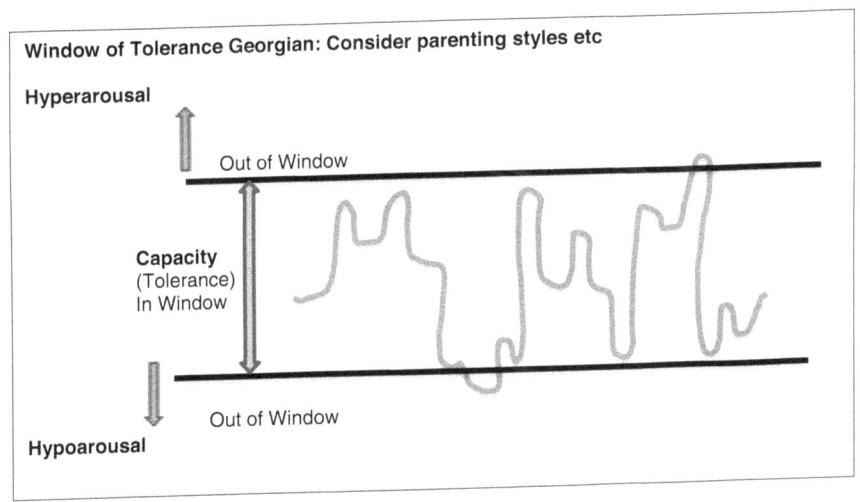

Figure 13.3 Window of Tolerance Georgian.

arousal. This can be done, for example, by playing games such as round about the garden to catch a teddy bear, statues, hide and seek, and snap, adapting these games and others as the child grows up. By stopping any game while still in their widening window, it enables learning through mirroring what enough feels like, when to stop, and how to re-regulate. With changes in breathing, the safe adult demonstrates and waits until there is re-regulation before continuing or playing again. The balance between mis-attunement and loving re-attunement also enables learning that the behaviour which caused the mis-attunement is the problem, and that the loving re-attunement shows that the child is not the problem but is still loved and lovable.

It would be very likely that any child in the care system will not have routinely experienced these crucial positive, window-widening interactions, and will therefore still require any adult, parent, teacher, or carer to externally manage their arousal and participation in any interviews, in interactions, especially in contact, where help will be needed by both parent and child to manage their individual non- or miss-attuned arousal.

Some Examples of Misattunement (Not Getting It Right)

The mum who plays peek-a-boo with the baby who at first boo gurgles immediately, on second boo a millisecond gap then gurgles, on 3rd boo has a quiet response with eyes fixed on mother, then on 4th boo cries. At this point, the mother is cross with the child for spoiling the game and leaves her crying.

The dad who throws his toddler in the air and catches him: first time the child laughs with delight, second time a quieter laugh, third time no laugh, fourth time cries and is sharply put down on his feet. The child reaches for dad's hand which is pulled away, is told off for being no fun, and dad walks away.

Both games are important when played with empathic attunement. This helps to widen the window, and also to know when to stop to prevent exiting the window.

Another example from 'Super Nanny' saying to sit the child on the naughty step for the same number of minutes as the child's age, with no differentiation for the 'crime' committed, and when the child is on the step, to walk away. How can the parent then judge when the child is still in their window and can still tolerate the level of stress caused by abandonment and thus enable the child to learn from the re-attunement that it is the behaviour that was not acceptable, but the child is still loved? If the level of distress takes the child out of their window, the child will then find a coping strategy to manage their own distress, to be naughtier, to draw on the wall, pick the wallpaper, begin to hum, sing, or rock to self-soothe. What is learned, when something happens out of the window, is to take care of yourself with your own invented coping strategy, sowing seeds and growing feelings of being unlovable and low self-esteem. How different the stretch and widening of the window when purposeful, developmentally appropriate mis-attunement and re-attunement are managed correctly.

One of the important ways of noticing when someone is moving from feeling stressed but still able to participate in an interview to experiencing the interview as traumatic and therefore intolerable is to pick up on early clues. These may not only appear in the tone or texture of the content, but more often in body movements, oftentimes micro-movements. Many siblings being interviewed will have experienced significant harm, often under threats that forced or maintained their secrecy. Keeping such secrets often results in learning to conceal any outward signs of physical pain, distress, or discomfort. As a result, obvious clues are rare, but when they do appear, they are often quickly retracted or denied out of fear of consequences. Micro-movements, therefore, are more likely indicators. Children who live with the impact of trauma develop coping strategies with the intention to ensure no one suspects their inner distress. It is less risky to appear calm, controlled, or unreadable than to endure further distress if the secret is exposed. For this reason, regulating arousal during interviews or interventions must involve confident but gentle empathic attunement, quietly noticing micro-movements, wondering about their meaning at any given moment, whilst resisting any urge to interpret them. This careful approach reduces the risk of triggering past terror, denial, or retraction.

There is a need to think very carefully about the impact that the words used will have on arousal. How often when telling a child about involvement in an assessment does the adult say, 'Hello, I am (name), my job is to talk to children.' An important difference is to say, 'Hello, I am (name), my job is to listen to children.' Sounds better? Maybe not? Why not? It is so important to observe and empathically attune to any impact the words are having. For one child being told someone will finally listen will be amazing and engaging; for another, terrifying that threats, containing that seed of truth to ensure silence, might be actioned if listening or talking is expected or required.

Active listening and careful observation are of increases or decreases in the child's arousal is needed. The interviewer is responsible for externally regulating this arousal. Careful monitoring will ensure that a small increase or decrease in arousal could enhance participation, but too much of either could stop empathic participation in both children and adults. Experiencing empathic disruption can result in the child or adult ending the interview, either by physically leaving by walking out, or psychologically by dissociating. For example:

The young person who shouted at his social worker, saying she was 'just fucking nosy' before he stomped out of the room,was then blamed for being uncooperative. He was not. The problem was the interviewer, who was anxious, in a hurry, and wanted to save his placement with his brother. This young person's behaviour had put his placement at risk. He had made violent comments to his male foster carer and then pushed him from behind while they were walking down the stairs.

The girl who was being asked for her wishes and feelings about having contact with her siblings, who sat twiddling with her hair and yawning. The interviewer, also trying to suppress a yawn and wondering how long it was since they both had eaten, offered to go to McDonalds. She failed to recognise that their right-brain to right-brain empathic attunement was causing infectious dissociation, psychological escape, and not the need for food.

In both interviews, there was significant empathic disruption, caused by the adults not ensuring both child and adult remained in their 'window of tolerance', activating out of the window responses.

Case example of siblings experiencing the same form of harm, the differences in their coping behaviours and the completely different impact of removal from home:

Susie aged 14 disclosed that her father was paying too much attention to her younger sister, Clare aged 12. She was worried that he might start sexually assaulting her just as he did when she was 12. She was praised many times by the professionals she met for speaking up and protecting her sister. Both sisters were removed from home and placed in foster care together. Both parents were charged with sexual offences against the younger sister. Susie made no disclosure in her ABE interview and refused to have a medical examination. Clare settled very quickly into her foster home, sleeping and eating well and enjoying her new school. Susie started self-harming which escalated alarmingly, putting her life at risk. The team around her responded to this with increasing panic and fear of doing the wrong thing, in case she died. This resulted in a significant reduction in their empathy, which prevented their curiosity to understand her behaviour and reduced their ability to intervene.

External advice was sought, and several hypotheses were raised about Susie's behaviour: her initial concern for her sister, her refusal to undergo a medical examination, her silence about her own experiences during the interview, and her reaction to removal from home. These hypotheses suggested extreme levels of distress, separation terror, and loss, indicating a trauma response to the intervention itself. Susie was interviewed in a gentle, empathic way, with the interviewer ensuring both she and Susie stayed in their WoT. Through this process, Susie was able to express that her relationship with her father was the most important one in her life. She had noticed him paying more attention to her sister and could not risk losing him. In her mind, raising the alarm would result in her sister's removal to safety, while maintaining nothing had happened to her and refusing the medical examination would mean she could return home and have her father to herself. Every time someone praised her for protecting her sister, she was consumed with self-hatred. She knew her true motivation was not to protect but to remove her sister, and this inner conflict drove her to self-harm. The complexities and paradoxes in the sisters' relationship with each other and their parents were now evident. A thorough assessment of this and the benefits and drawbacks of them continuing to live together resulted in Susie moving to a different foster home. With the support of individual and sibling therapy, the sisters were eventually able to shift from a complex, competitive, dysfunctional relationship to one that remained challenging but no longer undermined their relationship with each other or the stability of their placements.

Further Case Examples

The father of Andy aged nine made an application to the court to have contact with Andy and his twin baby siblings. Andy's father was serving a five-year prison sentence for violent offences within the home. The siblings were in foster care. Before making a decision, the judge required information about Andy's wishes and feelings about having contact with his father. The court-appointed assessor asked

Andy a question. 'What do you feel about seeing your dad?' Andy's immediate memory was Dad's violence towards his mother. Andy's somatic (body) response, triggered by this memory, makes his toes twitch (flight response), his fingers clench (fight response), and his tummy turn over (feed response or gut reaction). He puts one hand on his stomach; he states he has butterflies in his tummy. This reaction was caused by the release of chemicals to produce the energy needed for fight and flight.

Andy learned that when in danger he must not allow himself to make any noticeable movement, and if he must move, to only do so in a manner that will not bring unwanted attention. He was being interviewed, so could not escape. His level of anxiety continued to rise. He needed to take control of those feelings and prevent the interviewer from asking him any more questions. This triggered more memories of other times when he experienced this combination of bodily and emotional feelings increasing his distress. His response was to smile at the interviewer.

Why the smile? This is an attachment-seeking behaviour. One that he used when his father would ask him questions about his school day or what he and his mother had been doing. Just as he did when with his father, he hoped to evoke kindness and approval from the assessor and not more harm from more questions or consequences from his answers. With his smile came the words, 'I don't mind.' Again, as happened with his father, to say 'no' or not co-operate would be too scary; to say 'yes,' and co-operate also too scary, hence the disarming smile and the words, 'I don't mind.'

Andy was asked the question 'What do you feel about seeing your dad?' This, like other questions his dad used to ask him, does not have a simple 'yes' or 'no' answer. He knew from past experience every answer would have consequences, most likely negative consequences, for him and his mother. Just as he did in answer to his dad's interrogations, he answers questions with, 'I don't know,' 'I don't mind,' or 'I don't care.' It was not safe then and it is still not safe for him now to wonder about his own needs and feelings. In effect what he is saying is, 'What I am doing is not knowing,' 'What I am doing is not minding,' 'What I am doing is not caring,' because to know, mind, or care was and still is too painful and risky.

When Andy lived with his dad, he learned to know what answer Dad wanted to any question was more likely to ensure his safety and survival. Smiling at his dad would often lessen his dad's anger. Andy knew that his dad wanted him to behave as if he loved his dad. Andy's behavioural script or conditioned response when feeling frightened is to smile and meet the needs of the person making him feel frightened.

The assessor noticed the smile and assumed this was because he was pleased to be asked about seeing his dad. This confirmed their training, experience and belief that it is right and good for children to have contact. The assessor missed Andy's somatic (body's) indicators of his distress and terror, at the thought of just giving an opinion about seeing his dad. They did not understand the meaning of his, 'I don't know' response and she formed the wrong conclusion. This terror provoked by thinking about, or actually seeing dad, now needs further coping strategies resulting in further behavioural difficulties for Andy (Perry 1995).

For example: With a tone of interest and inviting his curiosity, the assessor asks, 'Andy do you know what happened when I asked you that question? Your toes moved and the muscles in your face twitched. I wonder what made that happen?' Andy then puts his hand over his tummy. With empathy and close observation of these movements and his slight nod of recognition, say to him, 'your hand moved to your tummy. I wonder if your tummy flipped at the same time? Hmm, I wonder if my question made you feel a bit worried because that can happen when someone is worried?' Attunement to his emotional and somatic responses is important, making sure the questions do not make him more anxious and create further dysregulation. Without this, his verbal answers would not be a true representation of his feelings or, therefore, his wishes.

Evoking his curiosity (an indicator of core self) enabled him to wonder about seeing his dad and the impact this had on him. He was then able to be curious and remember wanting to run away, his toes fidgeting and his tummy flipping when his dad got angry with him, and this happening when his foster mum told the interviewer about the visit. He agreed with the interviewer's wondering out loud whether or not his toes were telling him he did not want to answer questions about seeing his dad and just wanted to run out of the room. An amazed look passed between Andy and his toes, and the interviewer's face as he nodded his agreement that that was what had happened.

In the second interview, the interviewer noted Andy wore his wellingtons. He explained, 'They (his toes) are not talking today.' The interviewer wondered with them (his toes) what had made them come to that conclusion. Andy replied, 'It's not safe to talk.' His toes were then complimented on their being able to think ahead to wear their wellingtons to keep Andy safe. The tone used was validating and curious rather than negative, shaming, or dismissive of his way of protecting himself and managing his feelings. Comment was again made on how clever his toes were when they knew he should run to be safe, followed by wondering if this happened at any other time. He was then able to talk about several incidents when his toes had done this and how they tried to keep him and his mother safe. He was left feeling proud that his toes knew then, and now, that it was still not safe to see his dad even when his brain thought he ought to.

With the focus on the importance of contact, similar care must also be taken when a child asks to see a parent. While it is vitally important to work out whether or not the request is in the child's best interests, it is also important to assess whether or not a child is actually asking for contact and perhaps even more importantly what, if anything, is behind the child making that request now.

Clare, aged seven, was living at home whilst the subject of an interim care order. Her mother and two little sisters lived with her. Her father was serving three life sentences for violent offences within the family and in the community. Clare bounced into her therapy, saying with her tone and the tense state of her body (fight) that she had a question. The therapist responded with, 'Wow that must be a very important question.' Clare frowned, tightened her lips and said, 'I told my social worker I want to see my dad' (fight). Her therapist smiled and lowered their tone to bring Clare into her window of tolerance. Just before Clare could respond, the therapist asked her where that question about seeing her dad came from. Clare explained she had been having lots of nightmares in the last week about her dad escaping from prison and coming back to her home, getting in through a window and hurting her mummy, herself and her sisters again. She wanted to visit the prison to make sure he couldn't get out. When asked if she would want to visit her dad, she paled (flops), moved her head slowly from side to side whilst looking at the door to the room with eyes wide and rapid breathing (flight). She then looked terrified that something or someone was coming through the door of the therapy room (freeze).

When asked what frightened her, she asked, 'Daddy can get out?' The therapist quietly acknowledges her fear and, with a determined but calm tone, tells Clare they will talk to her social worker about visiting the prison to make sure her dad couldn't get out, but also to be clear that she didn't want to see him. Clare visibly relaxed and added that she has been getting up at night to check her mother had locked the doors and windows because sometimes her mum forgets to do this as she falls asleep after she has had a drink and taken her pills. By doing this, Clare took care of her mother and sisters by keeping them safe. This is too much responsibility for a child, which explains her bossy and challenging behaviours at home and falling asleep in school. The therapist repeated everyone will make sure her dad cannot escape and that this is a job for adults. Clare visibly relaxed (back in her window) and joined in a game.

Later the therapist telephoned the social worker, who immediately said that mother had phoned to pass on Clare's stated wish to see her father. As a result, the social worker had arranged a social visit to the prison for her. This visit was to be in a room used for such visits because it looked like an ordinary room and therefore wouldn't frighten children. The therapist explained that Clare's reason for wanting to see her dad was to check he couldn't escape. The social worker accepted she made an assumption that Clare's statement that she wanted to see her father was a straightforward request. This was the only way Clare knew how she could find out whether or not the prison was secure. A prison visit would have terrified this child. A subsequent home visit to assure her there was no escape would allow her not only to feel calmer but also to feel less responsible for the protection of her mother and siblings.

Chapter 14

Entwined and Unravelled
The Dynamics of Sibling Conversations

Communicating with siblings is not the same as communicating with individual children. If an individual child's communication is already skewed by their life experiences and therefore has impacted on their internal beliefs e.g. 'I'm a burden,' 'My sister is the favourite child,' 'It's my job to look after my brother,' 'I've got to keep us safe,' or 'I'm the broken one,' then these beliefs will be intensified when with their sibling, thinking about or being reminded of their sibling. Being asked about siblings may intensify these beliefs, causing a conflicted stress response. In the case of, 'My sister is the favourite child,' when together the siblings may become hyper-aroused, aggressive, jealous, or taunting, or they internalise, withdraw, give up by becoming hypo-aroused, or become competitive or a mixture of a range of conflicting behaviours compounding their held belief and confusing observers about how each child is feeling about the other. This intensity of emotion is not only discombobulating for the child but can be disorientating and dysregulating for the adult, bringing up the practitioner's own feelings of overwhelm or their own limiting belief, 'I am not good enough,' tapping into their own experiences, heightening the risk of projection or unhelpful counter transference.

Communicating with siblings is not simply a matter of talking. It is made up of many factors.

The reason for undertaking an intervention needs to be considered. The type of intervention and the context of the siblings' situation and the adult's role will all impact on the planned intervention. Whilst interventions may have similar issues, such as how to create safety, how to communicate will be influenced by age, developmental level, gender, disability, ability, resilience, and other individual factors which are not likely to provoke the same response in each sibling. Different interventions requiring different ways of communicating include the provision of therapy, the assessment of ascertaining a child's wishes and feelings in relation to contact, care proceedings, siblings' living arrangements, local authority care plans, achieving best evidence (ABE) interviews, reviews for looked after children, any manner of educational roles, therapeutic reviews, child in need meetings, MAPPA preparation and therapeutic life story work. The overarching and paradoxically underpinning factor for communications in all of these settings is safety.

Safety is key. Without it, trust cannot develop, and without trust, there can be no safety. In some situations, it will already be known that the children were not safe, but in others, it will not be known whether, or how safe or unsafe each child was. Even the belief that each child is now safe does not then automatically equate to each child feeling safe. Often, interventions heighten that feeling of a lack of safety, especially when one or more of the siblings has been threatened that something bad may happen if they talk to each other, other people, or if they talk at all, they are being disloyal. Being present with a professional or the experience of being heard may also have a profound and confounding impact.

Case Example: Larissa and Lila

Twins Larissa and Lila were the youngest of five children. Their mother had complex mental health issues including high anxiety, OCD, autism, and psychosis that led to her being sectioned under the Mental Health Act on a number of occasions. Their father also had mental health issues including schizophrenia and bipolar disorder. The parents' care of their children was impacted by inconsistency, unpredictability, a lack of attunement, an inability to model or ensure emotional regulation of either themselves or their children, the presence of frightening and bizarre behaviour, and an inability to recognise or meet their children's needs.

Larissa and Lila were seven years younger than their three older brothers, who appeared to have been cared for by a number of different but protective relatives and sometimes their parents during their most mentally and emotionally stable periods. Larissa and Lila were born prematurely with a low birth weight. As a result, they spent time separated in the Special Care Baby Unit (SCBU). Larissa was born first, was both bigger and stronger than her sister, who was born moments later. This was also the birth of Larissa's rite, as the older sibling, to be the caregiver. When they returned home to the care of their parents, the twin siblings experienced neglect, with poor household conditions and routines negatively impacting their attachments, attendance at nursery, medical appointments, and treatment. Larissa showed demonstrable developmental delay.

The parental relationship also included domestic violence, perpetrated and experienced by both parents, during periods of adverse mental health. In addition to their prescribed medication, the parents also self-medicated with alcohol, increasing their volatility and unpredictability, compromising even further their struggle with maintaining any sense of attunement or synchrony with their children.

The maternal grandmother was a significant protective resource. This aided the siblings to develop some resilience. This support ended with her death when Larissa and Lila were still young. Both children suffered in their parents' care, but there was a difference between the children: Larissa was the favoured child. This resilience factor for Larissa impacted on her relationship with her sister and indeed posed a psychological dilemma for both siblings: 'How can I be assured of my parents' love for me if their love for my sibling is not equal? If I accept the situation, then I am agreeing with my parents that my sibling is less worthy, or I am more lovable. If this is love, then love is conditional, inequitable or deserved. If I love my sister, how can I accept being loved more by my parents and yet maintain a relationship with my sister?'

Following the parental separation, the twin siblings lived with their mother. They were on the Child Protection Plan under the category of risk of emotional neglect and subsequently placed into their father's care. The two eldest siblings were living independently, while the next continued to live with extended family members. Larissa and Lila were finally removed from their father's care following a number of incidents where they were found in public places whilst their father was asleep as a result of alcohol consumption. The siblings were placed in foster care. By the time they were referred for therapy, aged fourteen, they were in their third placement. The first placement was short-term, the second ended when the female foster carer's mental health deteriorated, and the siblings moved into their third placement. The placement appeared to be relatively positive, but the foster carers' adult son became seriously ill, requiring a long period of treatment. The female foster carer supported him through this time. The care of the siblings fell on the male foster carer, a reserved man who found it hard to connect on an emotional level.

The messages the siblings received from these three placements reinforced their Internal Working Model that caregiving relationships were unreliable and further fuelled their belief that because no adult could commit to them, they had to rely on themselves (self-reliance), an indicator of their lack of trust, not only in caregiving/receiving relationships but in all relationships. Their older brothers, unusually for this type of parenting history, were all graduates who were successful in their chosen careers. Larissa and Lila had developed into self-reliant individuals who, despite early developmental delay, were successful in school and came across as mature, eloquent young people who appeared to know their own minds and needs.

The siblings appeared to know their minds and could articulate well. When asked for their opinion about school, they could give it; when asked their opinion about placements, they gave it; when asked their opinion about contact and a myriad of other issues, they could give it. Because the Children Act 1989 said it necessary to ascertain children's wishes and feelings and listen to children, the girls' responses were responded to. The legislation had been misunderstood, in that listening to children equated to enabling those wishes to be realised, regardless of whether this was in their best interests or not. For example, because the majority of children will say they want to live with their parents, despite the parents being the source of the abuse or harm, it becomes incoherent to agree to these wishes. There is often a colossal distance between what a child wishes for and what exactly should happen next. These girls' apparent maturity belied their actual needs.

Larissa had a resilience in that she could regulate and express herself through her artistic and creative bent. She had a sense of future. She had dreams of being a designer and yet her painfully low self-esteem affected how she thought, related to other people or acted. Her need to fit in was seen in her interest in mainstream fashion. Her friendships revolved around popularity. These friendships were transient and not maintained, never getting too close to people. She had dreams that she expressed but internally could not believe she would achieve them. She had an External Locus of Control believing that events that tripped her up were outside of her sphere of influence to change. Her self-efficacy: her ability to believe in her capacity to succeed is paradoxical and complex to describe. She appeared confident. As a result, the professionals around her took this as being confident and yet, self-efficacy is a mirror of self-belief and for Larissa this presentation was a hollow structure built to keep people from truly seeing her vulnerability and therefore kept at a distance. She believed that she would fail at everything she did, and because she was so negative about herself she was equally negative about those around her or came into contact with. She was highly anxious, lived in a state of high arousal and became preoccupied with illness, somatising her distress which sent her into acute sadness bordering on depression intensified by frequent nightmares.

Lila experienced the same familial environment as her twin sister Larissa. She presented as immaculate, with perfect self-care, and was always well prepared when she arrived at school. The school described her as someone who preferred her own company, spending time studying and reading books. She was perceived as mature and intelligent, with a passion for the arts. She was diligent, motivated, and had high aspirations. It was noted that occasionally she would be seen with her sister, ostensibly suggesting that this was an irregular occurrence. Unlike her sister, she was quieter and introverted; she was drawn to the 'alternative counterculture' in friendships and style. Larissa 'fit in,' whereas Lila's 'fit-out' resulted in her developing deeper relationships that endured, which paradoxically countered how she was seen by the school.

In her placements, she was described as quiet and calm in nature, with a fitness regime and had always participated in extra-curricular activities to the point that her carers felt she placed unprecedented pressure on herself to be active and achieve. This suggested she had a burdened-enduring character strategy. She fluctuated between rejecting or feeling rejected, implying inner conflict and ambivalence. She hid the anxiety that presented as hypochondria. She was seen to have significant trust issues in many professional, caregiving, and social relationships. Records included that, like her sister, purportedly as a result of her believed maturity, she had been involved in many potentially life-changing decisions from a young age.

Larissa was both the favoured child and the pseudo-parentified child, setting up a complex psychological dichotomy, in addition to all the other adversities they faced. A favoured child on the continuum with the scapegoated effects both children. A scapegoated child does not mean there has to be a favoured child and vice versa; the two challenges can exist independently. The favoured child may experience a level of relief in having some respite in complex and challenging environments, but this is not without implications. The favoured child needs to square being loved by someone who cannot treat the children equally. This creates implicit trust issues. To prevent one sibling resenting the other sibling's higher ranked position in the family and their relationship becoming stressed with resentment from one, and/or shame or entitlement from the other, both children need to make a psychological adaptation to square holding their relationship together. This means they develop an incongruent, paradoxical relationship; in other words, present differently to how they feel about each other. This functional strategy in a dysfunctional situation becomes a dysfunctional strategy if they are moved into a functional situation, such as foster care, where hopefully they will be treated equally. Another paradox is that in being treated equally, the favoured child may then feel a deep loss at the downgrading of status, and the scapegoated child may struggle with the upgrading of status. It forces both to see their parents in an alternate light, confirming their parents could not give unconditional love equally, further compromising the sibling relationship.

Larissa and Lila had a dislike of being homogenised, referred to as 'the twins' or 'the girls' (and how many times did those phrases have to be edited out of this case study?) and treated almost as if they were the same entity. This may have been annoying anyway as it depreciates the young people's individuality at a time (adolescence) when identity formation, growing autonomy and connectedness are key developmental features. The term 'twins' does not just negate individuality. It implicitly suggests sameness (even though only a small number of twins are 'identical,' which they were). The problem for Larissa and Lila was that they were not treated the same by their parents but were by everyone else. At high school, ironically, they found a mutual voice, and both vocalised their same desire to be seen and to be treated differently, at times rejecting each other in researching obscure and rare situations that could disprove, not just their identical twin status, but being twins at all. Yet they pendulumed from being fiercely protective of each other to being rejecting. They needed to be together, were inseparable, and created a safe world together. This safe world was unsafe. They were not kept safe by being together and their relationship became a distraction from everything around them.

Friends and carers alike noticed they would feel on the outside, the periphery, as though onlookers to the siblings' relationship. The siblings would be drawn equally to conflict as they would be to proximity with a giddiness that suggested hyper-arousal. Their relationship was experienced as exclusive and separatist as they became unaware of others around them. They worked hard to separate in their interests but emotionally they developed a co-dependency with a lack of clarity about where each sibling started or ended, entwined like a bramble around a rose bush, painful to join and painful to separate. Lila became subservient to her sister but used emotional extortion to try and get her needs met. Their relationship was blighted by occasional outbursts of violence and aggression towards each other. At other times they could present as regressed and immature, but these presentations were seldom witnessed by others outside of their placement. Even though Lila was the least favoured, she would be the first to come to the aid of her sister in any dispute and continued to support her even if Larissa was dismissive of her.

Their relationship with their 'high achieving' three brothers was equally paradoxical. Contact was seen as positive, partly as a result of their success and social standing, but messages received were to be more understanding towards their parents. It seemed the three older children had escaped the worst of the parents' decline into critical mental health issues or, having moved on, had redefined their experiences to maintain a relationship with their family. Regardless of the reason, the impact on Larissa and Lila was significant. They experienced their parents in one way and were being told by their siblings to see them in another, reinforcing the psychological split and denying their actual experience.

Contact

During school holidays (approx. every six weeks) the siblings had supervised contact with their mother, a woman who maintained her inability to connect with her children. This continually reinforced the message that it is fine to be emotionally disconnected and implicitly conveyed that this is the basis of human relationships and is therefore correct. This experience, or its confusing nature, was never processed with the siblings. Their separate contact with their father was a little more positive. He worked hard at trying to reciprocate. The parental contact, including overnight stays despite the unhelpful messages they received, was left to the siblings to negotiate, putting responsibility onto their shoulders.

Communicating with Larissa and Lila, Indeed All Sibling Pairs or Groups

To communicate with either of the siblings, those around them needed to know not just what was done to them but what those experiences did to them. Because they learned not to trust their primary caregivers to keep them safe, they subconsciously translated this into all caregivers are untrustworthy and then, all relationships are untrustworthy. Untrustworthy because they were not safe and therefore felt unsafe. This lack of safety provoked anxiety and anxiety led to complex behaviours. To feel safe, they needed to be in control of everything, but children cannot control their lives. As a result, they became self-sufficient in an insufficient way, pseudo-parentified or pseudo-mature. In addition, siblings who have to control everything cannot then have a successful or healthy relationship because they both need to maintain control, which leads to a battle of wills seen in many different ways.

This is crucial information. Regardless of role, trust is going to take time and without trust it is not possible to trust that what is heard is necessarily what is wanted, needed or even in the child's best interests. The children were seen to be unsafe, removed, and placed into a place of safety. Whilst they were safe, they felt unsafe. Their feeling of this lack of safety had not been processed because this was missed by those around them. It was almost as though the thinking was a new family equated to a job done. This was intensified over the following two moves. They had to develop their defences further to psychologically survive. Trust can only come about when feeling safe internally and then in the presence of another. How many agencies can admit to having the luxury of time to invest in building a relationship with not just one child, sibling group or all children to enable them to feel safe enough to lower their defences? When not feeling safe for long enough, ways of controlling emotions and environment are needed. Control prevents trust. Vulnerability follows when not being in control. To trust and let go is unsafe.

Lila had an external Locus of control which led to feelings of being out of control and believed there was nothing she could do to prevent life events impacting on her or to change her situation. This fatalistic belief compromised her ability to consider how life could be different. To alleviate this sense of hopelessness and helplessness, she turned to self-harm, giving her the impression of control.

A professional attempting to ascertain her wishes and feelings about the future may be faced with equally overwhelming feelings of hopelessness and helplessness in the transference and misread this as disinterest, depression or avoidance. What was required here was an acknowledgement that it can be hard to believe that life could be different, followed by presence and acceptance of those feelings.

One of her fears was that her personal information would be shared and, of course, sometimes it is an inevitable truth. It is easy to discount the impact of the need to know and downplay other professionals' need to know. The reality is that often it is necessary to share the very information the person does not want to be shared, which leads to other paradoxical interventions. Rather than avoid these complex situations, it is better to face them head on with empathic congruence and sensitivity. An expression of congruence might be, 'It must be hard to feel that personal information is not your own to control when everyone deserves privacy,' followed by, 'But to help you in the best way I can, I may sometimes need others to help me help you.' These reflections accept the person's experience and feelings, which are the tenets of being witnessed, heard and seen. They acknowledge that at times help, support or aid is needed. This also normalises and demonstrates reaching out to others and that it is not always necessary to be self-reliant; it is natural and healthy to rely on the availability of others. This feeds back into and provides the possibility of challenging Lila's self-reliant character strategy and also her belief that others cannot be available because her birth parents were not.

Lila's overwhelming anxiety was so profound she was unable to regulate through functional methods of arousal reduction, resorting to dual dysfunctional methods. One method was self-harm to bring respite to and alleviate her distress. This anxiety, if connected with, could also discombobulate the adults around her. The second method was overachieving to avoid feeling, and if professionals did not connect with this, they misread her behaviour as ambitiousness and a drive to be the best version of herself. Because Lila had an external Locus of control, she internalised her experiences, leading to low affect, hypo-arousal, withdrawal, somatic complaints, depression, anxiety, and paranoia. These levels of stress impacted on her decision-making, compounded her self-doubt, and further obstructed clear and cogent thinking. This negative impact induced shame, which, coupled with her self-critical stance, led to her covering up her shame by appearing confident. At school, she overcompensated by becoming a high achiever. Maths doesn't demand or elicit an emotional response, unlike families.

Larissa was equally self-reliant and took the responsibility away from the professionals trying to ascertain her wishes and feelings. She needed to hear, 'I hear what you are saying, but I need to spend time with you to ensure you are aware of the implications of your choices,' a time-consuming task. She would come across as dismissive and worked constantly to keep people at bay. Fundamentally, her experience was that adults could not help her, so why should she want to trust anyone now? Her need to develop a sense of safety and trust was the same as her sister's, not with her sister but in tandem. Providers are often asked to reduce financial quotes by requesting work with siblings on the basis they could be 'batched' together. Each review on each sibling needs to be undertaken separately with dedicated time to discuss the sibling relationships, not the siblings. Larissa, like every child, is unique and thus needed to be treated as such. She required consistency throughout her services, a TAC that gave the same messages, adapted to each service, that provided scripts to challenge her limiting beliefs and provide certainty in her daily life.

Larissa and Lila's relationship was paradoxical and complex. Typically, relationships between siblings who have had similar experiences can be multifarious and challenging. Their relationship on the surface looked solid, mature and supportive and yet was full of contradictions and inconsistency. The siblings could not live with each other, constantly triggering each other when they reminded each other of past emotional disruption, fear, and trauma. Equally, they could not manage separation, seeking each other out and at times appearing to have such an intense connection no one else could penetrate. The complexity stemmed from both their early shared trauma and the sense of worthlessness it created in each of them. What is more obvious than a mirror or reminder of your experiences than your twin sister? What feelings might then arise when you look at your own image reflected back at you in someone else? Anger, pain, fear, shame?

The difficulty of building relationships with two siblings simultaneously without provoking the stress response which increases their self-reliance is clear. The question most commonly asked is, should it be the same or a separate practitioner, in whatever role, involved to support the siblings. The pros and cons require weighing up. To have the same practitioner could create the danger of grouping and missing individual need or failing to see the nuances of the relationship. It could be that more is invested in one than the other or that they find it hard to have an open mind about what needs to be seen. The children may hold fantasies about what the practitioner shares and whether the practitioner can maintain confidentiality. To have separate practitioners may increase individual response to each young person or may create polarisation or an inequitable service based on the practitioner's ability, match, caseload resilience or availability, perhaps feeding into pre-experiences of scapegoating. To have clarity where there are two practitioners often needs a third person, not the clinical supervisor, to ensure there is an overview to prevent polarisation, blame or other transference issues. The positives come from good clinical supervision to ensure there is clear oversight of both young people's needs, maintaining continuity and consistency of service.

Larissa and Lila's relationship was clearly skewed, but neither they nor their support network could see or accept this despite clear indicators in their presenting behaviours. When Larissa stated that she wished to move away from her sister, not the placement, this was heard and acted upon. The placement was not the problem; the relationship was. Larissa had grown weary of her eternal conflict with and simultaneously draw to her sister and withdrew—but emotionally withdrawing didn't help and so subsequently saw the answer in moving placement. Lila's response was to threaten self-harm (emotional manipulation) if Larissa didn't agree to stay.

Practitioners struggled throughout their time with the siblings because, as research shows, the future outcomes for children are better when siblings are placed together and that the quality of sibling relationships is a predictor of positive mental health in later life, citing lower levels of depression and loneliness, higher self-esteem and life satisfaction, and that it can even compensate for low parental or peer support (Milvsky 2005). Yet, as Circirelli (1995) notes the sibling relationship is 'ascribed, rather than an earned' suggesting that this bond is not chosen and thus can be argued that it can hold together not just as a result of positive agency but negative too, as seen in a trauma bond. Larissa leaving the placement (her now fourth) had a significant impact on Larissa. She had to acknowledge that her relationship with her sister was keeping her tethered to the pain of her past, a choice that should not have been hers to make, because it fed constantly into self-reliance, that only she could ensure her needs were met and adults could neither be trusted nor relied upon. It also fed into her sense of responsibility and pseudo-parentification of her minutes-later younger sister.

The impact on Lila of this significant rejection was overwhelming. In order to hold the psychological impact of her sister leaving a secure placement, she needed to 'make-believe' it was the placement, rather than her sister, and requested a move. As a result, Lila was placed in an alternative foster placement, which again led to a similar sense of reinforcement of her character strategy.

Larissa struggled the most with the separation, an eventuality not anticipated. Whilst both siblings shared their experiences of therapy, Lila was able to share with her therapist that this was not a place that she wanted to bring the subject of her sister because this was the only place where she truly felt separate. Lila found space for herself in therapy, but the changes of placement made no discernible positive difference for either young person. She spiralled into a wretched place of despair believing that she was unworthy of empathy, kindness, sympathy, or love. The concern about the placement moves grew because the more placement moves a child has, the more placement moves a child will have. The past being a significant predictor of the future.

The siblings needed to hear the implications of their wishes and that it was unfair for them to make the decisions about their future because they had not been equipped to do so. They needed the TAC to take responsibility even if it meant that decisions were made that were not in line with their wishes.

Two months later, Larissa requested to be moved into a residential unit. The TAC, now therapeutically supported, were ready to decline the request (because not agreeing to a child's request can feel counter-intuitive, even though it may be basic good parenting). The TAC set a limit, knowing her outcomes of being in corporate care were not conducive to her best outcomes (this is not to say there is not a need for residential services—there absolutely is—just not for Larissa). This placed Larissa in a crisis as, for the first time in her life, she was experiencing being emotionally held by the team because it was undermining her predominant character strategy. Her work in therapy began to shift. She was forced to see her previous foster carers as good. They were leaving the placement open for either or both of the siblings in case their circumstances changed. This positive view of the foster carers meant she was in danger of seeing her parents' behaviour as negative and seeing her own parents negatively, which was overwhelming. A point she was, for the first time, in a position of having to contemplate.

Larissa was desperate. Lila jumped to her aid, berating professionals for not listening to her sister. Lila was not just jumping to her sister's aid, but to her own because it also impacted on Lila's worldview; something had changed. Her sister was not being listened to; she was, but the response was different. She therefore had to stand up for her sister (role reversal) and had to experience being emotionally held by proxy of her sister being emotionally held. Lila jumping to Alysia's aid was also problematic because it meant that Larissa was being pushed into the role of the protected rather than the protector, and both began to unravel. Lila asserted her sister knew her own mind, but what was unknown was how much of this was Lila's view and how much was her sister telling her to say these things could not be discounted because both were invested in maintaining the status quo.

Communication Issues between Practitioners

When communicating with children and young people, being clear about the context of one's role is important to ensure that the communication is coherent with that role. For example, it would be the social worker's role to ascertain the wishes and feelings of the child, but the therapist might explore the underlying drive and the foster carers may put in boundaries and limits in relation to the developmental and chronological level of the child. These three connected people must share their rationale, or conflicting messages may be given. If anyone oversteps their role, this impacts on both their role and everyone else.

A Venn diagram can be helpful to see the individual needs of the siblings and where these cross over. The cross-over component is not necessarily where their needs are the same but can be where their needs are enmeshed, complicated, the same or require separation or clarity.

Each professional is only in control of what that individual says. Even when pitch perfect, there is a difference between the outcomes from a statement, reflection, direction, sharing, or question because each elicits a different response. The volume, pitch, prosody, accent, tone, and lilt of the voice will have a bearing, as will the location, whether home, office, therapy space, bedroom, restaurant, or other geographical location. There is likely to be a difference between a police officer and a teacher, or a social worker and a doctor, or a therapist and a parent, or between a parent and a foster carer or adoptive parent. Gender, race, ability, or perhaps faith may also influence outcomes.

Being in control of what is said does not necessarily equate to how it is received by the recipient. How one recipient hears or receives information is not necessarily the same as another, especially in two or more siblings. How each individual then later processes the information may also change the message originally heard; a third meaning or understanding can be formed which can also vary markedly from the original meaning.

The moment something has been verbalised, the verbaliser has lost control. If a child is dissociative, it can be lost completely or have it stored somewhere that is hard to access or can recall when in a state of calm or dysregulation or in whose company or on their own. If further along the continuum of dissociation, one part may retrieve the information and another part may not, or even two parts understand the information received differently.

The need to ascertain how the individual child has heard the information is key, and as such repetition is important, but so too is linking it up with the child's other core organisers, such as their bodily or physical reaction, emotion, sense perception, thoughts, or memories. The ability to link core organisers suggests an ability to be present and to process and analyse information across the whole experience. A flow chart may help both child(ren) and any adult to see their similar and differing responses to the information or questions.

When needing to ask a question of siblings together, check out what they both heard to see if it matches up with each of their core organisers and then feedback what you heard both of them say. They then need time to process that information and their different perceptions. Then see the children apart and ask them both individually what they heard and then feedback what you heard them say. Then give them time to process what they heard. Then meet them again together and enable them to repeat what they had heard and respond and feedback any differing views of what had been said. Then end or repeat.

The sensorimotor psychotherapy mantra of 'titrate' is a luxury that no busy social worker, teacher or even therapist often has, and yet time is exactly what is needed. Slow down to go fast. If key services cannot provide this, it is not the service that is broken but society, and it is in society where change is needed. Harm is complex in growing children's experience; rectifying that harm is more so.

Chapter 15

Hold the Adult, Help the Child
Conversations with Parents and Carers

When adults become parents, the character of their care giving derives from their own experiences of care received as a child (Ainsworth et al. 1978, Grossman 1995, Howe et al. 1999). It is therefore necessary and responsible to consider the parents'/carers' experiences to cross-reference the children's presentation with their parents. It is therefore a requirement not only to look at the children's experience of harm and trauma but also their parents' experiences (Itzin 2000). Sroufe et al. (2005) build on this viewpoint, 'The assessment of the parents' own developmental histories… have notable predictive power… the stresses and other surrounding circumstances (e.g. violent neighbourhoods, substandard house and frequent moves) that impact on parenting also directly impact on the child.' This is seen when an anxious parent is triggered, so too can the child become anxious and vice versa. This becomes more complicated when children are living in an alternative-to-home placement such as foster care or adoption where another set of caregivers, or sets with multiple transitions are experienced.

Brazilian-born Marcia and her English husband Alistair brought their youngest son, ten-year-old Matheus, for therapy following his experience of sexual assault by a family friend's older son. Both parents brought their son to his sessions and did so without fail. Dad was on the somewhat reserved side and mum on the edge of worry. This led to frequent bouts of high externalised emotion that Matheus found occasionally intrusive. The initial information gathering established that one of Matheus' older brothers suffered from depression, causing Marcia further distress. It seemed both parents had been raised with all the supports and love that children require to develop a secure attachment, but mum's anxiety intimated this may not have been so certain.

After a relatively short intervention, Matheus, his parents, the therapist and school noted significant improvements in his overall well-being and outlook, which led to the agreed closure of the intervention. Some three years later, Marcia contacted the therapeutic service, sick with worry that during the COVID-19 crisis her son, now 13, had emotionally 'nose-dived' into a depression. The impact of this crisis on all children and their families was taken into consideration, as was his age and development. He had reached puberty and in many ways was responding the way many other young adolescents presented.

DOI: 10.4324/9781003724797-20

Further time with the parents enabled Marcia to share how she had always had the gift and curse of being a bright and driven young person. She left her family home at a relatively early age of fifteen to start university, much younger than her peers, in a major city that required her to be self-sufficient in many different ways. Following graduation and meeting Alistair, she moved to the UK where she was further separated from her close-knit family. Reaching middle age, she yearned to protect and keep her children around her, to fill the gap from her own geographically severed family. This led to fears of losing her own children in the way her parents had lost her. Her becoming overly concerned about their well-being had the adverse effect of pushing them away.

Matheus had certainly suffered a significant trauma, but it was not the memories of this that kept the trauma alive. It was two-fold: the level of his mother's concerns for his continuing well-being and the onset of puberty. Matheus could well have returned to therapy regardless of his mother's anxiety and/or the COVID-19 crisis because it is not unusual for adolescent boys sexually harmed in latency to need to do this. Adolescents question their identity, role, image, gender, sexuality, and a raft of other issues. Like many young males who have been sexually harmed by a male, particularly where they found it hard to see the power imbalance (Woodhouse 2019), additional complexity arises when questioning or exploring sexuality. Another developmental purpose of adolescence is to fragment, to cast aside parts of the self you were raised to be and then to reintegrate and become the person you desire to be.

Matheus had achieved integration in his first four years of life as a result of the positive (more than 'good-enough') parenting he received. Therefore, when he was sexually harmed, despite there being a delay of some months in his disclosing this to his parents and him being fragmented by this trauma, he knew what it was like to be integrated. He could therefore find his way back to this integrated state. The difficulty now was that he was close to the developmental task of adolescent fragmentation, creating further confusion. In addition, his mother's concerns and distress led him to struggle to manage his own feelings of culpability for the sexual assault because he was now questioning his sexuality and his feelings of guilt that he was causing his mother's distress.

By not regulating and stabilising parents, they will constantly be a potential threat to the progress of the child's therapy. Marcia and Alistair presented as loving parents on the continuum of secure attachment. However, Marcia's unresolved previously unexplored feelings of loss were leading her to become unintentionally enmeshed with her son's feelings and transferring her own concerns onto him. Alistair openly admitted to feeling overwhelmed and not knowing what to do for the best. He found himself either not doing anything or going along with Marcia's demands to keep checking on their son even though it felt wrong to him.

Adults are not always aware of their own actions or reactions. This is why all coherent therapeutic courses require their students to have a robust experience of their own therapeutic process. The mantra or aphorism, 'Don't do to others, that which you have not experienced yourself,' is also why all therapists are required to undertake, and practitioners should be provided with, their own supervision, clinical supervision, and further personal therapy when needed, to ensure their well-being and their ability to see any of their influences or issues in the work being undertaken. Through training and supervision, learning how to develop the capacity to engage caregivers enables them to share their experiences, to tap into the adult they are now with all the defences being used to avoid looking at painful areas. To also tap into their child parts who hold their doubts and vulnerabilities, hurts and pains, as well as their capacity to be playful, brave, and bold.

Marcia and Alistair were secure enough to be able to explore these aspects of their experiences. This is less easy to do when there have been deficits, harm, transition or abuse experienced in childhood. Marcia was struggling to come to terms with the source of her anxiety. Anxiety ultimately is about not feeling safe, often reflecting in a lack of trust, fear of not being in control or of being out of control. Trust is born out of safety, and questions must be asked about the validity of a secure relationship with primary caregivers where trust is absent. It was during this second bout of Matheus' therapy that Marcia disclosed her own experience of childhood sexual abuse, ironically by the son of a friend of the family. There was no irony. Marcia felt she needed to make contact with her older sister to tell her what had happened to Matheus and herself. The explanation of distance causing their fractured family needed to be revisited when her sister also disclosed sexual abuse by the same family friend's son. Their immediate reaction was anger, then hurt that they had not told each other and not protected each other or perhaps their younger sister. It is not uncommon that keeping secrets inhibits developing perception of, rather than an increased awareness of, or even at worst, generational vulnerability. This shift and raised awareness allowed the family to support Matheus' experience to be shared with his older brother and sister.

Parents/carers present themselves in a number of different ways depending on a range of factors, including how and why their child was referred to therapy and by whom their child was referred.

Karen was a prime example of a parent who, on discovering her child had been sexually abused by her husband, the child's father, dealt with the situation almost perfectly. Yet she was unaware of how her own experiences were unknowingly already impacting her daughter and had been even before her daughter had been sexually abused.

To help her daughter overcome her experiences, Karen needed support to overcome the defences she used, and still used, to keep her own experiences hidden. Vulnerability to Karen was abhorrent. She subconsciously kept herself guarded, building a framework of self-reliance and control in her work environment belying her inner experience. This strategy was functional in the dysfunctional situation in which she was raised but had become dysfunctional in her current functional situation. She loved and cared for her daughter. She was passionate about her job. Cutting off emotionally enabled her to become efficient in both her caregiving and employment. However, this also meant she did not fully connect on an emotional level with her daughter, leaving and keeping her and her clients slightly at a distance at best. Having established the harm Karen experienced, it was essential therefore that she was supported to stabilise before any reparative work was undertaken with her daughter.

There is no rule that states whether the adult needs to have started or completed a therapeutic process before the child does, or the child starts first, or they start in unison, but the decision does need to be considered carefully in each case.

In Karen's situation, she needed to come face to face, recognise and deal with her blunted emotional availability. This impacted on her right brain to right brain attunement with her daughter. If not, this lack would likely impact on her daughter, especially when her daughter started therapy and/or the process of criminal proceedings, when it would be likely her daughter would regress. Her need for increased emotional availability and empathic attunement would be so far out of Karen's reach that her daughter would be further disadvantaged. An intervention was therefore offered to Karen first. Therapeutic parenting support was not enough. She required a therapeutic service that both stabilised her, increased her awareness of her present moment experiences, raised her awareness of her limiting beliefs and rectified the harm she experienced whilst simultaneously enabling her to leave the therapy room regulated, able to meet her own needs and those of her daughter. When she completed her own therapy, Karen was able to have a conversation with her sister about their father's behaviour, the differences and similarities in their choice of partners, their career paths, her sister's alcohol misuse and their chronic avoidance of closeness within relationships. This prompted her sister to engage in her own therapy.

The foster carers of Becky and Tom were clearly presented as resistant. Becky and Tom had a trauma bond with their parents and each other. This is probably one of the most toxic combinations. The children's relationship with each other could not be addressed until the children's individual needs had been met. Despite years of offered training, Emmett continued to avoid, and Cicely remained ambivalent. Despite regular supervision from their supporting social worker, there was no change in their parenting or communication presentation. The foster carers were offered therapeutic foster care support. Another service Emmett evaded, and Cicely used to remain in her stuck cycle of negativity. This couple were stuck in an abusive or controlling relationship, one in which they felt 'comfortable.' Do not mistake comfort as OK. Comfort can be found in the known and familiar, even in abusive situations. The unknown, especially when this is safe, or safer, can be scarier. Being 'comfortable' must not translate as being in any way healthy, functional, or growth-inducing but instead be seen from the perspective of a child who has already experienced adverse control from their own parents or caregivers.

For professionals, carers, parents, indeed everyone, the known habitual behaviour experienced in childhood does not necessarily frighten anymore. It may even unconsciously or consciously feel like it fits or is fine because it is familiar. Trouble is likely to follow if the quality, the attributes or consequences of that familiarity need to be questioned. Trouble follows when having to consider seeing any caregiver in a negative light. Something that will be potentially psychologically unravelling. What better avoidance than to end up in a relationship that mirrors and confirms the, 'This is normal,' therefore, 'I am normal,' therefore, 'This is ok,' when the rest of the world is screaming, 'No it's not!'

This was the strategic block that kept Emmett away from services. If he had engaged and had been able to see himself as controlling, he would then have to look and reflect on his own care-receiving experience. Cicely was inconsistent. She would come to therapeutic foster care support and scroll through her presentations of irritation, ingratiation, sorrow, dismissiveness and withdrawal or fail to attend with avoidant rationale, followed quickly by debilitating guilt.

In order to see themselves as ok the foster carers had to come up with strategies to make sense of the children's behaviour that did not upset their own internal working model and view of the world. This is not uncommon. What is frequently seen is a demand from parents and carers for a diagnosis that alleviates the responsibility for looking inwards, i.e. the child's behaviour is not the carers' or the child's fault, and by placing the reasons behind the child's behaviours onto a psychopathological condition such as ASD, ODD, ADD, or ADHD, etc., it avoids blame or painful shame and allows the child and carers to be held as 'good.' This is then somewhat further endorsed if the child is subsequently diagnosed and medicated.

As stated at the beginning of this chapter, when adults become parents, the character of their care giving derives from their own experiences of attachment as a child (Ainsworth et al. 1978, Grossman 1995, Howe et al. 1999). If parents are not regulated and stabilised, they will be a potential threat to progress in the child's therapy. This statement is accepted by many fostering and adoption agencies who support those parents. The difficulties parents face can have been pre-existing or could have developed as a result of the demands of caring for a very distressed child or resulted from other catastrophic life events or a combination of events. Support provided is frequently practical even when the source is evidently emotional or psychological. This presents a dilemma for both those agencies who selected and recruited those adults and for the agencies overseeing funding. When a foster or adoptive parent has been recruited, a robust psychological profile is rarely part of that process. Interviewees already complain that the current accepted adoption and fostering process is already overly invasive. Agencies fear that further extending the rigour of that process will deter even more potential carers or parents from coming forward. Without this, it is not unusual to meet parents, foster carers, and adopters who bring siblings to therapy to present with their own debilitating depression or anxiety, or as highly dissociative, occasionally with symptoms as severe as Dissociative Identity Disorder, personality disorders, and clear indicators of developmental trauma. Putting aside overt reasons for fostering or adopting, it is known that hurt people, survivors, and thrivers have a comparatively high representation across the fields of social care.

The process of communicating with adults, as every adult-trained therapist or social worker will tell you, is well known. Add to this the dynamic taking place between the caregiver and their experiences and the siblings and their experiences. Regardless of the robustness of the assessments, there are still going to be times when there is no awareness of later triggered experiences.

Amy made contact with a therapeutic service to refer her two nieces for therapy following their mother's murder by their father, his arrest and the children's placement in her family. Amy presented as emotionally flat and with a burdened enduring character strategy. The development of safety is always the first task, but safety is born out of trust which is based on the individuals' primary relationships. As with children, meeting the adult client on their own territory prior to therapy is often the best option. Familiar surroundings are therefore the most likely to enhance feelings of safety. There is a colossal difference between being safe and feeling safe, with the former being measurable and the latter almost impossible to measure due to the multifarious ways this can be negatively influenced.

The work with Amy's nieces could not proceed until the source of her own flat affect and character strategy was fully understood and the implications this may have on her ability to support her nieces through a therapeutic process. Her presentation in sessions was consistent and unsurprising given she and her two sibling nieces were grieving the loss of the sister-in-law, mother and father they had, and the sister-in-law, mother and father they did not have.

Amy's nieces disclosed sexual abuse by their father. Amy spiralled further as she attempted to manage her family's competing needs: her nieces to be heard and her own children to be kept safe from the toxicity her nieces' disclosures brought into the house. Amy sat in therapy unable to speak. The therapist gave space (listening to the power of the silence and all that it says) before reflecting, 'This is so hard, it's as though it's almost impossible to share what is going on inside.' Moments of pure connection are a gift, a delight in many respects, but filled with pure pain that at the same time needs to be held. She stated, 'You know, don't you?' The sensorimotor psychotherapy magical stranger is a beautiful refrain in times like this, 'I wasn't there when you were growing up, but I do know this, I know that your nieces' father was your brother.' She sobbed in silence a while before sharing that she had no memory of her own experiences until her nieces disclosed, but had been flooded with memories since. She blamed herself for her nieces' experiences, stating 'I should have known.' 'I did not protect them.' This situation had put strain on her relationship with her husband, who told her he did not recognise the woman he had married and felt she had hidden this information from him.

People who have not processed their ACEs can sometimes require years of their own personal therapy. One of the major distributors of government funding to adoption services in the United Kingdom states that they will not fund support packages beyond, 'therapeutic parenting support.' They disallow direct therapy with parents, even when not doing so will impact on their parenting of an adoptive child in their care or where the parental need was so clearly missed in the recruitment of that individual and where not doing so may compromise the integrity, sustainability or viability of that placement. The information required from adults to adopt, foster, be connected carers or work in children's homes is notoriously hard to gather. Tanya, an adopter, retorted, 'Come on, when you want to adopt you are only going to show your shiny side,' demonstrating people choose not to share. Amy could not share because she could not recall, and others could not share because it had been so insufferably painful. Whether or not there is an underlying trauma, the impact of caring for a highly traumatised young person is exacerbated further where there are siblings. This can create vicarious traumatisation. If there is an underlying traumatic experience, this will be compounded. While this was being written, the therapist in a therapeutic review, following an assessment, watched as the social worker told the parents, 'We are not going to endorse the recommendations for your child's therapy because we are concerned about your marital relationship. We do not want to waste money on your child's therapy if you then split up.' The adopters accepted that their relationship was under significant strain but stated, 'But how do you know, when we don't, that our relationship has buckled with the additional tension of trying to cope with both brothers, our sons' very significant traumas?'

The aim of communicating with adults is not so different from communicating with children except that the adult has had many more years protecting themselves from acknowledging the impact of their formative experiences and adapting their worldview to accommodate those experiences. This must be softened to recognise the hurt child in the adults, and their siblings, to create better outcomes for children. Communication will then be more effective with the adults responsible for their care. There will always be a tension but to only see one child or only see one adult is, again, akin to one hand clapping.

Chapter 16

Between the Ship and the Anchor
The Pull of Sibling Ties

Sibling relationships are important. 'Maintaining links between siblings and acknowledging that, ' the relationship of siblings is likely to be the longest-lasting relationship of all family ties, likely to span nearly the entire lifetime of a sibling' (Smallbone 2014, p. 190). The Children Act 1989 has enshrined the view that siblings should be placed together, 'So long as reasonably practical and consistent with their welfare.' These two elements have almost inadvertently become the mantra that siblings must be placed together. Sibling relationships are important, not because of a rose-tinted view, but because positive, healthy sibling relationships equal security, identity, history, support, connection, understanding, unconditional love, tolerance, and a building block for other relationships.

Numerous factors influence children's ability to express their perspectives on their sibling experiences. Children do not just talk about being together or being separated through verbal communication. Their complex, paradoxical and pain-filled relationships can mean that what they do say is not always what they feel or what is in their short- or long-term best interest, nor does where they live automatically result in a positive relationship.

Additionally, various elements may impede the capacity of practitioners to hear, understand, and assess the significance of what children say in the decision-making processes.

Child Factors

History of protective influences or ACEs,
Ability to share rather than compete for affection,
Chronological versus developmental age,
Genetic factors creating or enabled ability or reinforce disability,
Acquired factors creating or enabled ability or reinforce disability,
Belief systems developed as a result of gender-assigned status,
Birth order of siblings,
Scapegoated or favoured or antagonist or agitator,
Sibling status: full sibling, half, foster, adopted, or other,
Intellectual acumen,

Sporting prowess,
Artistic bent,
Emotional intelligence or unknown or challenged skill sets,
Differences in ethnicity, cultural, or religious heritage from parents or change of parents and their beliefs,
Not just what was done or what it did, but what was missing and the impact of all three on global development,
Behavioural coping strategies and any medical or psychiatric diagnosis made because these strategies mimicked diagnostic criteria.

Adult Factors

History of protective influences of ACEs,
Adults' own sibling experiences and associated belief systems,
Adults' role with the child and/or their siblings,
Actual or percieved knowledge about the impact of developmental trauma,
Available support networks to test out and challenge beliefs: clinical supervision,
Case/management supervision, peer support, and consulation,
Knowledge, skills, and ability to hear and see what the child is expressing both verbally and non-verbally and its coherence in a range of settings,
Open questioning style without only listening for information to confirm preconceptions.

Lacey Aged Four and Eleanor Aged Two

'In the assessment of the parents' own developmental histories there are notable predictive powers and the stresses and other surrounding circumstances (e.g. violent neighbourhoods, substandard house, and frequent moves) that impact on parenting also directly impact on the child' (Itzin 2000, Richardson et al. 2002, Sroufe et al. 2005).

The children's 26-year-old mother, Judy, experienced parental alcohol misuse, father-to-mother domestic violence including witnessing parental rape, her mother tied up and beaten. She experienced profound neglect that led to alienation and isolation, developmental delay including delayed speech, and was witnessed negotiating busy roads unsupervised to attend primary school. The maternal grandmother admitted favouring her son, saying she found her daughter to be cold and distant. As a result, Judy developed anger-regulation issues, eating disorders, and was removed into care. Her brother disappeared from home in mid-adolescence and was never seen or heard from again.

A year after the birth of her second child, Judy was sectioned under the Mental Health Act following a 'nervous breakdown.' Research into depression indicates that women are particularly susceptible to depression as a consequence of the stresses of parenting and childhood abuse (Bifulco et al. 1998). Like her mother, Judy took prescribed medications. When these did not bring relief, she self-medicated using alcohol and illegal substances, and when these did not help, she self-harmed. Dereboy's study demonstrated that childhood traumatic events not only have effects on emotional regulation and the development of a sense of identity but are also associated with self-harming behaviours in later life (Dereboys et al. 2018). She was overwhelmed most of the time. She needed support and so left her children in the care of their violent and alcoholic father for respite. She had a history of being drawn to dangerous relationships that were violent or controlling. This included the children's father and explained her often intense compelling feeling, but never actioned, search for her brother. Like children who have been repeatedly traumatised, she had not developed much sense of self in relation to others. That is, she had not learned to be in tune with and trust her own mind's and body's responses to people or situations. Instead, she split off or dissociated aspects of herself. This once adaptive response to danger became destructive to further growth and development, resulting in more of her functioning being shut off and unavailable. Moreover, a 'small stressor' on this already traumatised child had a bigger, disproportionate impact on her brain and body because the impact of repeated traumas is cumulative (Siegel 1999).

It is evident that Judy experienced many ACEs. This trauma history, parental experience, and later corporate care led to a fragile dual insecure attachment style, having both ambivalence and avoidance in her strategy, which led to disorganisation. She used an external locus of control, believing she had no ability to prevent the adversities she was dealt, and so blamed herself and internalised the impact of her experiences to manage the psychic pain she endured. She was diagnosed with depression and bipolar disorder. She presented as emotionally flat, avoidant, and dissociative or disinterested, defensive, argumentative, and surly. 'Dyads with a depressed parent reveal significant effects on the emotional development of the child' (Siegel 1999). Ross also notes the frequency with which victims of multiple childhood traumas are given multiple diagnoses including or resulting in Unstable or Borderline Personality Disorder. Thankfully, it is now being recognised that a more appropriate diagnosis of Complex Post-Traumatic Stress Disorder is more accurate. This can lead to less blaming or shaming of behaviours that often accompany the BPD/UPD diagnosis and instead explore with more curiosity, 'What has happened to you?' rather than, 'What's wrong with you?' It can be seen that the children's mother bore the brunt of her own and her siblings' parenting experiences. This had not been rectified before becoming a parent, resulting in her repeating her own experiences with her own children.

The need for attachment-seeking behaviours increases where danger is prolonged and severe. Bonding to an in-group increases while distancing and 'dumping' on an out-group increases, even when that in-group itself involves abuse, neglect, and/or other forms of injury (Bloom 1997). This elevated attachment behaviour in dangerous, hostile environments is known as 'trauma-bonding.' Untrustworthy and destructive relationships are believed to be 'normal.' Trauma bonding results in separation or the threat of separation being so exquisitely painful it has to be avoided. The whole family group clings together in an effort to survive.

Judy was unable to provide consistency, structure, warmth, nurture, routine, or love. She did not know how to communicate, play with, supervise, or respond to her children. They experienced profound neglect and were reported to have bitten their mother. Bruises and bite marks were found on their bodies. The girls were failed in the same way their mother had been failed. Despite the fact that the children fought, bit, and kicked each other, services were adamant that the siblings should, if removed, remain together. The elder sibling took on the parenting role of her sister by giving her most of her food, but it was the younger sibling who dominated her sister and bit the most.

All the professionals agreed that the children should be placed together in foster care and Judy's siblings should be contacted and assessed as connected carers despite her disclosures about what had been done to them all. The children could not verbalise a view. It was believed the children's behaviours would improve in placement.

A parent's history significantly influences their children's behaviour. Neglect can turn siblings into rivals for resources or paradoxically force them to depend on each other to meet their needs. Van Der Kolk (2014) found that,

> Erratic caregiving produced kids who were chronically physiologically aroused. The children of unpredictable parents often clamoured for attention and became intensely frustrated in the face of small challenges. Their persistent arousal made them chronically anxious and constantly looking for reassurance which got in the way of playing and exploration.

Inconsistency is traumatic for the developing brain. Children have to develop strategies for managing the level of arousal caused by the unpredictable, the not known, the lack of security.

'Children of depressed mothers do not expect support, do not anticipate relief from distress and do not know how to regulate their feelings' (Howe 2005). In a similar way, 'Because they don't expect their ruptures to be repaired, they don't turn to others. Because they have not been taught to focus on solving problems step by step, they cannot imagine solutions' (Gerhardt 2004).

High rates of disorganised attachment have consistently been found in young children living in chronically and severely depressed households (Teti et al. 1995; van Ijzendoorn et al. 1999). The outcome for many children in this situation is role reversal. By becoming pseudo-parentified, they take on the care of the mother/father or sibling to avoid feeling nothing can be done to increase their sense of security. Archer and Gordon (2006) note, 'Parentified children (pseudo-adult), frequently need to be encouraged to relinquish their "adult" personae and be given permission to be children.'

Also useful to note, 'A child's troubled behaviour is so often a barometer for the parents' emotional states, parental stress, parental unprocessed trauma and loss and the emotional atmosphere in the home' (Sunderland 2017).

A sense of shared history is an important place to start or not. A shared history enables an anchor to fix who someone is or does not want to be. It creates a foundation upon which the roots of a family tree or a seedling can develop and grow. So many metaphors come to mind when thinking about how helpful a shared sense of history can be.

The Birth Family Context

Hannah and David's children remained supportive and interested in each other. They knew each other's likes and dislikes, wanted to share their successes, celebrated birthdays and other events but did not need to canvass each other's views on their personal decision-making. They were always there for each other when in need. Alison and Mark's children as adults had no contact and only spent time together at occasional family events, only able to share their history and not their current lives. Carla and Marcus' children shared family interests and often chose to attend events together but their contact with each other outside of the family events was sporadic. The largely unspoken knowledge that they are secure in their relationships enables children to get on with their lives. The difference between secure relationships and avoidant relationships is seen in their words and behaviours when they are comfortable on reunification or not.

The Fostering Context

Tom and Becky experienced protracted abuse and neglect. This was their history. Knowing this gives a backdrop to their relationship, a helpful sense of the children's now and potential relationships with each other. Their abuse led to a number of intrinsic beliefs which in turn led to strategies that enabled them to survive together in a dangerous situation. To survive in the role of a protective sibling, that sibling has to dissociate their fear and develop a sense of ability that is greater than their reality. By doing this, they create the belief that protecting oneself to survive in the situation makes it possible to 'protect' a sibling.

Larissa and Lila

Larissa and Lila had organised themselves into two young people who could present themselves with extraordinary maturity, intellectual capacity, and apparent self-reliance. They managed, or at least appeared to manage, because they held themselves with an uncanny aptitude that looked like resilience. Because they were articulate, they were able to express a view, and right from the start, their views were (rightly) sought and (unfortunately) acted upon. The children were seen as a combo, equal, and the same. It was easy to miss the complexity of their relationship. Their differences, communicated in so many ways, were manifold.

Hearing What Is Seen and What Is Heard

Listening to, ascertaining, and clarifying children's views about living together or not are the most complex, paradoxical tasks to undertake. A common thread for all children is the need to build a trusting relationship with a sense of both actual and perceived safety. Where the children's behaviour suggests that this sense of safety continues to be absent, through internalised or externalised markers of distress, it must be borne in mind that internalised markers can be devilishly difficult to discern. The factors may include contact, supervised or otherwise, the safety of the placement (short-term versus long-term versus permanent), the capacity and safety of the carers or caring environment, the number of carers, for example in a children's home, the presence or absence of pets, experiences in school, and the presence or absence of being bullied or bullying behaviour. When these factors have been explored and excluded, then the sibling experience and relationship must be assessed and whether there is a threat of physical or sexual harm, emotional harm, for example, by carrying over scapegoating experience, emotional, psychological, or psychic risk resulting from a trauma bond or indeed a combination of these factors.

Lacey and Eleanor were too young to be able to articulate their relationship or to know what the future implications would be, had they been able to express their views. This was not just as a result of their chronological age but their developmental age resulting from the adversity they had faced. Lacey was pseudo-parentified. She survived because she was ambulatory when she was at home and therefore, in her mind, she was the only person who could keep Eleanor alive, and that became her raison d'etre. Eleanor knew no different and continued to depend on Lacey. When left alone, even for a moment, they became aggressive. Under supervision, Lacey met Eleanor's needs; Eleanor responded by demanding more to keep her away from the foster carers, and Lacey did what Eleanor demanded. In Eleanor's fight to keep Lacey away from the foster carer, she became so preoccupied with Lacey's potential threat to take the foster carers' love away from her that she could not relax and accept the love she was fighting for. The solution frequently offered was that the foster carers reduce Lacey's responsibilities and by doing so could redirect Eleanor. The unspoken professional avoidance of seeing or accepting the presence or influence, in this sibling relationship, of the toxic power dynamics, sets of belief systems, hard-wired expectations of each child, and their view of caregiving relationships maintained the drive to keep them together. This overoptimistic viewpoint avoided making the unpalatable, unpopular, and bold decision to separate the siblings.

What the foster carers experienced was a greater capacity for reciprocation on a one-to-one basis with Lacey than with Eleanor. When Lacey was alone with the foster carers she could relax; her perceived role was in remission for the time they were apart. She could not take care of a sibling who was not present and relaxed. In her relaxation, she was able to connect, give and receive love, communicate, and play. When Eleanor was on her own with the carers she remained angry, controlling, demanding, and could not relax. As Eleanor found no respite in being on her own with the carers, she could not play and was preoccupied with when Lacey would return.

It is of note that the foster carers were so overwhelmed with the responsibility of caring for these two siblings that they could not identify either of these alternate presentations until they were given the opportunity to witness it from an 'outside' perspective. Eventually, the right decision, the least-worst, was reached to separate the siblings. On paper, without exception, professionals believed that the stronger of the two was Eleanor and that she would fare better, and yet it was Eleanor who was fighting the most because she felt the least safe and could not accept the love that was being freely given.

Tom and Becky's relationship was no less complex. The foster carers' presentation kept the professionals distracted from the siblings. When the young people were spoken to, Tom presented as non-committal, avoidant, apathetic, with emotionless responses and flat affect. He would take the line of least resistance, comply to meet the minimum requirements that hid his 'go slow' passive defiance, which enabled him to be largely left alone to his own devices and became a survival strategy, if existing can be seen as survival. The problem for Tom was that his original template of caregiving relationships was skewed and unhealthy, and his current experience, of which he was avoidant, was doing nothing to challenge or change that system. Worse, he was witnessing his sister utilise the very template he experienced in her relationship with their foster carers, deepening his belief that people are inherently dangerous and driving his own quietly deepening self-reliance, diffidence, and social avoidance.

Becky came out bickering, fighting and in conflict. She became so used to the opposition and defiance as a strategy that when someone did try to meet her on her terms, she could not recognise it, utilise it or trust the experience to connect with it. Her anger was misinterpreted as her being her, as opposed to the only viable answer to the overwhelming internal feelings she harboured and could not express in any other way. Her anger triggered her female foster carer, and her female foster carer's disinterest, blame, passive presentation, but passive-aggressive responses triggered Becky. They were caught in a spiral of helplessness and hopelessness that only ever had one ending: disruption.

On the way to this inevitable outcome, support services were ploughed into the family. The sibling relationship was ignored, quickly gave up on trying to engage Emmett, and were overwhelmed by the female foster carer's desperation to be heard and accepted, simultaneously with her inability to make any changes in her relationship to Becky. She would rant about Becky's behaviour, cry in desperation, comment on Becky's hard life whilst maintaining she was undertaking or had tried every conceivable strategy offered to her, which frustrated professionals but passively pushed them away, making the children as vulnerable and isolated as she was making herself.

The assessment of siblings is a desperately difficult task made harder when the children's context is not taken into consideration. Had this been done, Becky and Tom would never have been placed together. It is also clear that they should never have been placed in this foster family with so many unresolved issues. Warring parents struggle to establish their children's views because they often fail to see their own personal demons, and this blurred view becomes the lens through which they see their child.

The Residential Context

Fourteen-year-old Christian had raped his four-year-old half-sister on multiple occasions and escaping a custodial sentence was placed in a specialist facility. His father, an angry, inconsistent, and controlling man, demonstrated his ongoing power base and presence over his son by attempting to control the team around his child: the residential staff, social worker, therapist, school, and others, clearly showing Christian that if he could control all these professionals, he could continue to exert his influence over his son.

To determine Christian's wishes and feelings, professionals' primary task was to promote a sense of safety for Christian. He was physically safe in care from the experiences that developed into his harmful sexual behaviours, safe from the potential of harming others, and safe from the potential of neighbourhood vigilantism, but enabling him to feel safe was harder to promote and establish. Christian had lost his family, his home, his neighbourhood, his friendship group, and his liberty. He had also moved into a very contained environment with a group of carers who presented consistency, firm but sensitive boundaries, routines, limits, and nurture, an anathema for those that would vilify rather than understand and change behaviours. All of these were alien for Christian and therefore unsafe. His felt sense of safety was also undermined by his father's ongoing attempts to control him either directly during contact or indirectly through his control of professionals. If professionals could not contain his father, then they could not protect Christian.

Christian's mother had been isolated, alienated and finally excluded from her son's care by the time he was six years old. As a child, Christian's mother had experienced neglect, abuse, and intrafamilial sexual abuse. Alienation from her birth family had left her prone to depression, agoraphobia and the eventual diagnosis of Borderline Personality Disorder. Christian grew up in the care of his father and stepmother with the instilled belief that his mother had tried to kill his father before abandoning Christian. In his first therapy session, he was able to share his position in his family in a non-verbal creative psychometric test in which his mother was notably absent. Observation of this fact led to Christian spitting out a tirade of expletives to describe his disgust of a person who had no right to be referred to as his mother. He later recalled that some of these terms were the 'caller identity' on his father's mobile when she rang.

It was a year before he started to feel safe in the unit or in therapy. It was no surprise that this coincided with the reduction of contact and the increased containment of his father's behaviour. The more his father pushed boundaries, the tighter the team responded in the management of any contact with the plan that for contact to be meaningful it needed to be reduced to the point where Christian was not anxious and his father was neither angry nor inconsistent. When these dovetailed, a healthier contact emerged. It was at this point his mother made contact. She feared her ex-partner, worried that Christian would reject her, but wanted to try to develop a relationship with her son despite his behaviours. She agreed to being interviewed and was encouraged to write an initial letter which needed to be free of shame, blame, overwhelming content, self-pity, justification, or manipulation.

The introduction of another relative in contact when the existing contact was already overwhelming was a risk that needed to be carefully managed. Eventually, his mother was able to draft a letter that managed the tightrope of expectations. It was shared with him in therapy. The letter impacted him with enormity. He recalled some of the happy events his mother remembered and was touched by the memories. He was left speechless at the information that she still had some of his belongings, toys, and memorabilia. Things his stepmother had previously asserted had been thrown away by his mother. He thought for a while before wondering, 'She kept my stuff' (he paused), 'Why would she keep my stuff? Perhaps she struggles to throw things away' (he paused) 'Or, maybe, maybe she expected to see me again' (he paused), 'But if that's true then what my dad said was a lie' (he paused, 'I don't know what to believe anymore').

The power of enabling children and young people to make sense of their world takes time. The only people who know the truth cannot often tell us what had happened. Not just because of lies, deceit, manipulation, or misdirection, although these all become part of the mix, but because they believe the new life reality they have created or built up to protect themselves from their own experiences. It took a further nine weeks before Christian was ready to respond to his mother because this further truth sent him into a crisis when his previously believed reality was challenged with humility, love, and concern.

Further information was needed about Christian's half-siblings. How did they fit into the enquiries being made? What support services did they require? How were they seen by their parents or their half-brother? What do they believe happened to their half-brother? Why did he do the things he did or what do they know of the things that he did? What do they believe will happen to him in the future? Will he return home? Is he safe? Has he been punished? These and so many other complex questions with paradoxical answers.

The timescale for this work is not consistent with court or planning timescales. This does not mean going for what is second best. It means questioning the validity of any findings made when a child is seen on a few occasions to determine their desires or needs. This is indeed an uncomfortable truth. Young folk are met, multiple times, with questions, psychometric tests, or a whole raft of creative interventions, all valid, but do these really ascertain truth? Safety can only come out of a relationship that is mirrored by the development of trust, and yet trust is primarily based on the experience of being able to trust primary caregivers. When trust is not present, there is anxiety. Anxiety compromises the ability to be in connection with the self and others and to relate to what is felt, thought, remembered, or believed, all observed in what is said, heard, and not said, resulting in outcomes being equally impaired.

Chapter 17

Echoes of Separation

Adults Reflect on Siblings Lost and Togetherness

Effective communication is complex. In articulating perspectives on sibling relationships, or their absence, it remains challenging to view such dynamics from perspectives other than our own. Sibling relationships may vary significantly from how siblings characterise or describe their personal experiences of the same relationship. Society continues to push Western family ideals which often amount to stereotypes, sentimentality, and rose-tinted glasses. It is important to acknowledge position within one's own family; the support, the bonds, the subtle cues, the mild jellyfish stings, the glint in the eye of pride or anger, and the presence/absence of one parent or a sibling at events will be different for each sibling. Sibling rivalry leaves its mark.

It is impossible to look at all adults to understand or conclude their drive to have children: whether it is an innate genetic drive, a faith-bound principle, societal pressureor normalisation of behaviour, endorsed by siblings, cousins, friends or work colleagues etc., a lifestyle choice, a consequence of love, a trophy, accident, pressure, force, a completion of a sense of family, belonging, financial incentive, responsibility or a desire to provide a loving home. The context of adults' own childhood experience and their drive to have children is an important starting point.

The Adoptive Context

In the context of adopters, frequently but by no means universally, is the desire for a child to be part of their family either due to childlessness, an inability to complete their hoped-for family due to relationship breakdown, illness, accident, age-related phenomena, a change in circumstances or a choice not to have a/or another birth child, not to undertake artificial insemination, surrogacy, wanting or needing to provide what all children ideally should have—a loving family home.

It is a serious omission that the United Kingdom does not hold statistics on the number of adoptions that fail, or what caused them to fail, but it is anecdotally believed to be about 3%.

DOI: 10.4324/9781003724797-22

Tanya, a white middle-class adoptive mother of three children, was facing difficulties. Tanya herself was the middle child of three siblings. Whilst she often referred to her own siblings, the essence of the siblings' relationships had never been clearly ascertained. Tanya was struggling with her care of the children, her relationship with her partner, her interactions with and the expectations of her parents, and being the middle sibling. During a therapeutic parenting session, whilst reflecting on her own unresolved childhood issues, she agreed with the therapist's remark that this appeared to be the first time she had spoken of these events. In exploring the possible reasons these issues had not come up in her adoption assessment, Tanya stated, 'But of course people only show their shiny side if they want to succeed.' This statement highlighted her lack of information about her own siblings, demonstrating something missing in the practitioners' skills, knowledge, and ability to assist anyone investing in the process of securing a child for adoption. It is essential to enable individuals to be open and honest about their lived experiences, even when aware that disclosure may impact their chances of success.

Not all people are able to invest and make the changes necessary.

Although Tanya was able to express that she had been dishonest by omission, she could not take the next step which would enable her to change. Her therapeutic parenting sessions were to help her with her three troubled adopted children. The oldest two should never have been placed together. They had a trauma bond. These two were competing for survival and their presence reminded each other that the danger they were removed from was still very much alive within them. Tanya and her partner were then asked to take the children's younger sibling. There was no pre-existing relationship with this sibling. The problem was the assumption that siblings placed together do better together. Two parents were already failing with two siblings. The addition of a third sibling meant that no single child could have 100% attention, even if it was even possible or healthy for that to occur. The couple were geographically isolated from their wider family networks. When they saw their families, their families were at a loss as to how to make sense of the children's behaviour and labelled them as mad or bad. The children's behaviour intensified with intra-sibling violence, parental-targeted violence, and violence targeting the house and its contents. The parents were exhausted and needed respite. Their respite involved one of them visiting friends overnight, leaving the other to manage all three children, which resulted in that parent being exhausted and unable to present limits, boundaries, or safety.

The children's behaviour did not change because they were trauma-bonded and required parents to be exacting in their care. The parents were unable to be open and honest about their routines. Whilst these were carefully prepared, considered and agreed upon with the therapeutic team, they either could not, or would not, share their inability to carry these out. The parenting became increasingly inconsistent, negative, scapegoating, desperate, blaming and sometimes shaming. They were unable to explore why parenting deviated, when they deviated, or kept from the therapeutic team an accurate picture of the fluctuating and escalating levels of violence in the household. Without the levels of honesty and openness required, the family spiralled to the point of disruption. The children could not invest in the parents because the parents could not invest in the children.

The parents did not have additional health problems Mariela had, but they faced frequent adverse stresses that further eroded their capacity to cope. The biggest single negative factor to moving on was parental impulsivity and their need to make life-changing decisions without the support of the TAC. This was a double-edged sword; the parents were already feeling as if they had no autonomy and resented sharing their decision-making with the professionals around them, so made decisions in isolation. These decisions were contrary to either the children's needs or their capacity to finance their decisions, leading to greater insecurity, further financial hardship, spiralling family relationships and home conditions. The lack of sharing, consistency and close working relationships ultimately led to negative outcomes for the family.

Mariela, a white, professional woman and mother of one who had not been successful in four previous applications to adopt later succeeded by agreeing to have a child with multiple health issues placed with her. When applying for a second child she was accepted immediately. When the second child, a four-year-old girl, displayed sexualised behaviour on arrival, Mariela sought Local Authority, police, and therapeutic support for her daughter. Recognising a lack of connection with her child and feeling affected by her daughter's presence prompted her to seek therapeutic support for the child. During the child's therapy, Mariela began to experience fragmentation. Her own previously unrecognised trauma history resurfaced. It is possible that the previous adoption agencies that rejected her applications had an intuitive sense of this but were unable to identify, quantify, or substantiate their concerns.

She could not previously disclose information she had no memory of. She simply had not recalled or retained the memory of her experiences of early childhood sexual and physical abuse. These experiences directly led to her unhelpful responses to her children, particularly her adopted daughter whose behaviour indicated, and was later confirmed by disclosures of, child sexual abuse. Mariela's curiosity was piqued. She began to question why she reacted so negatively to her daughters' calls of distress. It was this curiosity and innate knowing that her manner and responses were not helpful, healthy, or conducive to healthy mother/daughter relationships that held the key to later success.

Mariela did not want to behave negatively towards her daughter. Rather than be shamed by it or ashamed of it, she brought her responses to her therapy. She had no cognitive rationale, and her memories of the flashpoints did not help her understand or change her responses. However, she was able to take note of her body, the recoil, disgust, blame and other physiological responses that held the answers to her verbal responses to her daughter's behaviour. She knew that she did not want to be that intolerant person, knew that if this was to continue then her relationship with her daughter would deteriorate and that her daughter's chances of recovery would diminish. Mariela made many mistakes in her care of her daughter and even repeated the same mistakes, but in her own therapeutic journey she was willing to share these experiences, explore them and seek to understand them.

Despite being diagnosed with a life-limiting illness and grappling with painful memories of abuse involving her parents, she remained focused on recovery and being the best parent for her children, striving for lasting change. Mariela showed commitment, openness, curiosity, creativity, honesty, and playfulness whilst seeking clarity, developing self- and other-directed compassion. She fought shame and blame and looked for the common triggers between her daughter and herself to attempt to alleviate, minimise, or avoid them.

Although initially given an 18-month life expectancy, she lived for an additional four years. During this time, she cultivated a strong and healthier relationship with her daughter, leaving a legacy all her children could then continue to build upon despite the loss.

Mariela had not realised the impact of her own childhood experiences because she could not recall them. They were normal to her. She needed to keep a belief that her parents were good and alive within herself. She also struggled with knowing that her own siblings had been abused and yet could not talk to them about their experiences.

Children and their siblings receive messages from what is said and not said by their parents or caregivers. The care received directly influences their worldview, self-beliefs, interactions with the world, and relationships.

When what is said or not said is positive, generally positive, or negative but with positive influences that actively counteract the negative experience, or there is robust repair, the child is more likely, to a greater or lesser degree, to experience safety and develop trust in their caregivers. These repeated experiences also contribute to a secure attachment, an internal Locus of Control, an integrated sense of self, self-efficacy, self-worth, and character strategies that are all in balance.

When what is said or not said is negative or generally negative with few if any repairs, the child experiences negative emotions. When fearful of caregivers or caregivers' ability to protect and are still reliant on them for survival, then two things happen simultaneously: feeling unsafe and trust fails to develop. Skewed or unbalanced character strategies, an external locus of control, insecure or disorganised attachment patterns, and poor self-worth develop.

The more harm or negative experiences, the greater the chance their presentations will become 'hard-wired.' Lack of integration increases the likelihood that the adopted child will fragment. Teenage challenges are more manageable when individuals reach adolescence having integrated. The process of identity formation is to undo some of what was learned in early childhood, to become who the individual wishes to be, not who it was wished they would be. If integration has not been previously experienced 'undoing,' 'falling apart,' or 'fragmenting' does not come from an integrated foundation but an already fragmented one. Determining who to become in adulthood when lacking a sense of identity during childhood potentially leads to further fragmentation, creating adults who see the world in a skewed, potentially dangerous and often unhelpful manner. The more internalised and integrated equates to how they respond to the world and everyone in it. Experiencing less than optimum conditions too often disables adults seeking to become caregivers of vulnerable children or adults, to share with openness, transparency, or complete honesty. The stakes are obviously too high.

Alfredo, an adoptive parent, was not a wished-for child. He had two significantly older brothers. His mother craved a daughter, a need his twin sister assuaged, leaving Alfredo as an unwelcome addition. As an adult he felt on the periphery. As a twin he could see the affection and love his sister was afforded. He could however also see, despite their affable relationship, that his sister was unable to allow herself to see the inequality in their parents' care not just of him, but also his brothers. He valued being seen as the rock, a pragmatist, deeply loyal man holding his own complex family together. He worked hard with his wife to ensure the children's recovery from their traumas but what was overlooked was that, at the same time, he was waiting to be asked about how this assigned role was re-opening the emotional and psychological burdens from his own childhood. The longer he had to wait for the right time to process his own developmental wounds was leaving him increasingly prone to the vicissitudes of life and at greater risk of vicarious trauma.

Martha and Ed adopted three children. The children had a trauma bond. The placement was on the verge of breakdown because the middle child was disruptive, violent, oppositional, and defiant. The couple were loving, caring, hardworking and desperate not to lose their child(ren) or fail, or both. They responded well to interventions and bought into the psychoeducation, support, refocusing and understanding what their children, especially the middle child, were trying to communicate by their behaviour. They had to alter their view from the children needing to be fixed to one of acceptance, and for Martha to accept her own therapeutic support after she was able to acknowledge in discussions about the children that it was her own unprocessed, developmental experiences in being triggered that were resulting in her less-than-optimal responses to the children. Breakdown was avoided because they, parents and children, all felt therapeutically held and therefore safe enough to learn to trust.

Learning to trust someone who is challenging the way you parent is a leap of faith. Working with people who engage can bring about other concerns. This family demonstrated their need and ability to invest in the therapeutic programme and support on offer but were not compliant or conforming, two traits which may lead to dependency and not lead to change or growth. Importantly then, to be able to tell the difference between a healthy cooperative relationship between practitioner and parent/carer versus a developing dependency. One example was that Martha and Ed did not yield; they fought to maintain their status quo. They were emotional, fearful, angry, ashamed, and confused about both historical and current conflicting professional advice. They were also able to challenge, resolve or accept differing advice from the team around the child. The intervention was centred around consistency, reliability, respectful, empathetic discussions, and debates, incorporating 'experiments' that permitted 'trial and error.'

These examples show how information can be withheld or hidden unconsciously or consciously, skewed, embellished, misrepresented, flawed, or freely given. The challenge is to enable adults to share their experiences, thoughts, feelings, and souls when there is fear the end result may be rejection. To be approved as an adopter without full disclosure adds to the relentless pain of smashed expectations, the real possibility of placement disruption, parental and sibling separation, or even further harm. One Local Authority, when challenged by a therapist about the quality of the assessment, stated that they psychometrically tested their adopters, a claim that held no substance, and brought into question their understanding of psychometric testing. Whilst stating this they simultaneously questioned whether psychometrics should even be included in an adopter assessment process suggesting they were conflicted and/or confused by their own views and procedures.

The Foster Carer Context

Foster carers have a different set of needs. Unlike adopters, their primary objective is not usually to become the child's legal parents. Fostering can provide short-term or long-term provision to children but does not always provide the commitment of support post eighteen. The initial goal of fostering is not to adopt, but this can and does happen. There are times in both fostering and adoption where this need has been mis-assessed, and the adult should have been counselled out of the role they were applying for. The wrong adult in the wrong role can have disastrous consequences.

Stan and Pleasance were rightly approved as foster carers but were coming towards the end of their career. The matching process was overoptimistic by both their supervising social worker and the child's social worker when placing Jacob. Jacob had multiple disabilities and an acute health challenge that, if not treated swiftly, was likely to be terminal. His treatment at this time was experimental. His future remained uncertain. The childcare social worker was desperate to place him. Time was of the essence, blurring objectivity, and the supervising social worker missed the ageing foster carers' unspoken but present resistance to retirement. They could not imagine a life without children. During Jacob's treatment, the foster carers' experience and commitment were very able to meet his needs, with the female foster carer electing to stay with him throughout his hospitalisation and lengthy treatment. They doted on him. However, when it came time to support him to move into adoption, they could not give him the permission to move on he required. They both actively and passively resisted the process because they did not want to lose him. Stan and Pleasance were unable to share their grief at having to let go of this child and instead became passive in their resistance. This had devastating consequences both for Jacob's ability to attach to his new adoptive parents,

Mariella and Alfredo, and his ability to share his new parents with the other children in their household.

Daria and Bart were experienced foster carers. They had twin daughters at university and a son studying A levels. They cared for Diego, aged seven, an extremely traumatised boy. His younger sister was placed in a specialist children's home and his baby brother remained in the care of his mother. Diego's behaviour was extreme; he was violent to property, people—mostly Daria and teaching staff at school—and animals alike, and yet, Daria did not give up. Her character strategy (Reich 1933, Kurtz 1990, Ogden 2006) enabled her to keep on keeping on despite the daily onslaught of terror that Diego brought. This strategy, 'Burdened-Enduring' (Kurtz 1990), superficially is a great strategy in a foster carer. A person with this type of presentation is unlikely to give up. Giving up is not an option. However, whilst this was good for Diego, it was not so good for Daria. The problem with an overriding character strategy is that is suggests an interruption(s) of or impairment(s) in the development of natural, social, and psychological functions and suggests a missing 'core experience.' The development of this strategy is between two and five years when the child's developmental task revolves around the expression of will, 'Can I have an impact on my environment?' or that period Erik Erikson described as 'initiative versus guilt.' When problematic, the child experiences undue pressure, responsibility beyond their developmental and/or chronological capacity, or being guilt-tripped into undertaking such tasks. The parenting the child experiences is that the parent's word is law; compliance is necessary. As an adult, they will be hardworking, unquestioning, and susceptible to over-compliance to those in authority but may harbour unspoken resentment. This double-edged sword means the carer will then do what is asked of them but be unable to express the toll it takes on their well-being. The practitioners had not enabled or supported Daria to communicate her experiences that led to this imbalance that supported her desire not to give up on Diego despite the increasing negative impact on her health.

Ruth and Richard raised four of their own boys successfully into adulthood. They had been fostering for years and had worked with a number of very complex children, seeing them successfully into permanence or providing a home into adulthood. When three-year-old Sky was placed, everyone saw it as business as usual, and the couple were left to get on with their role. Visiting the family, not to see Sky but to see two other children, siblings also in their care, it became immediately evident there was a problem in communicating with Sky and meeting her needs; Ruth was different with the other two children. She was irritated, cold, critical, lacking compassion, constantly misreading Sky's signals, misjudging her responses, and scapegoating her. Ruth struggled to nurture Sky, who 'at worst' was 'clingy' and 'needy,' behaviours Ruth had previously negotiated with other children with empathy and benevolence. When asked how she felt toward Sky, she looked shocked and stated, 'I don't know what to do with girls, every child I have ever had or cared for has been a boy.' Ruth's Achilles heel was Sky's gender. Ruth could not see the impact she was having on the child because she was overwhelmed with the impact caring for a girl was having on her, leaving her feeling inadequate and incompetent. This felt at odds with her ability to meet the needs of males and yet unable to know the needs of a girl. When asked about her own needs, she became resistant to further exploration, which may have contributed to Sky's placement breaking down soon afterwards.

The context of the carers is a significant key to their motivation towards children and the outcome of their communication with them. Thus, the starting point of those adults, be they adopters, foster carers, parents, connected carers, or stepparents, will vary considerably.

The context of young people moving into adulthood who are coming to terms with their sibling relationships is also key. They may be reinventing, renewing or developing unrealistic expectations of them, learning about them or building fantastical, unrealistic or idealistic images of how their future relationships may be.

The Young Adult or Care Leaver's Context

The backgrounds of the people presented here, on the cusp of independence, reflect the challenges they and services would face were they to go on and become parents themselves, and the changes in their relationships with their own siblings.

Leo, a 17-year-old male, had been living in a specialist residential unit for young people who had sexually harmed. He was moving toward his 18th birthday with frightening speed. He was contained and really needed to stay put in his current placement, a need rarely afforded to young folk in the care system in the UK. He had not had contact with his two adult brothers since he was seven. Services believed promoting contact between them would be a beneficial endeavour despite the dysfunctional family background they came from. Leo did not want his brothers to know why he was in the unit. This was agreed upon by some of the professionals in the team supporting him despite the brothers having young children of their own and would therefore be disadvantaged in their protection of them without this knowledge. Leo feared being rejected. The answer from Services was to promote contact without full disclosure. Contact was initiated despite advice to the contrary. The brothers, from the start, were verbally aggressive to residential staff and pushed boundaries and limits, threatened, and intimidated. A picture was being built of siblings who had taken on the same violent presentation they had endured as children. The argument for full disclosure was argued continuously by the therapeutic provider on the basis that:

- The lack of disclosure did not equip the brothers to make an informed decision about the relationship they were about to embark on with their younger brother.
- It did not enable them to make the safeguards to protect their own children.
- It did not enable them to provide Leo with the supervision to keep him and those around him safe from harm.

- That if (and importantly when) the siblings found out, it would not be possible to monitor their reaction towards their brother.
- That the siblings finding out the truth behind their brother's care status in an unplanned way would make it harder to manage any consequences than if the information were shared in a planned way.
- That disclosure was likely because their mother was not being discreet with the information about Leo.
- That young people who sexually harm do better when they understand that when triggered, and fear being unable to desist from acting out on their sexual responses, having a safe adult to share their feelings or sexual drives or fantasies is a key protective factor.
- That knowing if the siblings would be supportive or rejecting (albeit that their past experiences negated healthy attachment relationships) would be the best and safest way of future planning for Leo and, if rejected, enable him to be supported through this additional layer of loss.
- That it still was not even known if the siblings had harmed their brother, were aware of any harm he had experienced, been complicit in any harm he experienced, or failed to protect him due to their age, fear, ambivalence, avoidance, or perceived involvement in any harm.

Charlie was the second child in a family of five siblings. His mother was depressed, 'Children of depressed mothers don't expect support, don't anticipate relief from distress and don't know how to regulate their feelings' (Howe 2005) and 'Because they don't expect their ruptures to be repaired, they don't turn to others. Because they have not been taught to focus on solving problems step by step, they cannot imagine solutions' (Gerhart 2004). High rates of disorganised attachment have consistently been found in young children of chronically and severely depressed mothers (Teti et al. 1995; Ijzendoorn et al. 1999). In addition, they lived with the maternal grandfather who was a known political paedophile, perhaps the original source of their mother's depression. He preached society denied children the right to choose to have sex with him. He shared a bed with the oldest of Charlie's brothers. His father was violent; the level of neglect was extreme. It was the neglect that led the police to bring the children into care when Charlie was aged eight.

There was a significant age gap between Charlie, his two other similarly aged brothers and his four younger siblings. He knew nothing about his younger siblings and even struggled to recall their names with any accuracy because they were all adopted early to different adopters. He thought of himself as a middle child of three brothers.

Charlie was placed with his younger brother in a foster placement that, whilst lacklustre, was at least at that time safe. His older brother was placed separately where contact was not offered and where apparently neither brother asked to see him.

His foster carers were emotionally disconnected and physically absent, but Charlie and his brother appeared to be progressing in many aspects of their development. When Charlie was 12, his older brother's placement broke down. The reasons for this were never fully understood, or at least never documented or shared. Because the brothers seemed to be doing well despite the concerns relating to the foster carers' affect, it was decided to move the older brother in with his siblings based on the half-truth that siblings' outcomes are better when placed together.

The foster carers' disposition and the siblings' relationships had not been thoroughly examined. Within six months of his brother being placed, the foster carers separated. The male foster carer deregistered himself from fostering when he left the family home. Within a year of his brother being placed, Charlie and his older brother were convicted of having individually raped the same eight-year-old boy.

Placed in a specialist residential treatment centre, Charlie engaged in therapy where over a number of years he was able to gradually explore his experiences. He knew that he and his younger brother were doing ok prior to the placement of his older brother. This statement alone, of course, can never guarantee that their relationship was healthy because they did not have a 'healthy' template upon which to base this belief. He was clear he did not want to live with his older brother, could not recall being asked his opinion on whether he wished to live with his older brother, and reflected that even if he had been asked, he was not sure if he would have been able to articulate his wishes or even know why he held such a view.

Charlie knew sex was going to happen between him and his older brother as soon as his brother arrived in his foster home. It did, but was never seen. He recognised that the foster carers were not attuned to their needs but thought that this was normal. He accepted that he had raped the boy, something his brother denied. He was also able to disclose they had raped the boy multiple times and often raped the boy together. The brother's therapist believed that Charlie was the greater risk, that Charlie had influenced the older brother and that the assessment of risk of the older brother indicated there was low risk of recidivism. Despite this belief, the older brother went on to reoffend on multiple occasions.

Charlie, as a young adult, highlights a number of factors to help in understanding what adults tell us and what they do not.

- It can take years of personal therapy to realise that what was experienced as a child was not healthy.
- What is experienced as a child informs one's beliefs about oneself and the expectations of others.
- That a question may be asked about hopes, views or aspirations, but the ability to answer it in a meaningful or informed way may be compromised by developed beliefs about what constitutes normality or healthy or helpful.
- Charlie was aware that to truly progress he had to disclose information that was not going to be helpful for him in the short term and may lead him to be in greater trouble, indeed convicted or at least having his wishes denied. However, he saw this was the path to wellness.

- If neglected by birth parents, then being faced with emotionally illiterate foster carers is not going to seem alien and, in fact, will be familiar and reinforce belief about caregivers.
- If asked a question, the interviewee may tell the 'what is believed to be the truth' (but is not, e.g. sex between children and adults is normal), 'what is believed to be what the questioner wants to hear' (which constitutes a lie because the truth will not be heard or believed), 'tell a lie' (because the truth will not be heard, will induce shame, self-protection or ensure that needs will be met), 'embellish' (show the shiny side), 'avoid' (denial, shame, fear), 'stay silent' (avoids overwhelm, fear, shame), 'distract' (fear, shame, denial) 'or confuse' (dissociation, overwhelm, shame, fear).
- Charlie was originally open about his views on living with his older brother because he was not asked. Even if he had been asked, he could not have said he was afraid of sex because he thought sex was normal and consequently it was his fear of sex that was not normal. Also, the people who spent time with him, social workers/teachers/health staff, were the same people who spent time with his family and therefore he believed they knew what was going on implicitly; this confirmed his belief that sex was normal. Often, assessors' first mistake is to ask questions which paradoxically lead the child to believe there is only interest in data, not the person. Even when a question is asked it fails both the child and the interviewer because the purpose of the question is not clear, it is not asked in the right way, in the right circumstances or in the right location at the right time.

He was able to share, after a significant personal struggle through a lengthy therapeutic intervention in a contained environment, that his greatest fear was that he would be a paedophile and that he feared it because deep down he knew it, but he also knew he did not want it to be so.

Blocks versus Conduits to Change

The factors that support therapeutic change versus stagnation or compromise are all on a continuum that mirrors the children's experience and are clearly measurable. However, that measurement is commensurate with the time needed to do it, or find someone to do it, and then time saved by doing it against the time wasted by not doing it. The usefulness and value of a valid, peer-researched measurement of now and six months later are also in the balance.

Safety and trust are key elements. One is born out of the other and therefore are mutually inclusive. Safety, trust, and attachment are born and grow in a relationship where time, consistency, frequency, and regularity frame the relationship. The therapeutic relationship works because it mimics and mirrors a healthy attachment relationship, and in the same way, an attachment relationship, by creating security, does not result in dependency.

One of the major challenges, within any therapeutic relationship which relies on developing these very key foundations, is where time is rarely available due to the unrealistic demands and caseloads practitioners hold. Befriending individuals or families is a dangerous alternative. It is neither honest nor achievable. Despite the intentions of the practitioners, this will always doom the outcome of any intervention due to distrust, dependency, or stuckness. Safety and trust are born out of honesty, congruence, and openness. This means the family takes a risk by accepting our presence on their journey because what they may share may go beyond the realms of safety, child protection, or safeguarding, even if for a short time. It does mean the very risk endangered families need to take may lead to child protective services or others saying this is too dangerous a situation paradoxically at the time when the parents are invested and are taking the ultimate risk to generate change.

Perfection is not what is being sought; the opposite is true. The road to change is hard, and as imperfect humans, there should be an expectation of failure followed by learning. Individuals do get things wrong, and behaviours or presentations do not change as quickly as professionals would like them to. It is expected that parents reflect on their direct or indirect responses with their children and that these responses will vary from inspired and helpful to negative and potentially damaging. The parent will be stuck, or looking to be rescued, damned but curious, insightful, and prepared to reflect and revisit the experiences. One parent reflected, 'My daughter is progressing so well, and we can see the progress she is making, but she is now getting angry with her brother because he is refusing to move on and remaining stuck in the past.' Her shared reflection enabled her to recognise that her response to this situation, to over-identify with her daughter, would put her son in danger of being ostracised or scapegoated, and she adjusted her response to both her children as a result.

Another challenge, the need to identify each individual's ability to self-regulate. If parents cannot self-regulate, how can they be available to co-regulate or socially regulate their child? Tanya came religiously to her sessions as did her partner. They complained about their lives, the constant misery and how trapped they felt. Their response to advice was, 'We did that,' 'We tried that.' They were only superficially engaged and were closer to being in a state of disguised compliance than a mutually respectful relationship.

> Sometimes, during cycles of intermittent closure, a professional worker would decide to adopt a more controlling stance. However, this was defused by apparent co-operation from the family. We have called this disguised compliance because its effect was to neutralise the professional's authority and return the relationship to closure and the previous status quo.
> (Reder et al. 1993, pp. 106–107)

Tanya and her partner brought with them a palpable sense of hopelessness and helplessness that they couldn't allow themselves to admit, despite its presence in the room. Professionals can also start mirroring the family's chaos by being overly optimistic in relation to the family's ability to change or by accepting the rationales the family gives for the lack of change. The challenge when mirroring pessimism, at the opposite end of the spectrum, is often seen in being risk averse. Between these polar opposites is often stuckness, dependency, and lack of change in the family's functioning.

Therapists are sometimes accused of creating dependency. Not all will be aware that this is happening, and some will be consciously or unconsciously actively creating this unhealthy relationship for multiple reasons. If challenged, the therapist must demonstrate steps being taken to prevent this, through evidence in reviews, assessments, update reports, in explaining how their being reliable, consistent and caring are the corner stones for creating independence, in their clinical supervision or sometimes allowing the commissioner access to the therapist's own consultants or supervisors.

The importance of listening to what adults have to say about their sibling relationships, how they see and experience life, what their beliefs and limiting beliefs are and how attuned they are to their own core-self cannot be overstated. Whether accepting, rejecting, or questioning the premise that the sibling relationship is one of, if not the most important and long-lasting relationships, it brings with it both positive and negative short- and long-term impacts and consequences.

The danger of unprocessed feelings regarding any individual's experience of sibling relationships, an Achilles heel, which limits the ability to be aware of the difference between average sibling relationships and those siblings whose previous parenting has resulted in their paradoxical, complex, trauma-impacted sibling relationships.

References

Abuhatoum, S., Della Porta, S., Howe, N., and DeHart, G. (2020) A longitudinal examination of power in sibling and friend conflict. *Social Development*, 29(3), 903–919.

Abuhatoum, S. and Howe, N. (2013) Power in sibling conflict during early and middle childhood: Power in sibling conflict. *Social Development*, 22, 738–754.

Abuhatoum, S., Howe, N., Della Porta, S., Recchia, H., and Ross, H. (2016) Siblings' understanding of teaching in early and middle childhood: 'Watch me and you'll know how to do it.' *Journal of Cognition and Development*, 17(1), 180–196.

ACE (Adverse Childhood Experiences) Study. (2010) ACE reported by adults. *Centre for Disease Control and Prevention*, 59(49), 1609–1613.

Ainsworth, M. D. S., Blehar, M. C., Waters, E., and Wall, S. (1978) *Patterns of Attachment: A Psychological Study of the Strange Situation*. Hillsdale, NJ: Erlbaum.

Akhtar, A. (2019) *Our Symphony with Animals: On Health, Empathy, and Our Shared Destinies*. New York: Pegasus Books.

Albert, V. N. and King, R. (2008) Survival analyses of the dynamics of sibling experiences in foster care. *Families in Society*, 89(4), 533–540.

Anderson, A. (2016) The shocking abuse of toddler Liam Fee. *BBC Scotland News*, 31 May.

Andersson, Y., Holmqvist R., and Nilsson D. (2019) Child evacuations during World War 2: This should not happen again. *Journal of Loss and Trauma*, 24(3), 213–225.

Archer, C. and Gordon, C. (2006) *New Families, Old Scripts: A Guide to the Language of Trauma and Attachment in Adoptive Families*. London: Jessica Kingsley Publishers.

Arcos, E., Uarac, M, Molina, I., Repossi A., and Ulloa, M. (2001) Impact of domestic violence on reproductive and neonatal health. *Revista Médica de Chile*, 129(12), 1413–1424.

Ashley, J. (2013) Caring for my stroke victim husband Andrew Marr changed my life. *The Guardian*, 1 August, Opinion/Carers section.

Bank, S. P. and Kahn, M. D. (1997) *The Sibling Bond*. New York: Basic Books.

Barach, P. M. (1991) Multiple personality disorder as an attachment disorder. *Dissociation: Progress in the Dissociative Disorders*, 4(3), 117–123.

Beckett, S. (2018) *Beyond Together or Apart: Planning for, Assessing and Placing Sibling Groups*. London: Coram BAAF.

Beckett, S. (2021) *Beyond Together or Apart: Planning for, Assessing and Placing Sibling Groups*. Good Practice Guide. London: Coram BAAF.

Begley, S (2009) *The Plastic Mind*. London: Constable.

Bellis, M., Ashton, K., Hughes, K., Ford. K. et al. (2015) *Adverse Childhood Experiences and their Impact on Health-harming Behaviours in the Welsh Adult Population.* Public Health Wales NHS Trust.

Bhide, P. G. (2009) Dopamine, cocaine and the development of cerebral cortical cytoarchitecture: A review of current concepts. *Seminars in Cell and Developmental Biology*, 20, 395–402.

Bifulco, A., Brown, G. W., Moran P., Ball, C., and Campbell C. (1998) *Predicting Depression in Women: The Role of Past and Present Vulnerability.* Published online by Cambridge University Press.

Blom-Copper, L., Beal, J., Brown, B., Marshall, P., and Mason, M. (1985) *A Child in Trust: The Report of the Panel of Enquiry Into the Circumstances Surrounding the Death of Jasmine Beckford.* Wembley, Middx.: London Borough of Brent.

Bloom, S. L. (1997) *Creating Sanctuary: Toward the Evolution of Sane Societies.* New York: Routledge.

Bowlby, J. (1958) The nature of the child's tie to his mother. *The International Journal of Psycho-Analysis*, 39, 350–373.

Bowlby, J. (1969, 1973, 1980) *Attachment and Loss Vol 1 – Attachment 1–11.* London: Hogarth Press.

Braun, B. G. (1988) The BASK model of dissociation. *Dissociation*, 1(1), 4–23.

Bretherton, I. (1992) The origins of attachment theory: John Bowlby and Mary Ainsworth. *Developmental Psychology*, 28(5), 759–775. https://doi.org/10.1037/0012-1649.28.5.759

Briere, J. N. (1992) *Child Abuse Trauma: Theory and Treatment of the Lasting Effects.* London: Sage.

Briere, J. (1995) *Trauma Symptom Inventory: Professional Manual.* Odessa, FL: Psychological Assessment Resources.

Briere, J. (2005) *Trauma Symptom Checklist for Young Children (TSCYC): Professional Manual.* Odessa, FL: Psychological Assessment Resources.

Briere, J. (2011) *TSI-2: Trauma Symptom Inventory-2: Professional Manual.* Florida: PAR.

Buist, K. L., Deković, M., and Prinzie, P. (2013) Sibling relationship quality and psychopathology of children and adolescents: A meta-analysis. *Clinical Psychology Review*, 33(1), 97–106.

Bryson, B. (2019) *The Body. A Guide for its Occupants.* London: Penguin.

Cairns, K. (2002) *Attachment, Trauma and Resilience.* London: BAAF.

Campione-Barr, N. (2017) The changing nature of power, control, and influence in sibling relationships. In Campione-Barr, N. (ed.), *Power, Control, and Influence in Sibling Relationships across Developmen. New Directions for Child and Adolescent Development*, Vol. 156. San Francisco, CA: Jossey Bass, 7–14.

Carroll, J. (1998) *Introduction to Therapeutic Play: Working Together for Children, Young People and Their Families.* Oxford: Wiley-Blackwell.

Caspi, J. (2012) *Sibling Aggression: Assessment and Treatment.* New York: Springer.

Chapman, L. (2014) *Neurobiologically Informed Trauma Therapy with Children and Adolescents.* New York and London: W.W. Norton & Company.

Chess, S. and Thomas, A. (1995) *Temperament in Clinical Practice.* New York: Guilford Press.

Children Act 1989 (c. 41), London HMSO (or the Stationery Office). Schedule 7, para. 3. UK legislation.

Children and Young Persons Act 2008 (c. 23), London HMSO (or the Stationery Office). s. 8, inserting section 22C(8) into the Children Act 1989.

Children and Social Work Act 2017 (c. 16). London HMSO (or the Stationery Office). An Act to make provision about looked after children; to make other provision in relation to the welfare of children; and to make provision about the regulation of social workers. Received Royal Assent 27 April 2017. United Kingdom Parliament.

Chu, J. A. (2011) *Rebuilding Shattered Lives: Responsible Treatment of Complex Post-traumatic and Dissociative Disorders*. 2nd edn. London: John Wiley & Sons.

Cicirelli, V. (1995) *Sibling Relationships across the Lifespan*. New York: Plenum Press.

Cloitre, M., Courtois, C. A., Charuvastra, A., Carapezza, R., Stolbach, B. C., and Green, B. L. (2009) The need for a developmentally appropriate trauma category: Complex PTSD or disorders of extreme stress not otherwise specified (DESNOS). *European Journal of Psychotraumatology*, 1, Article 5.

Cole, P. and Putnam, F. (1992) Effect of incest on self and social functioning: A developmental psychopathology perspective. *Journal of Consulting and Clinical Psychology*, 60, 174–184.

Couper, S. and Mackie, P. (2016) *'Polishing the Diamonds' Addressing Adverse Childhood Experiences in Scotland*. Edinburgh: Scottish Public Health Network (ScotPHN); May 2016. www.scotphn.net/wp-content/uploads/2016/06/2016_05_26.

Cox, S. (2019) *Till the Cows Come Home*. London: Hodder & Stoughton.

Crenshaw, D. A. and Stewart, A. L (2015) *Play Therapy: A Comprehensive Guide to Theory and Practice*. New York: The Guilford Press.

Damasio, A. R. (1994) *Descartes' Error*. New York: Grossett/Putnam.

Dantchev, S., Hickman, M., Heron, J., Zammit, S., and Wolke, D. (2019) The independent and cumulative effects of sibling and peer bullying in childhood on depression, anxiety, suicidal ideation, and self-harm in adulthood. *Frontiers in Psychiatry*, 10, 651.

Della Porta, S., Howe, N., and Persram, R. J. (2019) Parents' and children's power effectiveness during polyadic family conflict: Process and outcome. *Social Development*, 28(1), 152–167.

Della Porta, S., Persram, R. J., Howe, N., and Ross, H. S. (2022) Young children's differential use of power during family conflict: A longitudinal study. *Social Development*, 31(1), 165–179.

Della Porta, S. and Howe, N. (2012) Mothers' and children's perceptions of power through personal, conventional, and prudential conflict situations. *Merrill-Palmer Quarterly*, 58(4), 507–529.

Department for Education (DoE) (2014) *Young Person's Guide to the Children and Families Act 2014*. London: DoE, 1.

Department for Education (2014) *The Young Person's Guide to the Children and Families Act 2014*. London: Department for Education.

Dereboy, C., Sahin Demirkapi, E., Sakiroglu, M., and Safak Ozturk, C. (2013/5) Department for Education Statutory Guidance on Adoption.

Dirks, M. A., Recchia, H. E., Estabrook, R., Howe, N., Petitclerc, A., Burns, J. L., Briggs-Gowan, M. J., and Wakschlag, L. S. (2019) Differentiating typical from atypical perpetration of sibling-directed aggression during the preschool years. *Journal of Child Psychology and Psychiatry, and Allied Disciplines*, 60(3), 267–276.

Doidge, N. (2007) *The Brain that Changes Itself*. London: Penguin.

Drapeau, S., Simard, M., Beaudry, M., and Charbonneau, S. (2000) Sibling placement patterns following foster care entry. *Children and Youth Services Review*, 22(7), 507–529.

Dunn J. (2002) Sibling relationships. In Smith, P. K. and Hart, C. H. (eds.), *Blackwell Handbook of Childhood Social Development*. Oxford, UK: Blackwell Publishing, 223–237.

Dunn, J. (2007) Siblings and socialization. In Grusec, J. E. and Hastings, P. D. (eds.), *Handbook of Socialization: Theory and Research*. New York: Guilford Press, 309–327.

Dunn J. (2015) Siblings. In Grusec, J. and Hastings, P. (eds.), *Handbook of Socialization: Theory and Research*. 2nd edn. New York: Guilford, 182–201.

Dunn, J. and Kendrick, C. (1982) *Siblings: Love, Envy, and Understanding*. Cambridge, MA: Harvard University Press.

El Marroun, H., White, T., Verhulst, F. C., and Tiemeier, H. (2014) Maternal use of antidepressant or anxiolytic medication during pregnancy and childhood neurodevelopmental outcomes: A systemic review. *European Child and Adolescent Psychiatry*, 23, 973–992.

Entringer, S., Buss, C., Andersen, J., Chicz Demet, A., and Wadhwa, P. D. (2011) Ecological momentary assessment of maternal cortisol profiles over a multiple-day period predicts the length of human gestation. *Psychosomatic Medicine*, 73, 469–474.

Felliti, J., Anda R. F., Nordenberg, D., Edwards V., Koss, M., and Marks, J. S. (1998) Relationship of childhood abuse and household dysfunction to many of the leading causes of death in adults. *American Journal of Preventive Medicine*, 14(4), P245–258.

Fenichel, O. (1945) *The Psychoanalytic Theory of Neurosis*. London: Routledge & K. Paul.

Finkelhor, D. (1995) The victimization of children: A developmental perspective. *American Journal of Orthopsychiatry*, 65(2), 177–193.

Firmin, C. E. (2017) *Contextual Safeguarding: An Overview of the Operational, Strategic and Conceptual Framework*. Bedford, UK: University of Bedfordshire.

Firmin, C. (2020) *Contextual Safeguarding and Child Protection: Rewriting the Rules*. London: Routledge.

Fisher, J. (2017) *Healing the Fragmented Selves of Trauma Survivors: Overcoming Internal Self-Alienation*. 1st edn. New York: Routledge.

Fisher, J. (2021) *Transforming the Living Legacy of Trauma: A Workbook for Survivors and Therapists*. Fort Washington, PA: PESI Publishing & Media.

Fonagy, P., Gergely, G., Jurist, E. L. and Target, M. (2004) *Affect Regulation, Mentalization, and the Development of the Self*. London: Karnac.

Fosha, D. (2003) Dyadic regulation and experiential work with emotion and relatedness in trauma and disorganized attachment. In Solomon, M. F. and Siegel, D. J. (eds.), *Healing Trauma: Attachment, Trauma, the Brain, and the Mind*. New York: W.W. Norton, 221–281.

Freedman, G. (2018) *Psychotherapy Reflections: Thoughts about Psychotherapy*. NC: Lulu.

Freud, S. (1905) *Three Essays on the Theory of Sexuality*. Verso Books.

Freud, S. (2010 ed) *Three Essays on the Theory of Sexuality*. London: Verso.

Galston, W. A. (1998) The torturer's apprentice. In Galston, W. A. (ed.), *Philosophy and Public Policy*. Boulder, CO: Westview Press, 17–31.

Gass, K., Jenkins, J., and Dunn, J. (2007) Are sibling relationships protective? A longitudinal study. *Journal of Child Psychology and Psychiatry*, 48(2), 167–175.

Gerhadt, S. (2004) *Why Love Matters: How Affection Shapes a Baby's Brain*. London: Routledge.

References

Gill, E. (2017) *Posttraumatic Play in Children: What Clinicians Need to Know*. London: The Guilford Press.

Gillick v West Norfolk & Wisbeck Area Health Authority [1986] AC 112 House of Lords.

Goddard, C. and Hiller, P. (1993) Child sexual abuse: Assault in a violent context. *Australian Journal of Social Issues*, 28, 20–33.

Grossman, K. (1995) Evolution and history of attachment research. In Goldberg, S., Muir, R., and Kerr, J. (eds.), *Attachment Theory: Social Developmental and Clinical Perspectives*. Hillsdale, NJ: Analytic Press, 85–122.

Haines, S. (2018) *Trauma is Really Strange*. London: Singing Dragon (Jessica Kinsley London).

Hart, S. (2008) *Brain, Attachment and Personality*. London: Karnac London.

Hegar, R. L. and Rosenthal, J. A. (2011) Foster children placed with or separated from siblings: Outcomes based on a national sample. *Children and Youth Services Review*, 33(7), 1245–1253.

Herman, J. L. (1992) *Trauma and Recovery*. New York: Basic Books.

Herrick, M. and Piccus, W. (2005) Sibling connections: The importance of nurturing sibling bonds in the foster care system. *Children and Youth Services Review*, 27, 845–961.

Hou, X. H., Wang, L. J., Li, M., Qin, Q. Z., Li, Y., and Chen, B. B. (2022) The roles of sibling status and sibling relationship quality on theory of mind among Chinese preschool children. *Personality and Individual Differences*, 185, 111273.

Howe, D. (2005) *Child Abuse and Neglect: Attachment, Development and Intervention*. Hampshire: Macmillan.

Howe, D., Brandon, M., Schofield, J. and Hinings, D. (1999) Attachment Theory, Child Maltreatment and Family Support: A Practice and Assessment Model. Basingstoke: Palgrave Macmillan.

Howe, N., Adrien, E., Della Porta, S., et al. (2016) 'Infinity means it goes on forever': Siblings' teaching of mathematics during naturalistic home interactions. *Infant and Child Development*, 25(2), 137–157.

Howe, N., Della Porta, S., Recchia, H., Funamoto, A., and Ross, H. (2015) This bird can't do it 'cause this bird doesn't swim in water: Sibling teaching during naturalistic home observations in early childhood. *Journal of Cognition and Development*, 16, 314–332.

Howe, N., Paine, A. L., Recchia, H., and Ross, H. (2022) Sibling relations in early childhood. In Hart, C. and Smith, P. K. (eds.), *Wiley-Blackwell Handbook of Childhood Social Development*. 3rd edn. Chichester, UK: Wiley, 443–458.

Howe, N., Recchia, H., and Kinsley, C. (2023) Sibling relations and their impact on children's development. In *Peer Relations in Early Childhood* (2nd revised ed.). March 2023. Concordia University, Department of Education & Centre for Research in Human Development. https://www.child-encyclopedia.com/peer-relations/according-experts/sibling-relations-and-their-impact-childrens-development.

Howe, N., Recchia, H., Porta, S. D., and Funamoto, A. (2012) 'The driver doesn't sit, he stands up like the Flintstones!': Sibling teaching during teacher-directed and self-guided tasks. *Journal of Cognition and Development*, 13(2), 208–231.

Howe, N., Rinaldi, C. M., Jennings, M., and Petrakos, H. (2002) 'No! The lambs can stay out because they got cozies': Constructive and destructive sibling conflict, pretend play, and social understanding. *Child Development*, 73(5), 1460–1473.

Howes, N. (2014) A Trauma model for Plannnin, Assessing and Reviewing Contact for Looked After Children. Community Care Inform, London.

Hughes, D. A. (2012) *Attachment-Focused Family Therapy Workbook*. New York: W.W. Norton.

Hughes, K., Bellis, M. A., Hardcastle, K. A., Sethi, D., Butchart, A., Mikton, C., Jones, L., and Dunne, M. P. (2017) The effect of multiple adverse childhood experiences on health: A systematic review and meta-analysis. *The Lancet Public Health*, 2(8), e356–e366.

Itzin, C. (2000) *Missing from the Agenda: The Role of Gender in Child Protection*. London: Whiting & Birch.

Jackson, S. and Martin, P. Y. (1998) Surviving the care system: Education and resilience. *Journal of Adolescence*, 21, 569–583.

James, A., Lawlor, M., and Brindle, P. (2008) Maintaining sibling relationships for children in foster and adoptive placements. *Children and Youth Services Review*, 30(12), 152–161.

James, B. (1994) *Handbook for Treatment of Attachment-trauma Problems in Children*. New York: Free Press.

Jewett, C. L. (1982) *Helping Children Cope with Separation and Loss*. Boston, MA: Harvard common Press.

Judd, T. (2001) Tragic tale of a child unwanted from day of her birth. *Independent*. Tuesday 2 October 2001 00:00.

Jung, C. G. (1967) *Two Essays on Analytical Psychology, Collected Works of C. G. Jung, Volume 7*. Princeton, NJ: Princeton University Press.

Kadushin, A. and Harkness, D. (1976, 2014) *Supervision in Social Work*. 5th edn. New York: Columbia University Press.

Kempe, C. H., Silverman, F. N., Steele, B. F., Droegemueller, W., and Silver, H. K. (1962) The battered-child syndrome. *Journal of the American Medical Association*, 181(1), 17–24.

Khan, R. and Rogers, P. (2015) The normalization of sibling violence: Does gender and personal experience of violence influence perceptions of physical assault against siblings? *Journal of Interpersonal Violence*, 30(3), 437–458.

Klaus and Kennell (1976) *Maternal-Infant Bonding: The Impact of Early Separation or Loss on Family Development*. Missouri: CV Mosby.

Klein, M. (1975) *Love, Guilt and Reparation and Other Works 1921–1945*. New York: The Free Press.

Klein, P. S., Feldman, R., and Zarur, S. (2002) Mediation in a sibling context: The relations of older siblings' mediating behaviour and younger siblings' task performance. *Infant and Child Development*, 11(4), 321–333.

Kolak, A. M. and Volling, B. L. (2011) Sibling jealousy in early childhood: Longitudinal links to sibling relationship quality. *Infant and Child Development*, 20(2), 213–226.

Kolawole, F. (2025) *The Role of Sibling Relationships in Shaping Emotional Resilience in Children*. SSRN.

Kothari, B., Sorensen, P., McBeath, B., and Steele, J. (2017) An intervention to improve sibling relationship quality among youth in foster care: Results of a randomised trial. *Child Abuse and Neglect*, 63, 19–29.

Kothari

Kosonen, M. (1996) Maintaining sibling relationships – neglected dimension in child care practice. *British Journal of Social Work*, 26, 809–822.

Kramer, L. (2014) Learning emotional understanding and emotion regulation through sibling interaction. *Early Education and Development*, 25(2), 160–184.

Kramer, L. and Hamilton, T. N. (2019) Sibling caregiving. In Bornstein, M. H. (ed.), *Handbook of Parenting. Vol 1. Children and Parenting.* 3rd edn. New York: Routledge, 372–408.

Kurtz, R. (1990) *Body-Centred Psychotherapy: The Hakomi Method.* Mendocino, CA: LifeRhythm Press.

Landreth, G. L. (2002) *Play Therapy: The Art of the Relationship.* 2nd edn. New York: Brunner-Routledge.

Lanius, R. A., Vermetten, E., and Pain, C. (eds.) (2013) *The Impact of Early Life Trauma on Health and Disease: The Hidden Epidemic.* Cambridge: Cambridge University Press.

Laing, R. D. (1970) *Knots.* London: Tavistock Publications.

Larzelere, R. E., Morris, A. S., & Harrist, A. W. (eds.) (2013) *Authoritative Parenting: Synthesizing Nurturance and Discipline for Optimal Child Development.* Washington, DC: American Psychological Association.

Law Commission (1988) *Review of Child Law: Guardianship and Custody.* Law Com. No. 172. London: HMSO.

Leach, J., Howe, N., and DeHart, G. (2017) Children's references to internal states with siblings and friends from early to middle childhood: Internal state language. *Infant and Child Development*, 26(5), e2015.

Leach, J., Howe, N., and DeHart, G. (2022) Children's connectedness with siblings and friends from early to middle childhood during play. *Early Education and Development*, 33(8), 1289–1303.

Leathers, S. J. (2005) Separation from siblings: Associations with placement adaptation and outcomes among adolescents in long-term foster care. *Children and Youth Services Review*, 27(7), 793–819.

Levine, P. A (1997) *Waking the Tiger.* Berkeley CA: North Atlantic Books.

Levine, P. A. (2010) *In an Unspoken Voice: How the Body Releases Trauma and Restores Goodness.* Berkeley, CA: North Atlantic Books.

Levy, A., and B. Kahan. (1991). *The Pindown experience and the protection of children.* Staffordshire County Council, Stafford, UK.

Linares, L., Jimenez, J., Nesci, C., Pearson, E., Beller, S., Edwards, N., and Levin-Rector, A. (2015) Reducing sibling conflict in maltreated children placed in foster homes. *Prevention Science*, 39, 1–10.

Linares, L. O., Schneider, C. R., Shrout, P., Li, M., Pettit, G., and Brody, G. (2015) Promoting sibling bonds: Pilot randomized trial of an intervention for siblings in foster care. *Children and Youth Services Review*, 57, 39–51.

Liotti, G. (2011) Attachment disorganization and the controlling strategies: An illustration of the contributions of attachment theory to developmental pychopathology and to psychotherapy integration. *Journal of Psychotherapy Integration*, 21(3), 232–252.

Liotti, G. (1992) Disorganized attachment and dissociative experiences: An illustration of the developmental-ethological approach to cognitive therapy. In Rosen, H. and Kuehlwein, K.T. (eds.), *Cognitive Therapy in Action.* San Francisco, CA: Jossey-Bass, 196–204.

Lord, J. and Borthwick, S. (2008, 2014) *Together or Apart? Assessing Siblings for Permanent Placement.* 2nd edn. London: Coram BAAF.

Main, M. and Hesse, E. (1992) Attaccamento disorganizzato/disorientato Nell infanzia e stati mentali dissociati nei genitori (Disorganized/ disoriented infant behavior in the strange situation, lapses in the monitoring of reasoning and discourse during the parents' Adult Attachment Interview, and dissociative states: In support of Liotti's hypothesis.)

Translated [into Italian] by V. Chiarini and published in Ammaniti, M. and Stern, D. (eds.), *Attaccamento e psicoanalisi(Attachment and Psychoanalysis)*. Bari: Laterza, 86–140.

Main, M. and Solomon, J. (1990) Procedures for identifying infants as disorganized/disoriented during the Ainsworth Strange Situation. In Greenberg, M. T., Cicchetti, D., and Cummings, E. M. (eds.), *Attachment in the Preschool Years: Theory, Research, and Intervention*. Chicago: University of Chicago Press, 121–160.

Mandela, N. (1995) Address at the launch of his children's fund in Pretoria. Nelson Mandella Fund Archive.

Marley, B. (1962) *Judge Not*. On: Songs of Freedom [album]. Island Records, 1992.

Maslow, A. H. (1954) *Motivation and Personality*. New York: Harper & Row.

McCarthy, J. BBC Archives Parkinson Interviews.

McConnell, S. (2020) *Somatic Internal Family Systems Therapy: Awareness, Breath, Resonance, Movement and Touch in Practice*. Berkeley, CA: North Atlantic Books.

McDowall, J. J. (2015) *Sibling Placement and Contact in Out-of-home Care*. Canberra & Sydney: CREATE Foundation.

McEwen, B. (2015) *Experience Shapes the Brain Across the Life-course: Epigenetics, Biological Embedding and Cumulative Change*. GCPH Seminar Series 11, lecture 6; 21 April 2015. Bruce S. McEwen, Glasgow Centre for Population Health.

Meakings, S., Sebba, J., and Luke, N. (2017) *What is Known about Placement Outcomes of Siblings in Foster Care? An International Literature Review*. London, UK: London Rees Centre, University of Oxford and DfE.

Meunier, J. C., Roskam, I., Stievenart, M., De Moortele, G. V., Browne, D. T., and Wade, M. (2012) Parental differential treatment, child's externalizing behavior and sibling relationships: Bridging links with child's perception of favoritism and personality, and parents' self-efficacy. *Journal of Social and Personal Relationships*, 29(5), 612–638.

Milevesky, A. (2005) Compensatory patterns of sibling support in emerging adulthood: Variations in loneliness, depression, self-esteem, depression and life satisfaction. *Journal of Social and Personal Relationships*, 22(6), 743–755.

Minnis, H. and Devine, C. (2001) The effect of foster carer training on the emotional and behavioural functioning of looked after children. *Adoption and Fostering*, 1(Spring), 44–54.

Monk, D. and Macvarish, J. (2018) Siblings, contact and the law: An overlooked relationship? *Family Law*, 50, 180–187.

Monk, C., Georgieff, M. K., and Osterholm, E. A. (2013) Research review: Maternal prenatal distress and poor nutriyion – Mutually influencing risk factors affecting infant neurocognitive development. *Journal of Child Psychology and Psychiatry*, 54, 115–130.

Munro, E. (2011) *The Munro Review of Child Protection: A Child-centred System*. London: Department for Education.

Music, G. (2011) *Nurturing Natures: Attachment and Children's Emotional, Sociocultural and Brain Development*. Hove: Psychology Press.

National Commission of Inquiry into the Prevention of Child Abuse (1994) *Childhood Matters: Report of the National Commission of Inquiry into the Prevention of Child Abuse*. London: HMSO.

Neulinger and Shuruk v Switzerland App. No. 41615/07, (2011) 1 FLR 122, European Court of Human Rights.

Newberry, J. J. and Stubbs, C. A. (1990) *Advanced Interviewing Techniques*. Glynco, Georgia: Bureau of Alcohol Tobacco and Firearms National Academy.

Nijenhuis, E. (2015) *The Trinity of Trauma: Ignorance, Fragility, and Control*. Göttingen: Vandenhoeck & Ruprecht.

NSPCC (2024) *Child Deaths Due to Abuse or Neglect: Statistics Briefing*. London: NSPCC Learning. Available at: https://learning.nspcc.org.uk/research-resources/statistics-briefings/child-deaths-abuse-neglect (Accessed: 24 July 2025).

Ogden, P., Minton, K., and Pain, C. (2006) *Trauma and the Body: A Sensorimotor Approach to Psychotherapy*. London: W.W. Norton.

O'Neill, T. (2000) *A Place Called Hope*. 2nd edn. Blackburn: Educational Printing Services.

Paine, A. L., Howe, N., Karajian, G., Hay, D. F., and DeHart, G. (2019) 'H, I, J, K, L, M, N, O, PEE! Get it? Pee!': Siblings' shared humour in childhood. *British Journal of Developmental Psychology*, 37(3), 336–353.

Paine, A. L., Karajian, G., Hashmi, S., Persram, R. J., and Howe N. (2021) 'Where's your bum brain?' Humor, social understanding, and sibling relationship quality in early childhood. *Social Development*, 30(2), 592–611.

Perlman, M., Garfinkel, D. A., and Turrell, S. L. (2007) Parent and sibling influences on the quality of children's conflict behaviours across the preschool period. *Social Development*, 16(4), 619–641.

Peck, M. S. (1978, 2006 print) *The Road Less Travelled*. London: Arrow Books.

Perry, B. D. (1997) Incubated in terror: Neurodevelopmental factors in cycle of violence. In Osofskyed, D. J. (ed.), *Children in a Violent Society*. New York: Guildford, 124–149.

Perry, B. D., Pollard, R. A., Blakley, T. L., Baker, W. L., and Vigilante, D. (1995) Childhood trauma, the neurobiology of adaptation & use-dependent development of the brain: How states become traits. *Journal of Infant Mental Health*, 16(4), 271–291.

Perry, B. D. and Szalavitz, M. (2017) *The Boy Who Was Raised as a Dog: And Other Stories from a Child Psychiatrist's Notebook – What Traumatized Children Can Teach Us About Loss, Love and Healing* (Revised & Updated Second Trade Paperback ed.). New York: Basic Books.

Pike, A. and Oliver, B. R. (2017) Child behavior and sibling relationship quality: A cross-lagged analysis. *Journal of Family Psychology*, 31(2), 250–255.

Porges, S. (2011) *The Polyvagal Theory: Neurophysiological Foundations of Emotions, Attachment, Communication, Self-regulation*. New York: W. W. Norton.

Putnam, F. W. (1997) *Dissociation in Children and Adolescents: A Developmental Perspective*. London: Guilford.

Rauchfuss, M. and Gauger, U. (2003) Biopsychosocial predictors of preterm labor and preterm delivery? Results of a prospective study. *Zentralbl Gynakol*, 125(5), 167–178.

Reamer, F. C. (2013) *Social Work Values and Ethics: Foundations of Social Work Knowledge Series*. 4th edn. New York: Columbia University Press.

Rees Centre. (2017) *What is Known about the Placement and Outcomes of Siblings in Foster Care?* Oxford: University of Oxford.

Recchia, H. E. and Howe, N. (2009) When do siblings compromise? Associations with children's descriptions of conflict issues, culpability, and emotions: When do siblings compromise? *Social Development*, 19(4), 838–857.

Recchia, H. E. and Howe, N. (2008) Family talk about internal states and children's relative appraisals of self and sibling. *Social Development*, 17(4), 776–794.

Reder, P., Duncan, S., and Gray, M. (1993) *Beyond Blame: Child Abuse Tragedies Revisited*. London: Routledge.

Reich, W. (1933) *Character Analysis*. New York: Orgone Institute Press.

Reiland, R. (2002) *I'm Not Supposed to Be Here: My Recovery from Borderline Personality Disorder*. Center City, MN: Hazelden Information & Education

Richardson, J., Coid, J., Petruckevitch, A., Shan Chung, W., Moorey, S., and Feder, G. (2002) Identifying domestic violence: Cross sectional study in primary care. *British Medical Journal*, 325, 1417.

Richardson, S. M. and Yates, T. M. (2014) Siblings in foster care: A relational path to resilience for emancipated foster youth. *Children and Youth Services Review*, 47, 378–388.1

Richmond, M. K., Stocker, C. M., and Rienks, S. L. (2005) Longitudinal associations between sibling relationship quality, parental differential treatment, and children's adjustment. *Journal of Family Psychology*, 19(4), 550–559.

Rogers, C. (1951) *Client-centered Therapy*. London: Constable.

Ross, H. S., Filyer, R. E., Lollis, S. P., Perlman, M., and Martin, J. L. (1994) Administering justice in the family. *Journal of Family Psychology*, 8(3), 254–273.

Rossetti, C. G. (1862) *Goblin Market and Other Poems*. London: Macmillan.

Rowe, J. and Lambert (1975) *Children Who Wait*. London, UK: Association of British Adoption Agencies.

Rushton, A. (2003) *Sibling Placement in Foster Care and Adoption: An Overview of International Research*. London: British Association for Adoption and Fostering (BAAF).

Ryan, V. and Wilson, K. (1996, 2000) *Case Studies in Non-directive Play Therapy*. London: JKP.

Sapolsky, R. M., Romero, L. M., and Munck, A. J. (2000) How to glucocortoids influence stress responses? Integrating permissive, suppressive, stimulatory and preparative actions. *Endocrine Reviews*, 21(1), 55–89.

Saunders, H. and Selwyn, J. (2010) *Adoptions from Care in the UK: A Study of Adoption Policy and Practice*. London: BAAF (British Association for Adoption and Fostering).

Scaer, R. (2014) *The Body Bears the Burden*. 3rd edn. Hove: Routledge.

Schore, A. (1994) *Affect Regulation and the Origin of the Self*. Hillsdale, N.J.: L. Erlbaum Associates.

Schore, A. N. (2001) The effects of early relational trauma on right brain development, affect regulation, and infant mental health. *Infant Mental Health Journal*, 22(1–2), 201–269.

Schore, A. N. (2003) *Affect Regulation and the Repair of the Self*. New York: Norton.

Schore, A. N. (2010) Relational trauma and the developing right brain: The neurobiology of broken attachment bonds. In Baradon, T. (ed.), *Relational Trauma in Infancy: Psychoanalytic, Attachment and Neuropsychological Contributions to Parent–Infant Psychotherapy*. London: Routledge, 19–47.

Schwartz, R. C. (1997) *Internal Family Systems Therapy*. New York: Guilford Press.

Schwartz, R. C. (2001) *Internal Family Systems Therapy: New Dimensions*. 2nd edn. New York: Guilford Press, 33.

Sellars, E., Oliver, B. R., and Bowes, L. (2024) Children's resilience to sibling victimization: The role of family, peer, school, and neighborhood factors. *Development and Psychopathology*, 36(4), 1–15.

Selwyn, J., Wijedasa, D., and Meakings, S. University of Bristol School for Policy Studies Hadley Centre for Adoption and Foster Care Studies (2014) *Beyond the Adoption Order: Challenges, Interventions and Adoption Disruption*, Research report. DfE: London.
Seuss, Dr. (1954) *Horton Hears a Who!* New York: Random House.
Shemmings, D. and Shemmings, Y. (2011) *Understanding Disorganised Attachment: Theory and Practice of Working with Children and Families*. London: Jessica Kingsley.
Siegel, D. J. (1999) *The Developing Mind: How Relationships and the Brain Interact to Shape Who We Are*. London: Guilford.
Siegel, D. J. (2012) *Pocket Guide to Interpersonal Neurobiology*. London: Norton.
Siegel, D. J. (2002) *The Developing Mind*. London: Guilford.
Silberg, J. L. (2012) *The Child Survivor: Healing Developmental Trauma and Dissociation*. New York: Routledge.
Sinclair, I. (2005) *Fostering Now: Messages from Research*. London: Jessica Kingsley.
Sinclair, I., Baker, C., Wilson, K., and Gibbs, I. (2003) *What Happens to Foster Children? Report Three*. York: University of York.
Smallbone, M. (2014) Brothers and sisters in care. In Hindle, D. and Sherwin-White, S. (eds.), *Sibling Matters: A Psychoanalytic, Developmental, and Systemic Approach*. London: Karnac Books, 190–204.
Smarius, L. J. C. A., Strieder, T. G. A., Loomans, E. M., Doreliegers, T. A. H., Vrijkotte, T. G. M., Gemke, R. J., and Van Eijsden, M. (2017) Excessive infant crying doubles the risk of mood and behavioral problems at age 5: Evidence for mediation by maternal characteristics. *Our Child Adolescent Psychiatry*, 26(3), 293–302. Published online 2016 Jul 15.
Solomon, E. P. and Heide, K. M. (1999) Type III trauma: Toward a more effective conceptualization of psychological trauma. *International Journal of Offender Therapy and Comparative Criminology*, 43(2), 202–210. Sage Journals.
Spiegel, L. (2017) *Internal Family Systems Therapy with Children*. 1st edn. New York: Routledge.
Sroufe, L. A., Egeland, B., Carlson, E. A., and Collins, W. A. (2005) *The Development of the Person: The Minnesota Study of Risk and Adaptation from Birth to Adulthood*. New York: Guilford Press.
Stevenson, O. (1986) Guest editorial on the Jasmine Beckford Inquiry. *British Journal of Social Work*, 16, 501–510.
Summers, J. (2011) *When Children Came Home: Stories of Wartime Evacuees*. New York: Simon and Schuster.
Summit, R. (1983) Beyond belief: The child sexual abuse accommodation syndrome. *Child Abuse and Neglect*, 7, 177–193.
Sunderland, M. (2007) *What Every Parent Needs to Know: The incredible Effects of Love, Nurture and Play on Your Child's Development*. London: DK.
Sunderland, M. (2017) *Good Every Day: The Science of Parenting*. London: DK Publishing.
Tan, L., Volling, B. L., Gonzalez, R., LaBounty, J., and Rosenberg, L. (2022) Growth in emotion understanding across early childhood: A cohort-sequential model of firstborn children across the transition to siblinghood. *Child Development*, 93(3), 101095.
Tarren-Sweeney, M. and Hazell, P. (2005) Mental health of children in foster and kinship care in New South Wales, Australia. *Children and Youth Services Review*, 27(3), 259–282.

Tavassoli, N., Dunfield, K., Kleis, A., Recchia, H., and Conto, L. P. (2023) Preschoolers' responses to prosocial opportunities during naturalistic interactions with peers: A cross-cultural comparison. *Social Development*, 32(1), 204–222.

Tavassoli, N., Howe, N., and DeHart, G. (2020) Investigating the development of prosociality through the lens of refusals: Children's prosocial refusals with siblings and friends. *Merrill-Palmer Quarterly*, 66(4), 421.

Tavassoli, N., Recchia, H., and Ross, H. (2019) Preschool children's prosocial responsiveness to their siblings' needs in naturalistic interactions: A longitudinal study. *Early Education and Development*, 30(6), 724–742.

Terr, L. C. (1991) Childhood traumas: An outline and overview. *American Journal of Psychiatry*, 148(1), 10–20.

Teti, D. M., Gelfand, D. M., Messinger, D. S., and Isabella, R. (1995) Maternal depression and the quality of early attachment relationships: A study of infants, preschoolers, and their mothers. *Developmental Psychology*, 31(2), 364–370.

The Department of Health (2001) Achieving Best Evidence in Criminal Proceedings: Guidance for Vulnerable or Intimidated Witnesses, including Children.

Toseeb, U. and Wolke, D. (2022) Sibling bullying: A prospective longitudinal study of associations with positive and negative mental health during adolescence. *Journal of Youth and Adolescence*, 51(5), 940–955.

United Nations Committee on the Rights of the Child (2016) *Concluding Observations on the Fifth Periodic Report of the United Kingdom of Great Britain and Northern Ireland*. CRC/C/GBR/CO/5. Geneva: United Nations.

UN General Assembly (2010) *Guidelines for the Alternative Care of Children: Resolution Adopted by the General Assembly*, A/RES/64/142, 24 February (annex). United Nations, New York.

van der Hart, O., Nijenhuis, E. R. S., and Steele, K. (2006) *The Haunted Self: Structural Dissociation of the Personality and the Treatment of Chronic Traumatization*. New York: W. W. Norton & Company.

Van der Kolk, B. A., McFarlane, A. C., and Weisaeth, L. (eds.) (1996) *Traumatic Stress: The Effects of Overwhelming Experience on Mind, Body, and Society*. New York: Guilford, 880–905.

Van der Kolk B. A. (2014) *The Body Keeps the Score: Brain, Mind and Body in the Healing of Trauma*. New York: Viking.

VanFleet, R., Sywulak, A., and Sniscak, C. (2010) *Child-centered Play Therapy*. New York: Guilford Press.

Van Ijzendoorn, M. and Sagi, A. (1999) Cross-Cultural patterns of attachment: Universal and contextual dimensions. In Cassidy, J. and Shaver, P. (eds.), *Handbook of Attachment*. London: Guilford Press.

Volling, B. L. and Belsky, J. (1992) The contribution of mother–child and father–child relationships to the quality of sibling interaction: A longitudinal study. *Child Development*, 63(5), 1209–1222.

Volling, B. L., Howe, H., and Kramer, L. (2025) The development of sibling relationships across childhood and adolescence: Recommendations for parents and practitioners. In Bornstein, M. H. and Shah, P. E. (eds.), *Handbook of Pediatric Psychology*. American Psychological Association, 267–287.

Volling, B. L., Kennedy, D. E., and Jackey, L. M. H. (2010) The development of sibling jealousy. In Legerstee, M. and Hart, S. (eds.), *Handbook of Jealousy: Theory, Research, and Multidisciplinary Approaches*. Malden, MA: Blackwell Publishers, 387–417.

Wade, J., Sinclair, I., Stuttard, L., and Simmonds, J. (2014) *Investigating Special Guardianship: Experiences, Challenges and Outcomes*. London: Department for Education.

Waid, J. and Wojciak, A. (2017) Evaluation of a multi–site program designed to strengthen relational bonds for siblings separated by foster care. *Evaluation and Program Planning*, 64, 69–77.

Ward, H. (ed.) (1995) *Looked after Children: Research into Practice*. London: HMSO.

Weiland, S. (2011) *Dissociative Identity Disorder: Diagnosis, Clinical Features, and Treatment of Multiple Personality*. New York: Routledge.

Wilbarger, P. and Wilbarger, J. (1997) *Sensory Defensiveness and Related Social/emotional and Neurological Problems*. Van Nuys, CA: Wilbarger Press.

Wilkinson, J. and Bowyer, S. (2017) *The Impacts of Abuse and Neglect on Children; and Comparison of Different Placement Options*. Evidence Review, Dartington: Research in Practice.

Wilson, K. (ed.) (2004) *Fostering Success: An Exploration of the Research Literature in Foster Care*. Social Care Institute for Excellence (SCIE), Nottingham: The Policy Press.

White, N., Ensor, R., Marks, A., Jacobs, L., and Hughes, C. (2014) 'It's mine!' Does sharing with siblings at age 3 predict sharing with siblings, friends, and unfamiliar peers at age 6? *Early Education and Development*, 25(2), 185–201.

Williams, J. H. and Ross, L. (2007) Consequences of prenatal toxin exposure for mental health in children and adolescents: A systemic review. *European Child and Adolescent Psychiatry*, 16, 243–253.

Winnicott, D. W. (1971) *Playing and Reality*. London: Routledge.

Wojciak, A. S., McWey, L. M., and Waid, J. (2018) Siblings in foster care: A relational path to resilience. *Child & Family Social Work*, 23(1), 70–78.

Wolfensberger, W. (1999) A contribution to the history of Normalisation, with primary emphasis on the establishment of Normalisation in North America between 1967 – 1975. In R. J. Flynn and R. A. Lemay (eds.), *A Quarter-century of Normalisation and Social Role Valorisation: Evolution and Impact*. Ottawa, ON: University of Ottawa Press, 125–159.

Woodhouse, T. (2019) Play therapy with children affected by sexual abuse: Developing awareness, safety and trust. In Ayling, P., Armstrong, H., and Gordon Clark, L. (eds.), *Becoming and Being a Play Therapist: Play Therapy in Practice*. London: Routledge, 189–202.

Wulczyn, F. and Zimmerman, E. (2005) Sibling placements in longitudinal perspective. *Children and Youth Services Review*, 27(7), 741–763.

Yahuda, R. and Bowers, H. E. (2017) *Neurochronology and Neurobiology of PTSD*, Chapter 10, 2, 165–172.

Zoia, S., Blason, L., D'Ottavio, G, Bulgheroni, M., Pezzetta, E., Scabar, A., and Castiello, U. (2007) Evidence of early development of action planning in the human foetus: A kinematic study. *Experimental Brain Research*, 176, 217–226.

Index

Abuhatoum, S. 59
abuse, emotional 38, 104; emotional neglect 18, 38, 44, 91, 139–140, 150; neglect 43; physical 17, 112, 177; sexual 10, 21, 33, 43–44, 164, 173, 177
achieving best evidence (ABE) 19, 132, 148
adolescence 38, 63, 130–131, 138, 152,148
adoption 61, 128–131, 139–140, 176–178, 180
adrenalin 98
adverse childhood experiences (ACEs) 3, 37
adversity 17, 27–28, 78–79, 171–172
age, chronological 38, 171; developmental 166, 171
aggression 60, 85, 109
Ainsworth, M.D.S. 159, 163
Akhtar, A. 51
Albert, V.N. 49
alcohol misuse 162
amygdala 106, 138–139
Anderson, A. 30
Andersson, Y. 59
Anger 4–5, 45, 53, 111–112, 139, 145, 172
Anxiety 41, 45, 60, 77, 84, 144–146, 153–155, 161–163
Archer, C. 31
Arcos, E. 75
Ashley, J 90
assessment 90; attachment 54, 65, 139; parent 51, 59, 167; sibling 49–51, 69, 112–113, 184–186; trauma informed 49
attachment, disorganised 45, 62, 78, 80, 96–98, 167–168; insecure 44, 78, 168
attention deficit disorder (ADD) 44, 84

attention deficit hyperactivity disorder (ADHD) 44, 84
attunement, empathic 35–36, 132, 140–143, 152

Bank, S.P. 58
Barach, P.M. 92
Beckett, S. 5
Begley, S. 90, 104
behaviour, age-appropriate 42, 54, 77, 92, 102–103, 106; externalising 7, 82; internalising 60, 104; trauma-informed 166–167, 171
belief systems 97; anecdotal 3, 16, 40, 42; internal 148; limiting beliefs 148, 155, 162, 187
Bellis, M. 39
best interests of the child 65–67, 153
Bhide, P. G. 77
bias 65, 127
Bifulco, A. 167
Blom-Cooper, L. 14, 32
Bloom, S.L. 168
boarding school 49
bond, trauma *see* trauma
Bowlby, J. 59
brain function 116–117; amygdala 126, 158, 159; cortex 110–111; higher cortex 62, 91, 130; limbic system 35, 90; new-cortex 90; sub-cortex 90
Braun, B.G. 93
Bretherton, I. 37
Briere, J.N. 20, 39, 98, 109, 188–189
Bryson, B. 104, 132
Buist, K.L. 58

Cairns, K. 84, 113
Campione-Barr, N. 59
capacity to care 19, 181; change 124; consent 153; intellectual 57, 82; tolerate stress 157–158
care, connected 31, 71, 177; kinship 87; proceedings 78, 84
caregiving, failure to protect 155; frightened 61, 99, 165–167; frightening 61, 99
Carroll, J. 52
Caspi, J. 60
Chapman, L. 84
Chess, S. 44
child development, biological 4, 73, 80; neurological 33
Children Act 1989 48, 64, 67, 150, 166
Children and Social Work Act 2017 66
Children and Young Person's Act 2008 65
Chu, J.A. 31
Cicirelli, V. 60, 107
Cloitre, M. 88
Cole, P. 45
competence, Frazer/Gillick 19
compliance 107, 181; disguised 7, 186; non-compliance 130
congruence 7, 19; empathic congruence 154; incongruence 9, 93, 115
contact, assessing 89, 90, 95; planning 19–20; purpose 104; reducing 84; sibling 59, 67, 112–113
context, cultural 57, 59; adoptive 175; developmental 112; fostering 180; professional 157; relational 114; residential 173; young adult/care leaver 12
Couper, S. 58
Cox, S. 51
Crenshaw, D. 131
curiosity, empathic 17, 82, 134; mindful 103; non-empathic 18, 38, 99, 105, 136, 197–198

Damasio, A.R. 35
Dantchev, S. 60
death 47–54; children's concept of 82–83
defiance 54; as a strategy 66
Della Porta, S. 59
denial 29, 63, 95, 143, 185
Dereboys, C. 148
development trauma *see* trauma

diagnosis/misdiagnosis 44, 47, 84, 92, 96, 140, 163, 167–168
Dirks, M.A. 58
disability 34, 64, 115, 148, 168
disruption, family 49, 177; placement 40, 88–89, 125, 133
dissociation 37–46, 92, 100, 133–134, 143; dissociative identity disorder (DID) 20, 158, 185
Doidge, N. 90
domestic violence 15, 21, 23, 43–45, 149, 167; coercive control 15
dopamine 98
Drapeau, S. 49
Dunn, J. 58–60, 107

El Marroun, H. 76
empathy 35–38, 91, 99, 105–106, 110, 156
engagement 16, 112, 132
Entringer, S. 76
evidence 57–59, 79, 187
externalisation 7, 60, 102

family systems 38, 59
fault 61, 85–86, 88, 91–95, 111, 115, 165
Felitti, J. 39
Fenichel, O. 80
Finkelhor, D. 80
Firmin, C.E. 8, 26
Fisher, J. 36–37
Fonagy, P. 14, 92
Fosha, D. 35
fragmentation 39–40, 133, 160, 175–179
Freedman, G. 77
Freud, S. 14, 28
'fs' 61, 90, 98, 145–147

Galston, W.A. 101
Gass, K. 109
Gerhardt, S. 34, 74, 76, 169
Gill, E. 132
Gillick *v* West Norfolk 133
Grief 61–63
Grossman, K. 159, 163

Haines, S. 84
Hart, S. 92
Hegar, R.I. 49
Herman, J.I. 39, 86
Herrick, M. 58, 107
hierarchy of needs 41, 74

holding, emotional 88, 152, 179; environment 35–36; in-mind
hope 46, 93, 118, 134, 145
hopelessness 5, 98, 186; professional 154
Hou, X.H. 59
Howe, D. 58
Howe, N. 58
Howes, N. 84, 85
Hughes, D. 56, 104, 126
hyper-arousal 152
hypo-arousal 90, 154
hypotheses 54, 92, 127–128, 130, 132, 135

identity 4, 42, 51, 110, 116, 152, 160, 166, 168, 178–179
individuation 38, 99
integration 37–40, 178
Internal Family Systems (IFS) 38
internal working model 9, 31, 40, 45, 78–79, 90, 150, 163
intrusive experiences 8
Itzin, C. 159, 167

Judd, T. 29
Jung, C.G. 38, 40

Kadushin, A. 6
Kempe, C.H. 26
Khan, R. 60
Klaus, M.H. 74
Klein, M. 36
Klein, P.S. 59
Kolak, A.M. 59
Kolawole, F. 60
Kosonen, M. 107
Kothari, B. 68
Kramer, L. 59

Laing, R.D. 99
Landreth, G.L. 50
Lanius, R.A. 84
Larzelere, R.E. 44
Law Commission 64
Leach, J. 58, 59
Leathers, S. 49
Levine, P.A. 93, 96
life story work 39; therapeutic 148
Linares, L.O. 49, 68
Liotti, G. 79, 92
locus of control: internal 178, external 151, 154, 168, 178
Lord, J. 64

loss 43, 49, 53, 61, 96, 120–122, 164

Main, M. 88, 92, 109
Mandela, N. 3
Marley, B. 17, 18
Maslow, A.H. 41, 43, 44, 74
Meakings, S. 68
memory, psychic 129; state-dependent 138; traumatic 89, 119, 145, 177
mentalisation 35–36, 85, 92, 140
Meunier, J.C. 59
Minnis, H. 68
model coherency 8, 13, 17, 34
Monk, C. 48, 69
Monk, D. 76
Munro, E. 32
Music, G. 74, 76

Neulinger, I. 66
neurobiology 83, 93, 96
neuroscience 4, 27, 33
Newberry, J.J. 131
Nijenhuis, E. 39, 73, 75, 132
non-compliance 110, 130
nor-adrenalin 98
NSPCC 27

Ogden, P. 36, 80, 181
O'Neill, T. 28, 31, 33
opiates 98
oppositional behaviour 179
optimum arousal zone 137
oxytocin 98

Paine, A.L. 59
Paradox, sibling, (20 references) professional 34, 63, 171, 186
paramountcy principle 64
parentification 40, 156
parenting, capacity 74, 177; corporate 66, 157, 168; good-enough 44, 73, 74, 160; style 15, 16, 19, 38, 44, 78; unavailable 88, 89
parts 37, 57, 158, 160, 161
Peck, M.S. 3, 19, 21
Perlman, M. 58
Perry, B.D. 9, 51, 76, 84, 91, 96, 146
Pike, A. 60
placement, disruption 4, 7, 40, 65, 68, 69, 105, 112, 113, 180; stability 64, 144; viability 165
polyvagal theory 137

Porges, S. 130, 137
power, adult 15, 121; authority 17; control 40, 45, 59, 78, 79, 95, 103, 108, 128, 145, 153, 154, 161, 163, 175
practice, curious 17, 31, 82, 105, 134, 136, 139, 144, 146, 168, 177; ethical 12, 43, 55; humility 174; neutral 36; forensic neutrality 127; professional stance 13, 33, 57, 186; reflective practice 33
present moment 162
proximity 10, 35, 36, 45, 74, 76, 79, 99, 100, 152
Putman, F.W. 35, 40, 58, 84, 85, 92, 93, 95, 113, 138

Rauchfuss, M. 75
Reamer, F.C. 5
Recchia, H.E. 59
Reder, P. 23
Rees Centre 48
regulation, relational 76; physiological 130; self 35; social 58, 60, 78
Reich, W. 80, 81
Reiland, R. 100
repair 25, 77, 78, 137
resilience 17, 22, 35, 137, 148–150, 155
resistant 9, 111, 162, 182
Richardson, J. 167
Richardson, S. 49
Richmond, M.K. 59
Rogers, C. 60, 132
Rowe, J. 68
rupture 77; empathic 86; relational 183
Rushton, A. 57
Ryan, V. 132

safeguarding 8, 27, 128, 186
safety, signs of 69
Sapolsky, R.M. 96
Saunders, H. 64
Scaer, R. 75, 76
scapegoating 8, 53, 101, 155, 171, 176, 181
Schore, A.N. 26, 35, 36, 41, 89, 96, 98, 106
Schwartz, R.C. 4, 38, 80
self, sense of 31, 38, 42, 92–93, 110, 168, 178; reliance 40, 45, 76, 78, 150, 155, 161, 170, 172; self-blame 85–86, 91, 93, 103–104; wise 38
Sellers, E. 60
Selwyn, J. 54
separation anxiety 63, 77
Seuss, Dr. 3
seven 'fs' 61, 91, 98, 147

sexual exploitation 34, 43, 86, 88, 131; trafficking 87
shame, toxic 58, 96
Shemmings, D. 88
sibling adoptive 49–50, 52, 67, 166
sibling, bereavement/death 15, 18, 28, 29, 32
sibling biological 48–52, 149, 166, 170, 175
sibling contact 15, 50, 54, 59, 65, 67–68, 103–104, 106–108, 111–113, 118, 122, 139, 143–145, 161, 170, 182, 183
sibling foster 8, 10, 12, 27, 48–49, 65, 166, 181
sibling half 28–29, 49, 166, 174
sibling placement 4, 6, 10, 26, 44, 48–49, 54, 58, 61, 64–65, 67–69, 105, 113, 156
sibling reunion 61; rivalry 52, 59–60, 65, 109, 175
sibling separation 27, 54, 61–67, 102, 104, 117, 119, 138, 154, 178, 187
sibling step 14, 29, 31, 48, 65, 67, 166
sibling twin 51, 144, 150–152, 155, 179, 181
sibling victimisation 60
sibling violence 60, 152, 176
Siegel, D.J. 86, 137, 168
Silberg, J.L. 33
Sinclair, I. 67, 68
Smallbone, M. 166
Solomon, E.P. 65, 109
Spiegel, L. 38
Sroufe, L.A. 159, 167, 198
Stevenson, O. 32
stress response 25, 26, 40–41, 51, 76–77, 83–84, 90, 148, 155
stress toxic 57–59
Summers, J. 59
Summit, R. 85
Sunderland, M. 96, 169
supervision 6–7, 22, 30–34, 42, 113, 156, 161–162, 167, 187
supervision reflective 33, 63

Tarren-Sweeney, M. 48
Tavassoli, N. 59
Team Around the Child (TAC) 13, 135, 180
Terr, L.C. 85
Teti, D.M. 169, 183
therapeutic, alliance 150; parenting 66, 162, 164, 176; relationship 185–186
Toseeb, U. 90

transitions 28, 38, 43, 61, 131
trauma, bonds 3, 53, 62, 65, 100, 103, 106, 114; complex 80; cumulative 168; developmental 36, 59–60, 73, 80–82, 131, 163, 167; relational 96; types and 4, 36, 165, 179
trauma informed, assessment 44–46, 82; considerations 61–62; lens 31; observation 112; parenting 6; practice 64; responses 108, 114

unconditional positive regard 103

van der Hart, O. 93
van der Kolk, B.A. 39, 94, 104
vicarious trauma 36, 165, 179
voice, pitch 17; prosody 158; silent, tone 91, 134
Volling, B.L. 58

Wade, J. 69

Waid, J. 68
Ward, H. 68
Weiland, S. 93
White, N. 59
Wilbarger, P. 137
Wilkinson, J. 57–59
Williams, J.H. 76
Wilson, K. 132
window of tolerance 35, 76, 84, 98, 137–147
Winnicott, D.W. 35, 36
wishes and feelings, said, unsaid, not yet said 50, 66, 114, 136, 144, 148, 150
Wolfensberger, W. 8
Woodhouse, T. 160
Wulczyn, F. 48

Yahuda, R. 98

Zoia, S. 75

For Product Safety Concerns and Information please contact our EU
representative GPSR@taylorandfrancis.com
Taylor & Francis Verlag GmbH, Kaufingerstraße 24, 80331 München, Germany

www.ingramcontent.com/pod-product-compliance
Ingram Content Group UK Ltd.
Pitfield, Milton Keynes, MK11 3LW, UK
UKHW020435240426
470322UK00017B/529